The Syntax of
(In)dependence

Linguistic Inquiry Monographs
Samuel Jay Keyser, general editor

The Syntax of (In)dependence

Ken Safir

The MIT Press
Cambridge, Massachusetts
London, England

This book was set in Times New Roman on 3B2 by Asco Typesetters, Hong Kong and was printed and bound in the United States of America.

Library of Congress Control Number: 2004102965

ISBN : 0-262-19500-3 (hc)
      : 0-262-69300-3 (pb)

10 9 8 7 6 5 4 3 2 1

For my father, Marshall Safir

Contents

Contents

Series Foreword

We are pleased to present the forty-fourth in the series *Linguistic Inquiry Monographs*. These monographs present new and original research beyond the scope of the article. We hope they will benefit our field by bringing to it perspectives that will stimulate further research and insight.

Originally published in a limited edition, the *Linguistic Inquiry Monographs* are now more widely available. This change is due to the great interest engendered by the series and by the needs of a growing readership. The editors thank the readers for their support and welcome suggestions about future directions for the series.

Samuel Jay Keyser
for the Editorial Board

Preface

For more than a decade, my research has focused on the nature of linguistic anaphora, and when the opportunity arose, in the form of a commission to write a state-of-the-art book on the topic, I felt I was ready for the task. However, as I became engrossed in the project, it eventually expanded to the point that the original publishers no longer recognized it as the project they had in mind. Moreover, parts of the book long finished were languishing as I tried to complete other parts. On the advice of almost everyone, I finally decided to break the project into smaller parts, of which the book before you is one of at least two.

The largest part, *The Syntax of Anaphora* (Safir 2004), is devoted to rethinking the binding theory effects in terms of a competitive algorithm for computing the distribution of dependent forms, as discussed here in chapter 1. As part of the division of labor, I have tried to sever the lines of argument developed here from those in *The Syntax of Anaphora*, but the cuts are awkward at times. Although a certain unity of purpose is somewhat disguised by the division, presenting the central ideas of the original vision separately has, I hope, clarified the central themes. Those especially interested in the small portion of this book that addresses the issues that overlap can consult the discussion of the first book. Nonetheless, both *The Syntax of Anaphora* and this book can be read independently. A third manuscript drawn from the original book, currently in preparation, addresses perspective anaphora and person, the relations between the two, and other discourse-influenced phenomena, and that too can be read independently.

Most of the ideas presented here were developed in one chapter of the original book and parts of other chapters, all of which were first circulated in my fall 2000 seminar at Rutgers University and revised in spring

2001. The delays I have faced in getting this material into print have required me to avoid too much updating to address recent work. Essentially, I comment on nothing that was not in my hands before January 2002 (and probably not all that was). Developments in our field happen fast, and so I freeze a moment at my peril, but I do so in the hope that some of the results presented here are substantive enough that they are not likely to be so rapidly undercut.

Acknowledgments

A number of people were very helpful in the development, improvement, and completion of this book, and it is a pleasure, too long deferred, to thank them now. I would like to thank those who witnessed the manuscript in process during the course of two graduate seminars at Rutgers University, spring 1999 and fall 2000, and helped me to separate the metal from the dross. In particular, I would like to thank Caroline Heycock and Lynn Nichols, visitors in fall 2000, who provided many valuable suggestions. Among those who commented on drafts of this book in earlier stages, I would also like to thank Marcel den Dikken and Dave Lebeaux. At a later stage, Judy Bauer provided invaluable comments that helped improve the presentation. I would also like to thank several of my colleagues, both in and out of my seminars, for criticisms and suggestions that led to improvements: Mark Baker, Veneeta Dayal, and Roger Schwarzschild (although the usual disclaimers apply). Thanks to Jane Grimshaw for some timely help at the end. I would also like to thank Hamida Demirdache, Robert Fiengo, Richard Kayne, and Tanya Reinhart for particularly useful conversations in which they disagreed thoroughly with various parts of what I have had to say.

Finally I would like to thank my family, for whom this project has only meant less of my time, and in particular my wife Susan Sidlauskas, who made some suggestions about writing this thing and getting it published that turned out to be crucial.

Chapter 1

Introduction

One of the most important discoveries in modern linguistics has been that abstract structural properties of utterances place subtle restrictions on how speakers can use a given form or description to pick out entities in a discourse. In the last thirty years, these restrictions on acceptable interpretations for sentences have been mined for clues to the exact nature of the structural properties in question, and the vein shows no signs of giving out. This book is an attempt to streamline and rearrange our commitment to syntactically determined principles of interpretation while revealing new empirical generalizations that we are led to discover by looking at things in the way I propose.

The influence of the theory developed here will be demonstrated to range across a wide class of empirical phenomena, including the distribution of crossover effects, bound variable ellipsis, functional answers to questions, resumptive pronoun constructions, (anti)reconstruction effects, and proxy readings. All of these effects are primarily interpretive, which is to say that in almost every case, the linguistic constructions in question are grammatical under some interpretation, but certain coconstrual interpretations between nominals in these structures are excluded by the principle under investigation.

I approach the interpretive issues with some theoretical commitments that should be made clear at the outset. First, I assume that all natural languages are a reflection of a linguistic capacity innate to human beings, often referred to as Universal Grammar (UG). The structures that are revealed by research into natural language grammars are thus structures that are generated by UG, and in constructing theories of how these structures are generated, the linguist is positing principles that are to be understood as psychologically real. This ensures that there is a fact of the matter and that the intuitions of adult native speakers, among other sorts of evidence, may be brought to bear as evidence to support or refute a theory the linguist proposes. Linguistic data, like any other sort, must be interpreted and controlled as they must be in any science; and as in any science, data can mislead or later be reinterpreted in light of better understanding. Many of the data discussed in this book have been interpreted and reinterpreted, and so part of the argumentation is based on defending one interpretation of the data against another.

I will take it as uncontroversial that a sentence can be computed to express a meaning independent of any particular context, which determines what it can be used to say (I set aside extralinguistic codes; for example, *The eagle has landed* means 'I have received the money'). To a large extent, the interpretation of a sentence is guided by lexical selection and the syntactic representation that serves as a guide to semantic constituency. In other words, the meaning of a syntactic phrase is computed from composition of its immediate daughters. To most linguists, these assumptions are familiar and standard. What I explore here is the way a particular syntactic restriction limits the range of dependent identity interpretations a sentence can have, and hence the range of possible entailments it can have on the basis of these anaphoric interpretations. I lightly touch on how one or another of these possible anaphoric interpretations may be favored by manipulating a discourse, but mainly I focus on interpretive restrictions that cannot be repaired by discourse accommodation.

1.1 The Proposal and the Plan

My main proposal, one with historical antecedents I will mention later, is that dependent identity interpretations are restricted by a c-command prohibition and not by a c-command licensing condition. This goes against the grain of most work (in particular, the very influential work of Reinhart (1983a,b) and Grodzinsky and Reinhart (1993), for example, and slight extensions of it by linguists such as Hornstein (1995)) that assumes that a c-commanding antecedent is needed to license a dependent identity interpretation. Apart from the role that c-command plays in licensing syntactic anaphors, I argue that dependent readings are otherwise generally available where they are not excluded by a c-command prohibition. In other words, c-command does not license dependencies, but instead plays a role in ruling them out. I also assume that scope, perhaps determined by c-command at LF, plays a licensing role, but quantifier-bound interpretations are only a subset of dependency relations. This means I will be focusing on (a) cases where a dependent identity reading is not induced by a quantified antecedent, but relations between antecedent and dependent form are still c-command sensitive (and not on account of the binding theory or its descendants; see chapter 2); (b) cases where scopal licensing conditions are met, but bound interpretation still fails (as in the case of crossover in chapter 3); and (c) cases where surface forms appear not to c-command their antecedents, but sometimes behave as though they do (as in the discussion of reconstruction and antireconstruction in chapter 4).

The c-command prohibition I propose is one I adapt from Higginbotham (1983, 402) (see also Evans 1980, 355). It can be fairly simply stated (though provisionally) as in (1), which is to be compared with what I take to be the core assumption of the c-command licensing approach stated in (2). I will henceforth refer to (1) as the *Independence Principle* and (2) as the *C-command Licensing Principle*.[1]

(1) *Independence Principle (INP)*
    If *x* depends on *y*, then *x* cannot c-command *y*.

(2) *C-command Licensing Principle (CLP)*
    If *x* depends on *y*, then *y* must c-command *x*.

Let us suppose that c-command is defined as it most commonly is (e.g., roughly as in Reinhart 1976).

(3) *C-command*
    A c-commands B if the first branching node dominating A also dominates B and A does not dominate B.[2]

The difference between these two approaches can immediately be observed with respect to the contrast in (5) (which is a contrast of type (b) mentioned above).[3]

(4) a. Someone loves everyone's mother.
    b. ∃y∀x (y loves x's mother)
    c. ∀x∃y (y loves x's mother)

(5) a. *Everyone's* mother loves *him*.
    b. **He* loves *everyone's* mother.
    c. Every x, x's mother loves x
    d. Every x, x loves x's mother

Any theory must assume that *everyone* can have wide scope over the subject *someone* insofar as (4c) is a possible interpretation for (4a).

However, if we attempt to construe the pronouns in (5a) and (5b) to be bound variables of the universal quantifier in each case (as in (5c) and (5d), respectively), only (5a) is acceptable (where coconstrual in (5a,b) is marked by italics). For this contrast, the CLP makes the wrong prediction, namely, that both (5a) and (5b) should be excluded—in neither case does the quantifier c-command the pronoun. However, the INP correctly distinguishes between (5a) and (5b). In (5a), *him* does not c-command the surface position of *everyone*, and *him* can be in the scope of *everyone*. In (5b), by contrast, where the quantifier can also have wide scope, the pronoun *he* c-commands the quantifier on which it depends, a relationship the INP correctly prohibits under the dependent reading.

This argument based on the bound variable phenomena in (5), long known in the literature (and more recently characterized as cases of "almost c-command" by Hornstein (1995, 108–110)), is oversimplified for the purposes of presentation (e.g., if we assume LF movement of quantifiers, the nature of c-commanding antecedents must be reconsidered thoroughly) and in some respects, it is not the most interesting one, but it illustrates how one might distinguish the INP and the CLP on the basis of empirical contrasts.

Closely related to the contrast between the INP and the CLP is the nature of how coconstruals are represented. The term *coconstrual* is one I use when I want to be neutral about the nature of the relationship between forms that results in the identity of the referential value assigned to the nominal argument positions those forms represent. Starting in section 1.2, I argue that the only form of coconstrual influenced by the structures of formal syntax is dependent identity and that dependent identity is an asymmetric relation, such that if A depends on B, then B does not depend on A. These claims resonate throughout my presentation, and I return to them in the concluding chapter. Although it is not likely that the dependency relation itself requires representations relevant to syntax, the distribution of such relations is sensitive to c-command and is crucial for determining what sort of dependent identity readings a sentence can have.

It is not possible to discuss the nature of syntax-influenced coconstrual without reviewing the nature of morphologically specific anaphora and the effects related to it, which is my way of referring to the binding theory principles developed in Chomsky 1981 (henceforth, *LGB*). These effects are presented first with respect to the nature of the noncoreference effects they induce (section 1.2), though I later reinterpret the *LGB* binding theory in terms of a competitive theory of anaphora (section 1.4).

In chapter 2, I further distinguish my approach from others that examine the role of c-command in determining the class of possible coconstruals. Some of these are more like the INP (e.g., Higginbotham 1983; Fiengo and May 1994; Williams 1997), and others are more committed to the CLP (associated with Reinhart 1976, 1983a,b, as extended to almost c-command as a licensing factor in Hornstein 1995, 108). I argue in chapter 2 that freeing dependent identity interpretations from sentence-bound restrictions not only accounts for bound readings where c-command does not hold, but also permits a simpler account of the absence of third party readings in ellipsis contexts (readings that are neither strict nor sloppy), while providing an account of the restrictions on proxy readings (identity readings between arguments interpreted as noncoextensive). Rule H (Fox 1999, 2000) is presented and defended in chapter 2 as well, although I take it up again in chapter 5.

A major result of my approach, to be explored in chapter 3, is that all crossover effects (weak, strong, weakest), empirical patterns of bound anaphora that have been explored by linguists for over thirty years since Postal's (1971) seminal work, follow, without any stipulation specific to crossover, from the proper formulation of the INP as presented in chapter 2. In chapter 4, I explore this result, and the ancillary hypotheses that support it (including my reformulation of the binding theory and Rule H), with respect to some well-known and not so well-known reconstruction asymmetries that yield detailed support for my approach and for the copy theory of the Minimalist Program. In chapter 5, I examine the principles I have proposed in the context of a wider perspective on the architecture of UG with respect to the relation among formal syntax, interpretation, and pragmatics. In so doing, I compare my theory of these relations with alternative accounts of coconstrual, particularly the coconstrual-as-movement theory proposed by Kayne (2002), which I argue is conceptually inferior to the proposals made here.

Chapters 2 and 3 are thoroughly Anglocentric and even chapter 4 is largely so. This is partly a presentational convenience in that English is the language that has been studied in the most detail and the facts are most familiar to me and to my readers. However, since the principles I propose are universal and unparameterized, the structure of my arguments for English should serve as an adequate model for arguments based on the facts in other languages. Insofar as my arguments for English cannot be transparently extended to languages that permit scrambling, I have included an analysis of scrambling in Hindi in the appendix as a model for the line of argument I must take to extend my theory, without any revision, to scrambling languages. In other words, however languages may differ in their input to the principles that I propose (e.g., in the range of movements they allow, in the distribution of resumptive pronouns they allow, or in the variety of dependent forms their lexicons contain), the principles that regulate dependencies act on whatever their inputs may be in the same way for any grammar.

1.2 Dependent Identity and (Non)coreference

Although the difference between dependent identity and coreferent readings are fairly well known to those familiar with the anaphora literature, not everyone agrees on the consequences of this distinction for syntactic representation. When the referential value of a linguistic expression x can only be determined as a function of the interpretive content of the linguistic expression y, then x depends on y. When I speak of *coreference* or *covaluation*, I mean that the value of x and the value of y are the same— which typically means that they pick out the same referent in discourse or else that they covary. *Covariation* is typically part of the dependent identity reading with respect to a quantified antecedent. In chapter 2, I will introduce *codependent covariation*, where two nominals A and B independently depend on C, but A does not depend on B and B does not depend on A. As remarked at the outset, when I want to be neutral or noncommittal about the nature of an identity relation between x and y, I will say that x and y are *coconstrued*.

The contrast in truth-conditions for (6) evidenced by the implications in (6a,b) has often been used to illustrate differences between dependent reference and independent coreference.

(6) Of all the women, only Mara believes Sean loves her.
    a. None of the other women believe that they are loved by Sean.
    b. None of the other women believe that Sean loves Mara.

The reading that permits the implication in (6a) is the *dependent* or *bound* (covariant) reading, the one where the pronoun covaries with the choice of women believers who might antecede it. The reading that permits the implication in (6b) is the *strict* or *independent* reading, where the reference of the pronoun remains Mara even if the choice of believer varies. As Lasnik (1976) and Reinhart (1983a,b) have pointed out, a similar distinction is also observed in ellipsis contexts.[4]

(7) Mara believes Sean loves her and Sheila does too.
   a. Sheila believes that Sean loves her = Sheila.
   b. Sheila believes that Sean loves Mara.

The "sloppy" reading, as it is known in the literature, is illustrated by the "filled-in ellipsis" in (7a) and corresponds to the dependent/bound reading (like the interpretation of (6) with the implication in (6a)). The "strict" reading, illustrated in (7b), is taken to be an independent reading (which corresponds to the reading of (6) with the implication in (6b)).

Since the late 1970s, the distinction between dependent identity and coreference has played a role in what it means to claim that coreference (or covaluation) is blocked between two nominals. For example, consider Principles B and C of the binding theory, first presented in *LGB*.

(8) *Binding theory*
   a. *Principle A*
      An anaphor must be bound in domain D.
   b. *Principle B*
      A pronoun must be free in domain D.
   c. *Principle C*
      A name must be free.

(9) *Binding*
   x binds y if x c-commands y and x and y are coindexed. If x is not bound, it is free.

The exact nature of the locality restriction imposed by domain D was variously defined, though the different proposals fall largely outside the concerns of this book (but see Safir 2004, sec. 5.1, for a discussion of the locality of A-movement). In fact, the issues surrounding the binding theory, which I will reformulate in section 1.4 (in accordance with Safir 2004), play a secondary role altogether in the task I have set for myself. My main line of argument most directly addresses the distribution of bound (dependent identity) readings of pronouns that are not necessarily morphological anaphors (i.e., forms subject to Principle A). However, where the empirical effects that the binding theory is designed to account for obscure the more general pattern of dependent identity, I explore the relevance of binding theory effects and my theory of them in slightly more detail.

With respect to the interpretive effects the binding theory addresses, if we say that coreference is blocked by Principle C, then we should expect that copular sentences should not permit identity statements, since the copular subject c-commands the object of *be*.

(10) a. We only saw Oscar once and that guy has his back to us, but *he* is definitely *Oscar*.
     b. We only saw Oscar once and that guy has his back to us, but *he* is definitely *him*.
     c. *We only saw Oscar once and that guy has his back to us, but *he* is definitely *himself*.

In (10a), it would appear that Principle C is violated, and in (10b), Principle B, yet in each case coconstrual is possible. What seems to have gone wrong is that the c-commanded name or pronoun in these cases is possible because the relation involved is one of coreference, not dependent identity. The copular cases assert a coreference relation between two independently established referents (the Oscar we know and the guy we see). In fact, as the weirdness of (10c) attests, using a true dependent, *himself*, does not permit the intended reading at all for these equative copular contexts. If Principles B and C only regulate dependent identity, not coreference, then independent coreference asserted by equative *be* is unproblematic. Alternatively, if Principle C blocks coreference, then we must assume that where there is a conflict between Principle C and equative *be*, the latter trumps Principle C to allow coreference. The second position seems far more awkward.

Yet if Principles B and C only block dependent reference, why don't they allow covaluation even where dependent reference is blocked? After all, coconstrual between *he* and *Oscar* in (11a) appears to be blocked when the sentence is taken in isolation. Moreover, independent identities established in the discourse and then equated do not appear to allow *he* and *Oscar* to take their reference from different sources that just *happen* to be covalued (sometimes called accidental coreference).

(11) a. *He* is unaware that *Oscar* is incompetent.
     b. *We only saw Oscar once and that guy has his back to us, but *he* is *Oscar* and *he* is unaware that *Oscar* is incompetent.

Moreover, (11b) is no improvement over (11a), since adding the context provided in (10) still does not allow the last *Oscar* to corefer with the last *he*. This indicates that if dependent reference is what is blocked, this blockage must have a consequence for the failure of coreference, or else Principles B and C will fail miserably.

The line I will take here, justified at greater length in Safir 2004 (where the intellectual lineage of this reasoning is traced to Evans 1980, Higginbotham 1983, and Reinhart 1983a,b, among others), is that the binding theory only blocks dependency, and a pragmatic strategy or principle of obviation separate from the binding theory itself blocks coreference. In other words, where dependent reference is blocked by Principles B and C, coreference is unexpected unless it is emphasized or asserted (as it is in equative contexts).

Consider first (12), an example of a sort discussed by Higginbotham (1980a, 234–235; 1985, 570).

(12) You may not think that that guy is John, but he put on John's
       coat.

In this case, the individual in question, who is identifiable by both parties as salient in discourse (whether he is John or not), is posited by the speaker as having met a criterion for being identified as John. Moreover, the criterion in question ("puts on John's coat") is also in the common ground. If the listener does not accept the relevant presuppositions, he or she might ask the speaker how one can be certain that the coat in question is John's or why one should be certain that the person who puts on John's coat should be John. What is important for our discussion is that the referential values for *he* and for *John* are established separately, and the listener must draw his or her own logical conclusion (see also Fiengo and May 1994, 10) based on whether or not an appropriate criterion has been met—namely, whoever puts on John's coat must be John.

Crucial to this argument is (a) that coreference, not dependent identity, is involved, but also (b) that coreference for (12) is formally determined to be contrary to expectation. The statement in (12) is ironic because the speaker has stated the criterion of identity for *John* as if accepting the addressee's assumption that *he* does not refer to John. The example would be quite transformed if putting on a coat (any coat) was to be our indication that the secret spy we are meeting is John, in which case one of us might turn to the other and say, "He put on his coat, so he must be John." This reading, which could be a dependent one for *his*, is avoided by using *John's* in place of *his* in (12). Similar reasoning applies to Evans's (1980, 357) example given in (13).

(13) Everyone has finally realized that Oscar is incompetent. Even *he*
       has finally realized that *Oscar* is incompetent.

Insofar as words like *even* adjust our expectations, such that *he*, namely, Oscar, is the least likely individual to realize that Oscar is incompetent, the Principle C effect is neutralized here. Independent coreference arises from the frozen criterion for set membership, "realized Oscar is incompetent," and the assertion that Oscar is also in that set.

Although the expectation of noncoreference induced by whatever derives Principles B and C can be overcome by a strong context (called a context of instantiation in Safir 2004, or a context of structured meanings in Heim 1993) or assertion, the ban on dependent identity interpretation cannot be pragmatically overcome. Consider examples like (14a).

(14) a. Even Alfred says that Alfred is crazy.
     b. Even Alfred says that he is crazy.

The use of *even Alfred* indicates that Alfred, though one would not expect him to be in this set, is also one of the individuals who has the property of considering Alfred crazy (where the instances of *Alfred* are coconstrued) and so a coreferent interpretation is possible. Compare (14b), which, in addition to a coreferent interpretation, permits a dependent (bound) interpretation whereby Alfred is one of the x's who consider x crazy. The accommodation that permits a coreferent reading in (14a), however, does not license a sloppy reading in ellipsis contexts like (15b), even given the context in (15a).

(15) a. Almost every doctor is willing to say that Alfred and Maurice
        are crazy.
     b. Even Alfred says that Alfred is crazy, and more surprising still,
        even Maurice does.
     c. Even Alfred says that he is crazy, and more surprising still, even
        Maurice does.

While (15c) permits a reading where each of the men thinks about himself that he is crazy, (15b) can only mean that even Maurice thinks that Alfred is crazy, not that Maurice thinks that Maurice is crazy. The fact that the first conjunct in (15b) permits coreference (however clumsily), but blocks the sloppy dependent reading, follows from the force of Principle C as, on the one hand, an absolute prohibition on dependent identity interpretation and, on the other, merely the source of an expectation of noncoreference that can be accommodated.

By contrast, the INP, which also blocks dependencies, does not carry with it any presumption that coreference is unexpected. In (16), *he* c-commands *him*, so *he* cannot depend on *him*, but this does not create an expectation one way or the other about whether *he* and *him* should be coreferent or not. (Of course, *him* could depend on *he*, but that is not at issue here.)

(16) *He* said Sylvia saw *him*.

This difference goes part of the way toward distinguishing the force of the INP from that of Principles B and C, though in this case the difference appears theory internal, since an account based on the CLP would not predict anything different for these cases (i.e., *he* cannot depend on *him* because *him* does not c-command *he*). However, in section 2.4 I will revisit the INP's prediction that *he* cannot depend on *him* in such cases, showing that it has interesting empirical consequences.

1.3   The Formal Representation of Dependent Identity

If syntax directly restricts only dependent identity, not coreference, then some syntactic representation of dependency may be necessary, but there must not be any syntactic representation of coreference. Traditionally, indices have been used to represent the coreference or covaluation relation, but we must now ask whether this notation is appropriate to the dependency relation. Since dependency is an asymmetric relation (if x depends on y, then y does not depend on x) while coreference is a fully symmetric one, we would expect any notation of dependency to indicate the asymmetry.

1.3.1   Indices and Asymmetry

No property of simplex indices, however, indicates that of two or more coindexed elements, one has primacy over the other in any way. Additional statements must be made about indices, or else another diacritic (or diacritics) must be added to them to allow them to represent dependencies. This has spawned at least three strategies:

(17) a. Abandon indices in favor of an asymmetric diacritic.
　　 b. Use indices only where a dependency relation holds augmented by c-command.
　　 c. Augment indices with an asymmetric diacritic.

The first strategy is developed by Higginbotham (1983, 1985), who introduces arrows that connect dependents with their antecedents. I notate this relationship as in (18), where the anchor "⊢" represents the antecedent on which the term marked with the hook "⌐" depends.

(18) *Everyone* loves *his* mother.

As I remarked at the outset, the dependency relation does not have to be licensed by c-command in my theory, so dependency on a non-c-commanding antecedent is possible (19a), as is backward dependency (19b), although I will reconsider the well-formedness of (19b) in section 2.5.

(19) a. *Everyone's* mother loves *him*.

   b. *His* mother loves *Bill*.

I reserve discussion of the dependency relations that are blocked by the INP for section 2.4.

As Higginbotham pointed out when he introduced these arrows, they are inherently relational: the arrows do not express inherent properties of the nominals they relate, but only how they relate to one another. Indices, by comparison, are not inherently relational unless they are stipulated to be so: a nominal x with index i picks out the individual i in discourse whether or not another nominal y is also indexed i.

The second strategy (17b) is developed by Grodzinsky and Reinhart (1993) (henceforth, G&R), building on a proposal by Reinhart (1983a, 71) wherein indices are generated freely but are "interpretable" only where they mark a relation of dependency on an antecedent that binds the dependent. The binding theory and the "translation rule" in (20) along with Rule I stated in (21) are the heart of their theory.

(20) a. *Definition*
     A node α is *bound* by a node β iff α and β are coindexed and β c-commands α.
   b. *Conditions*
     A. An anaphor is bound in its governing category.
     B. A pronoun is free in its governing category.
   c. An NP is a variable iff either
      i. it is empty and Ā-bound, or
      ii. it is A-bound and lacks lexical content.
     Other cases of NP coindexation are uninterpretable.

(21) *Rule I: Intrasentential Coreference*

NP A cannot corefer with NP B if replacing A with *x*, *x* a variable A-bound by B, yields an indistinguishable interpretation.

Notice that the use of indices is somewhat vestigial in this account except where they serve to introduce c-command via the definition of binding, since indices are not interpretable otherwise. The stipulation that binding is asymmetric dependency of A on B only if B c-commands A (as in (20a)) is an accretion on the indices—a statement that compensates for what they do not naturally express.

However, the c-command condition in (20a) along with the stipulation that "other cases of NP coindexation are uninterpretable" is essentially what I have been calling the CLP, and I will argue directly against it in the next chapter. There are significant negative consequences for G&R's theory if the CLP is false, because the conditions under which bound readings are possible feed Rule I. Consider cases like (22) (hereafter, italics mark coconstrual).

(22) a. *No one's* mother thinks *he* is smart.
     b. *His/The boy's* mother doesn't think *he* is smart.
     c. *His* mother doesn't think *the boy* is smart.

If a bound variable reading is available in (22a), where *no one* does not c-command the pronoun *he*, then a bound variable reading should be available for (22b) for the pronoun *he* anteceded by *his/the boy's*. If so, *the boy* should not be able to corefer with *his* in (22c), since if coreference were intended, then (22b) would have to be used, because (22b) permits a bound reading. Unfortunately for Rule I, (22c) is perfectly acceptable.

The existence of a bound reading in (22a) and the possibility of a co-referent one in (22c) is predicted by the INP theory. First, all of these (so far) are instances of permitted dependency, since *his* does not c-command *he* or *the boy*; and second, even if *his* can be dependent on *the boy*, there is no obviation where there is no c-commanding antecedent (a point further developed in section 1.4). In other words, the availability of a bound reading does not require an obviative relation between *his* and *the boy* in a theory without Rule I, since only obviation requires c-command. C-command can, of course, be built into Rule I (as it is in Reinhart 1999), but then there is no direct relation between the logical notion of binding, in which c-command has no place, and linguistic obviation.[5] A further critique of Rule I is presented in Safir 2004, so I will not belabor the point here.

G&R's theory explicitly assumes that there is no role for indices in syntax beyond representing dependency. Indeed, Reinhart (1983a, 160) does not see indices as specifically necessary to represent the relations she posits. If the compensating statement, the one requiring interpretable indices to mark a relation between c-commander and c-commandee, is wrong, then it would appear that G&R, to maintain this view, must change the statement to whatever characterizes all the cases where dependency can be represented (and abandon or amend their account of Principle C effects). In either case, if the compensating statement is entirely responsible for the interpretable distribution of the indices, then there is no significant role for indices themselves.[6]

G&R (1993, 76–77n8) do allow for the possibility that covaluation can exist outside of binding in that "the system proposed here does not rule out the possibility of obligatory (unbound) coreference, but only rules out the possibility of its being enforced by the binding theory, or other syntactic conditions on coindexation." However, it is not obvious that covaluation of this sort has any important role to play in their theory.[7]

Fiengo and May (1994) (henceforth, F&M) take the third alternative in (17c). They employ indices with two forms of diacritic, one for dependency and one for covaluation. When a form is coindexed with another form and the index bears a β diacritic, then the form with the β diacritic is dependent on its antecedent; but when a form bears an index with an α diacritic, it has merely a covalued interpretation with any form bearing the same index. Both forms of indices are part of linguistic representation, Fiengo and May argue; but unlike the Evans-Reinhart-Higginbotham line of reasoning, theirs assumes that the binding theory applies to both α and β indices.[8]

The system allows for two ways of notating coconstrual and three ways in which it can arise. The sentence in (23) can be indexed in any one of three ways. If there is coindexation, the coindexation can either be dependent (β) or covalued (α) or else there can be the absence of coindexation, in which case covaluation can be extralinguistic.

(23) a. John$_{i\alpha}$ said he$_{i\alpha}$ was late
    b. John$_{i\beta}$ said he$_{i\beta}$ was late
    c. John$_i$ said he$_j$ was late

Coindexation means that there is a linguistic commitment to coreference, and the absence of coindexation means that there is an absence of commitment to coreference, where coreference is covaluation here. Thus, absence of dependency does not indicate noncoreference, but absence of coindexing indicates noncoreference as far as matters of linguistic form go. F&M assume that identity statements are instances where there is no coindexation, not simply the absence of dependency between the arguments, and thus if covaluation is possible, it is extralinguistic. Perhaps if we are slowly putting it together that the person John is describing, a person we know as "the mysterious stranger," is in fact John, then we might utter (23c) in our process of deducing that John is the mysterious stranger (e.g., John said the mysterious stranger was late and John himself was late and no one else was late; so when John said, "*He was late*," using *he* to refer to the mysterious stranger, he was in fact referring to himself). However, we are not linguistically committed to that covaluation.

At least one case suggesting that some covaluations must be linguistically marked is the existence of strict and sloppy readings permitted in ellipsis environments. While (24) could have a sloppy reading (i.e., a dependent one, as in (25a), or a strict one, as in (25b)), it is not at all possible for (24) to have the structurally parallel interpretation in (25c), in which *John* and *he* are coconstrued, but the elided pronoun (in brackets) refers to someone other than Bill or John.

(24) John said he was late before Bill did.

(25) a.   *John* said *he* was late before **Bill** [said **he** was late]
      b.   *John* said *he* was late before Bill [said *he* was late]
      c.   **John* said *he* was late before **Bill** [said he was late]

Only if there is a positive requirement that the value for the pronoun in the antecedent constituent of the elision must match the value of the pronoun in the elision can this fact be captured. Insofar as indices are part of the representation that must be copied, F&M's system captures this fact. However, I do not believe one must resort to more than dependency arrows to explain the absence of (25c). I present my account of this fact in section 2.3.2.

Of the three coconstrual relations that F&M's theory permits, only two seem necessary. F&M's β indices appear to express the dependency relation expressed here with arrows. The lack of commitment to coreference does not require indices in either theory, but it does seem necessary, as it is what characterizes (what I take to be) the independent covaluation reading for the copula, as in *That guy is John* in (12) (see note 13 of chapter 2). However, there is apparently no evidence that requires an α-indexing account and, furthermore, there is evidence that such an account predicts relations that do not exist.

For example, F&M's account predicts that some anaphors should be bound by coreferent antecedents with which they are independently covalued; in other words, they are covalued with antecedents on which they do not depend. This is because F&M assume the *LGB* binding theory, hence the indexing inherent to binding; further, they assume that the binding theory applies to any coindexation, and so it will apply to both α and β indices coindexed with c-commanding antecedents. Thus, if a form is anaphoric, whether it bears an α or β occurrence of an index, it is subject to Principle A; that is, if a pronoun is marked with a SELF form, then its binding requirement can be satisfied by either α or β coindexation with its binder.

The reason that F&M treat both sorts of indices as subject to the binding theory is that they are committed to saying that in every instance where the binding theory applies to block dependency, not only dependency is ruled out but covaluation as well. For their account, the connection between the failure of dependency and the failure of coreference is a formal restriction on syntactic binding, not a pragmatic inference of any sort that could arise from an otherwise possible dependent interpretation that blocks an independent coreferent one. Thus, the connection between failure of dependency (β coindexation) and failure of covaluation (α coindexation) in the same contexts is stipulated as a property of the failure of coindexation, but the stipulation removes the need for any additional rule of noncoreference.

Treating both kinds of indices the same way for Principles B and C also requires treating them the same way for Principle A. If, however, there are no anaphors bound solely by α indices, then F&M's account of binding-theory-induced noncoreference for Principles B and C is more ad hoc than they contend. To put it as a question, when does Principle A have to be stated on anything other than dependencies? The cases that could distinguish between an anaphor uniquely bound by an α index and one bound by a β index require the following scenario: dependency must be independently blocked and coreference must be linguistically enforced. F&M suggest that the strict reading for the elided portion in (26) may be an instance where an anaphoric form is not dependent, but must bear an α index.

(26) Who slashed the samurai? *The samurai* must have slashed *himself*.
     Clearly the shogun couldn't have.

The last sentence does not involve a self-slashing, so the interpretation appears to be strict—that is, the shogun couldn't have slashed the samurai. The α index on the object of the elided verb (i.e., [*slashed x*]) is supposed to be what enforces identity of x with *himself*, which is bound by *the samurai*. On F&M's reasoning, the x of *slashed x* is elided *himself* bound by an α index on *himself* in the second sentence.

However, the assumption that an α-indexed reflexive is involved for the second sentence in (26) is undercut by F&M's assumption that in elision contexts, it is not necessary to reconstruct the SELF portion of English pronoun-SELF forms (for further discussion of this process with respect to vehicle change, see section 2.1). Without the SELF portion reconstructed in the elided portion, the reconstructed pronoun (i.e., '... the shogun couldn't have [slashed him]') does not fall under Principle A; rather, it falls under Principle B, which does not rule it out (see F&M 1994, 213n17). The availability of this analysis within F&M's theory undermines their claim that the ellipsis in this context must preserve α indices on a SELF form as opposed to a pronoun. F&M's claim that there are reflexives that are uniquely α-index bound then reduces, in this case, to the assertion that *himself*, emphatically stressed (F&M 1994, 208n14), is an α-indexed form (as in the object in *The samurai must have slashed himsélf*). I see no compelling reason beyond those internal to their theory to suppose that α-indexed SELF forms exist.

In any case, the elision in (26) does not take *slashed himself* as its antecedent; if it did, F&M's theory would be straightforwardly disconfirmed. Consider (27).

(27) Who slashed those samurai? *Each samurai* must have slashed *himsélf*.
       Clearly the shogun couldn't have.

It appears that the elided portion takes *slashed those samurai* as its antecedent; otherwise, the stressed purported α-occurrence *himself* would not be dependent on *each samurai*, contrary to fact. If the last sentence is slightly odd, it is because the intervening sentence suggests a different VP antecedent (*slashed himself*), but one that clashes with the presuppositions of the question (we are talking about slashed samurai, not slashed shoguns).[9]

Thus, the claim that there are α-indexed anaphors subject to the binding theory is suspect, and along with it, F&M's account of noncoreference induced by the binding theory. I will argue in section 2.3 that there are in fact cases where Principle A is satisfied by an antecedent that the anaphor does not depend on; but the dependencies that hold in those cases would not correspond to α coindexation either, since they are not cases of independent covaluation.[10]

In what follows, I will assume there is no need for a coindexation relation in formal grammar to express (linguistic commitment to) independent covaluation, nor any reason to introduce indices contingent on a c-command relation as in G&R's version of the CLP theory. All that needs to be represented to achieve the proper interpretations is a dependent identity relation, and this relation will be represented henceforth with the arrow notation.

1.3.2 Numeration Indices and Inclusiveness

One argument occasionally invoked for the existence of indices was that movement theory requires indices anyway, thus they can also be used to express coconstrual. With the modern reemergence of the copy theory, the view that indices arise independently from movement operations, and thus are already in the theory, is no longer valid. Chomsky (1995) does propose a new class of indices, numeration indices, which arise as a result of copying, but these indices refer to the number of selections from the lexicon in forming a numeration (the lexical items to be used in a derivation), not to referential properties. Relations of identity posited to hold between copies and what they are copies of arise from the identity of numeration indices matching word for word (not phrase to phrase).

Since I will have a great deal to say in the chapters that follow about how numeration indices are propagated, it is useful to pause here to illustrate what they represent. A minimalist derivation begins with a selection from the lexicon of forms to be used in the derivation. This set of selected forms is called the numeration. Suppose, for example, we are to derive the surface sentence in (28a). If so, we will need the lexical selections in (28b), including two selections of the word *the* and two selections of the word *brown*.

(28) a. A brown dog bit the brown fox in the neck.
   b. the_1, the_2, $brown_3$, $brown_4$, dog_5, $PAST_6$, bit_7, a_8, fox_9, in_{10}, $neck_{11}$

The derivation proceeds by merging one word with another to form a phrase, and then by attaching another word from the numeration to the ones already merged, forming a larger syntactic constituent. A minimalist derivation is complete when every lexical item in the numeration has been used in the derivation (thereby introduced into the syntactic tree structure) and all lexical requirements and features of the lexical items have been satisfied. The numeration indices indicate that the selection of forms is finite, and they permit distinctions between one instance of a form (e.g., *brown*) and another.

Minimalist derivations are ruled by an economy principle or principles, variously stated; but in all accounts, using the same form in a derivation more than once is uneconomical unless it is necessary to satisfy lexical requirements or syntactic features. Thus, in (28), it is also possible to select *the* more than two times in the derivation, but to do so would not be economical, since the third use of *the* would not be some newly indexed form, the_{12}, but a selection of either the_1 or the_2 again. Forms that bear the same numeration index are copies and are indistinct in their syntactic and semantic values, though they may occupy different positions in a syntactic structure and hence participate in distinct structural relations with other forms.

Appealing to a formulation of the movement relation from early versions of syntactic theory, Chomsky (1995) proposes that movement is a copying relation, such that displaced phrases contain copies of the forms in the launching site of movement. For example, consider (29a). (29a) has the numeration shown in (29b), which differs from that for (29c), let us suppose, by virtue of the presence of a topic marker (TOP) that attracts *Tom* to the fronted position.

(29) a. Tom, Bill likes.
   b. Tom_1, $Bill_2$, $PRES_3$, $like_4$, TOP_5
   c. Bill likes Tom.

Let us assume for the purposes of presentation that TOP is a phonologically null lexical item consisting of a feature that must be satisfied. The feature can be satisfied by the presence of an appropriate phrase in the specifier relation to the Top head (e.g., specifier-head agreement or a feature-checking relation). The derivation (simplified for presentation) proceeds as follows:

(30) a. $[like_4\ Tom_1]$
   b. $[PRES_3\ [like_4\ Tom_1]]$
   c. $[Bill_2\ [PRES_3\ [like_4\ Tom_1]]]$
   d. $[TOP_5\ [Bill_2\ [PRES_3\ [like_4\ Tom_1]]]]$
   e. $[Tom_1\ [TOP_5\ [Bill_2\ [PRES_3\ [like_4\ Tom_1]]]]]$

The two copies of *Tom* are necessary, since one satisfies the thematic selection of the verb *like* while the other satisfies the feature of TOP. Which copy is pronounced is a function of which copy is preserved in phonological form (assuming that not all copies are preserved). The copy preserved in LF is semantically interpreted in its structural position (again assuming that not all copies are preserved).

It is clear for cases like (29a), however, that there is no sense in which forms that share the same numeration index are in a relation of referential identity in any sense. The fact that the form Tom_1 in Spec,Top picks out an individual indistinct from Tom_1 in the complement position of *like* is incidental in (30e), since only one of these forms is interpreted at LF; rather, what the common numeration index marks is an identity of forms that could hold as well between adjectives or determiners and their copies arising from movement. These relations will be examined in some detail in chapter 4. What matters at this point is that numeration indices are not referential indices.

Chomsky (1995, 228) suggests further that (referential) indices should be eliminated from syntactic theory entirely as a consequence of his principle of Inclusiveness:

A "perfect language" should meet the condition of inclusiveness: any structure formed by the computation (in particular, [PF and LF]) is constituted of elements already present in the lexical items selected for [the numeration]; no new objects are added in the course of computation apart from rearrangements of lexical properties (in particular, no indices ...) ...

The dependency arrows I propose also would violate Inclusiveness since they represent relations that are not lexical properties and they do not correspond to numeration indices. However, a slightly weaker version of inclusion would permit dependency arrows but still be forceful enough to exclude symmetric indices. Suppose Inclusiveness is considered more as a ban on new individual properties assigned to lexical forms or phrases in the derivation than as a ban on new relations between forms and/or phrases. An index is a property assigned to a head or phrase that could happen to be the same index as that of some other head or phrase, in which case an unwanted (accidental) coincidence of indices could create a commitment to covalued interpretation that is reminiscent of features that happen to match. By contrast, arrows are inherently relational: one end of an arrow has no meaning; hence, it could not accidentally match some other end of an arrow in any meaningful way (as Higginbotham pointed out when he invented them).

An alternative view would be to treat the arrows in the same way that G&R treat indices, that is, as the mere notation of a class of relations, the distribution of which is entirely determined by principled constraints. If so, the arrow notation is nothing more than a convenient presentational description, not itself part of UG. To put it another way, dependent identity, like covaluation, may be a semantic notion that is functionally necessary outside of sentence grammar or, for that matter, outside UG, but only dependent identity is specifically restricted by the nature of natural language. It is a separate question whether the representation of dependent identity must be part of actual representations, rather than just a set of options for relations that the semantics can compute. Only if the notational form of arrows is crucial to the statement of syntactic constraints or principles must we treat them as part of UG. The issue will hover in the background in the chapters that follow, but I know of no compelling evidence that the patterns of dependency I examine require representation with arrows. Rather, I will use the dependency arrows in presentation over indices because the dependencies with syntactic consequences are more precisely represented that way.

1.3.3 Obviation

Once we eliminate indices, hence the notion "binding," Principles B and C must be reformulated, not only to rule out dependency, but also to block covaluation where dependency fails.[11] As an intermediate step (before I reformulate Principles B and C as a single principle in section 1.4), we could assume a binding theory like that of Higginbotham (1985, 572), as in (31).

(31) a. An anaphor is locally linked.
     b. A pronominal is locally obviative.
     c. An r-expression is obviative.

Higginbotham assumes that (31a–c) only hold under c-command by an antecedent. He defines *obviative* as in (32), and he uses *linked* to mean 'connected by the hook end of a dependency arrow'.

(32) If x and y are obviative, then they cannot be determined by the structure in which they occur to share a value.

Principle B as given in (31b) determines that *Jack* and *him* must be "obviative" in (33a), and Principle C determines that *Jack* in object position in both (33a) and (33b) is obviative with respect to the matrix subject *Jack*.

(33) a. *Jack saw *him/Jack*.

     b. *Jack* said that Jacky saw *him/*Jack*.

Notice that obviativity is part of the syntactic binding theory, but not
defined on arrows at all. This appears necessary within the dependency
arrow account to avoid permitting examples like (34a–c) where two elements that must not be coconstrued are not blocked from coconstrual
with a third term.

(34) a. *He said that the woman *he* loves saw *Phil*.

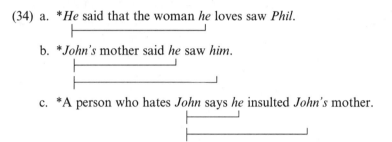

     b. **John's* mother said *he* saw *him*.

     c. *A person who hates *John* says *he* insulted *John's* mother.

In (34a), *Phil* cannot be dependent on the matrix *he* because of Principle
C, but Principle C does not rule out coreference between *Phil* and the
second *he*. In (34b), both *he* and *him* can be dependent on *John*, but *him*
cannot be covalued with *he*. Similarly, dependency of *John's* on *John* is
permitted, as is dependency of *he* on *John* in (34c), but all three cannot be
covalued.[12] Examples (34a–c) illustrate a transitivity problem originally
raised by Lasnik (1976). Lasnik points out for examples like (34a,c) that
it is not enough for Principle C (as Lasnik's noncoreference principle
came to be known) to simply require that the name and its c-commanding
antecedent are not marked coreferent. Elements not marked coreferent by
rule could then "accidentally" happen to have the same referent. Lasnik
concludes that failure of coreference is not strong enough and so for-
mulates his principle to require noncoreference between *he* and *John's*.
This is captured in Higginbotham's system by the force of obviation,
which does not permit x and y, once they are obviative, to share a value;
hence, the transitivity relation is ensured.[13]

     However, examples like those in (35), pointed out by Heim (1993),
show that Higginbotham's theory is too strong, since (35a) is acceptable
under a reading like that in given (36a).

(35) a. *Each female candidate* believes *only she* voted for *her*.

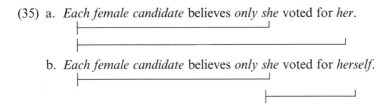

b. *Each female candidate* believes *only she* voted for *herself*.

(36) a. Each x, x a female candidate (x believes (only y (y = x) (y voted for x)))
b. Each x, x a female candidate (x believes (only x (x voted for x)))

The reading that is impossible for (35a) is the one where *her* depends on *she*, which is presumably blocked by Principle B (*she* and *her* should be obviative), but it is indeed possible for *she* and *her* to share a value, both of them depending on *each female candidate* (or its trace at LF), a reading that may be described as "codependent" (and to which I will return in section 2.3). The existence of this codependent reading is part of the reason why I have characterized the empirical force of Principles B and C (for interpretation) to be one of expected noncoreference, which can be overcome when there is a marker of exceptional expectations, such as *only*, or an instantiation context like those discussed earlier.

Notice also that (36b) permits dependency of *herself* on *only she* because the choice of form in (35b), *herself*, does not exclude the dependency in question, but *her* in (35a) cannot support that dependency. We may now ask whether or not failure of dependency and the obviation effect (which I now take to be expectation of noncovaluation) are induced by the same principle, or whether they are distinct effects. Examples like (36a) suggest they are distinct effects, since even where obviativity is overcome by the right sort of adjustment of expectation, dependency of *her* on the subject *only she* is still blocked (an effect noted earlier with respect to ellipsis).

Suppose we separate the obviation effect and the blocked dependency effect by treating them separately, as in (37) and (38), now explicitly incorporating c-command since it is no longer folded into binding.

(37) a. *Principle A*
An anaphor is locally linked to a c-commanding antecedent.
b. *Principle B*
A pronominal cannot be locally linked to a c-commanding antecedent.

c. *Principle C*
An r-expression cannot be linked to a c-commanding antecedent.

(38) a. If a pronoun x cannot be linked to y by Principle B, then x and
y are obviative.

b. If an r-expression x cannot be linked to y by Principle C, then x
and y are obviative.

Even if obviativity can be neutralized when coreference is contrary to expectation, (37) ensures that blocked dependency cannot be so neutralized.

There is much to be suspicious of in (37) and (38), particularly (a) the separate appeals to c-command in (37a–c), which are the residue of what was formerly folded into "binding" based on indexing and (b) the separate injunctions in (38a,b) necessary to connect both Principles B and C to the obviativity effect. The latter inelegance dates back to the binding theory itself, insofar as the noncoreference enforced by that theory treats Principles B and C as separate. It is time to eliminate the need to posit distinct Principles B and C.

1.4   The Form-to-Interpretation Principle and Pragmatic Obviation

I have just concluded that Principles B and C feed obviation in the same way, which suggests that the two principles can be unified. In this section, I briefly introduce a theory I defend in Safir 2004, which reduces Principles B and C to the outcome of a competition between more and less dependent forms. However, the main purpose of introducing my competition theory is to distinguish its effects more thoroughly from those induced by the INP, which returns as our primary focus in chapter 2.

The elimination of a distinct Principle B would be desirable for a number of reasons, besides the general scientific desideratum of eliminating unneeded principles. Conceptually, Principle B has always had a rather odd status, in that it singles out as a lexical class a set of forms that are specified for an environment where they cannot occur. Normally pronouns can pick up antecedents in the sentence or not (unless they are also anaphors susceptible to Principle A). It seems similarly odd to say of r-expressions that they have a lexical property of being specified for an environment where they cannot occur (where they would have a c-commanding antecedent). It is further suspicious that pronouns are excluded in exactly those environments where anaphors are available; that is, they are in complementary distribution, at least for the most part.

The complementary distribution of pronouns and anaphors was en-shrined in the binding theory (and crucial to the PRO Theorem, aban-doned by most linguists since the early 1990s; see Chomsky and Lasnik 1995). Yet the binding theory achieved that complementarity by pro-posing separate statements for Principles A and B, rendering largely ac-cidental the fact that the domains in which they apply overlap. Indeed, C.-T. J. Huang (1983) exploits the accidental enforcement of comple-mentarity in the *LGB* binding theory by assigning different domains for Principles A and B in order to account for cases where complementarity appears to break down.

By contrast, some have argued that the complementarity between pro-nouns and anaphors, on the one hand, and between pronouns and names, on the other, is absolute under the right interpretation of the data and have proposed that the complementarity effect should be derived. Most typically, it is proposed that Principle B effects should be derived from the distribution of Principle A effects. In other words, pronouns are ex-cluded where anaphors are available, and, at least where the antecedent c-commands, r-expressions are excluded where pronouns are available.

Among the various derived complementarity theories that have been proposed, those put forth by Hellan (1988), Burzio (1989, 1991, 1996), Levinson (1987, 1991), and Y. Huang (1991, 1994) have been developed in some detail. Burzio's approach treats the complementarity effect as determined by a syntactic theory of competition, and in this respect it is the immediate ancestor of mine, as opposed to proposals based on pragmatic principles developed from Gricean maxims, such as those of Levinson and Y. Huang. Reinhart's (1983a) proposal that names are excluded where a c-commanded bound variable pronoun is possible is another ancestor, though her theory is based on the CLP, which I reject, as well as some assumptions about the role of pragmatic strategies that I also reject (for reasons related to the primary reason I reject the Gricean-maxim-based proposals). I will not review here my reasons for formulating my approach in terms different from these antecedents; for details, see Safir 2004, where I also defend my contention that comple-mentary distribution between anaphors and pronouns and between pro-nouns and names holds empirically, once apparent deviance from this norm is understood in the proper light.[14]

The essential idea behind my version of the derived complementarity approach is that dependent readings with c-commanding antecedents are only possible if the form that is used to achieve the dependent reading is the "most dependent form available" in a given context. A form is available if the lexicon contains it and nothing prevents it from occurring in a given position. From this perspective, consider the operation of Principle A, which I reformulate within my approach as *Local Antecedent Licensing* (LAL). (I will not explore the details of domain D here as they will not affect my later reasoning—most standard versions of the domain for Principle A of the binding theory will do.)

(39) *Local Antecedent Licensing (LAL) (provisional)*
      An anaphor must be anteceded in domain D.

(40) *Most dependent hierarchy*
      Anaphor > pronoun > r-expression

If a given form, such as an English pronoun-SELF form, is an anaphor, then it is always more dependent than either a pronoun or a name, as indicated in the dependency hierarchy assumed in (40). However, since I do not assume Principle B, both pronouns and anaphors are available in the local domain; but in that domain, a pronoun will always lose to an anaphor in the competition to represent the dependent reading. Similarly, where both pronouns and r-expressions are available, a pronoun will always win the competition to represent the dependent reading. The principle that rules this competition is the Form-to-Interpretation Principle.

(41) *Form-to-Interpretation Principle (FTIP)*
      If x c-commands y and z is not the most dependent form available in position y with respect to x, then y cannot be directly dependent on x.

One of the advantages of the FTIP is that it reduces Principles B and C to a single principle. There is now no lexical statement about where otherwise independent forms cannot appear; rather, it is just a question of whether or not a form has lost the competition on the most-dependent scale to represent the dependent identity interpretation. The obviation effect can now be directly keyed to the output of the FTIP.

(42) *Pragmatic Obviation*
      If the FTIP does not permit y to be interpreted as directly
      dependent on x, then x and y form an obviative pair.

Notice that in this formulation, Pragmatic Obviation simply characterizes a relation between two nominals without determining their structural relation to one another. The structural relation is entirely expressed by the

FTIP, which only identifies which nominal is blocked from depending on which other, and it is only this relation that Pragmatic Obviation enhances. Thus, the c-command effect on coreference is indirect since Pragmatic Obviation makes no direct appeal to syntactic structure.

This division of labor permits Pragmatic Obviation to be overcome where unexpected coreference is focused, while the effect of the syntactic constraint is not; blocked dependency is impervious to any accommodating pragmatic factor. This is worth illustrating again. As Lasnik (1976) has pointed out, epithets can be used as bound variables, but they are still sensitive to his c-command restriction.

(43) a. *Every bastard's* mother thinks *the bastard* is crazy.
     b. **Every bastard* thinks *the bastard* is crazy.

(44) a. **Every bastard* raised *the bastard's* hand.
     b. Every bastard raised a bastard's hand.

In (43a), the bound variable interpretation succeeds because the quantified expression does not c-command it from an A-position, in contrast to (43b), which can only succeed with a bound reading if *the bastard* is replaced by a more dependent form, namely, the pronoun *he*.[15] Example (44a) shows, just like (43b), that *the bastard* does not permit a bound reading, even in a context that heavily favors a gestural interpretation, such that the hand in question might be expected to be the one that belongs to the bastard who raises it. Rather, the gestural reading that expresses the sort of accidental correlation of hands and bastards is achieved with the use of the indefinite, *a bastard's hand*, in (44b). A more natural bound reading for (44b) is only achieved where *his* replaces *a bastard's*.

The competitive approach has a wide variety of other advantages, some of them pointed out as support for some of the ancestors to my theory (as cited above). For example, it follows from the FTIP that no language that has antisubject orientation for pronouns fails to have subject orientation for anaphors in the same positions. Moreover, anaphors can compete against each other on the most-dependent scale, and if so, an anaphor that cannot be anteceded locally (because another anaphoric competitor is available) may still outcompete pronouns and names in a wider anaphoric domain; this explains why some anaphors have a locality gap in their distribution (i.e., it is unnecessary to say of these forms that they act like pronouns in one domain and like anaphors in a wider one). Thus, differences in the inventory of potentially dependent forms in a language can result in different patterns, even though the principle determining their distribution, the FTIP, is invariant and universal. Quite a few other results are explored in Safir 2004.

Let's consider more concretely now how FTIP competitions are constructed. In (45a), for example, a reflexive pronoun is available (would be licensed by LAL) and so it wins over *him* and *Larry*. In (45b), *himself* is not available because it would not be licensed by LAL, so the only competitors are *him* and *Larry* and *him* wins. *Larry* cannot support the dependent reading and will be marked obviative with respect to *he* by Pragmatic Obviation.

(45) a. *Larry* loves *himself/*him/*Larry*.
    b. *He* says Malva loves **himself/him/*Larry*.

Cases like (45a), for example, where the matrix subject is marked as part of an obviative pair with either *Larry* or *him*, disguise a second effect, an INP effect, that I will distinguish later. After all, nothing in the FTIP precludes dependency of the matrix subject on *himself/him/Larry*. As we will see, the INP does ensure that the subject could not be anteceded by its c-commandees, but failure of a dependency relation under the INP, unlike under the FTIP, does not feed Pragmatic Obviation. If it did, then the only successful competitor in (45b), the lower pronoun *him*, would also be marked obviative with *he* (because dependency of *him* on *he* would fail, even if the opposite dependency can succeed). This would be the wrong result (a matter I will return to from time to time).

The notion of obviative pairs proposed here does involve a kind of relational recordkeeping that is presumably added to recordkeeping in a discourse, as in any theory of discourse tracking.[16] I am assuming that if x is obviative with y and y is covalued with z, then x is obviative with z. Since obviativity is a relation, not an inherent property (like a referential index), marking it would be consistent with the reinterpretation of Inclusiveness suggested in section 1.3.2; but there is no obvious reason to suppose that this sort of recordkeeping is any part of syntactic representation. I know of no syntactic condition that refers to the obviativity relation; moreover, such relations seem to be necessary external to grammar, unless one assumes that all presupposition of identity (or the lack of it) is linguistic, a view that few if any would support.

This presentation of the intuitive idea behind the FTIP competition approach will do for what I have to say in later chapters, and so I will not argue further for it here. Interested readers can explore the FTIP and its effects in Safir 2004.

However, what will be important in later chapters is that the FTIP effect can be neutralized in certain contexts by a mechanism that also has (indirect) consequences for the INP. The exact nature of these cases I take up in chapter 4, but the neutralization mechanism deserves discussion here. As F&M (1994) note, examples like (46) permit coconstrual between *Orville* and the object of the elided verb *praise* in the second conjunct.

(46) a. Ollie expects that the boss will talk to *Orville*, but *Orville* hopes she won't [talk to *Orville*]

   b. We knew the boss would fire *Orville*, but *Orville* didn't [know the boss would fire *Orville*]

If the material in brackets is reconstructed with the name in strict parallel fashion, then Principle C will predict (46a,b) to be ill formed, and so would the FTIP. F&M propose that in contexts of ellipsis, parallelism can be relaxed in the following sense: names can undergo so-called vehicle change to become pronouns, in which case, Principle C will not apply in (46a) and (46b). As F&M observe, vehicle change does not neutralize Principle B, since a pronoun is still a pronoun even if it undergoes vehicle change (see F&M 1994, 222).

(47) *Malva aggravates *him/Nigel*, but *Nigel* doesn't [aggravate *him/ Nigel*]

Here a pronoun copied or vehicle-changed in the second conjunct does not improve its acceptability.

Consider how the difference between (46a,b) and (47) plays out with respect to the FTIP. Suppose that the second conjunct, though unpronounced, has exactly the same lexical selection (a fairly strict notion of structural parallelism) as the first conjunct except that in the second conjunct, pronouns are always available in lieu of exactly matched nominals from corresponding positions in the first conjunct. Since a pronoun is always possible in the second conjunct, there is no more dependent form than a pronoun that could have been selected for cases like (46a,b), and so the object of *talk to* or *fire* in the second conjunct is not obviative with the c-commanding *Orville*. In (47), once again a pronoun is a possible alternative for the elided object of *aggravate*, but the most dependent form in that position for that clause would be a reflexive, and that is not available for the second clause—only *Nigel* or the vehicle-changed pronoun is. Thus, neither *Nigel* nor the pronoun *him* is the most dependent form with respect to the subject *Nigel*, and the result is obviation in (47).

Now consider that parallelism can also apply to overt conjuncts (e.g., see Chomsky and Lasnik 1995, 125). With parallelism forced on overt conjuncts, as in (48a), there is no vehicle-changed option, as there is in (48b), to submit to the FTIP competition; thus, the FTIP rules that the last *John* is obviative with the second one, since a competing numeration with a pronoun in place of the name was not selected.[17]

(48) a. *Mary loves *John* and *John* admits she loves *John*, too.
      b.   Mary loves *John* and *John* admits she does [love *him*], too

I am not assuming, however, that vehicle change can provide an alternative nominal other than a simple pronoun. If a reflexive could replace a pronoun in (47), then we would predict, contrary to fact, that (47) would be acceptable with *aggravate* understood reflexively with respect to the subject *Nigel*. On the other hand, a reflexive can be vehicle-changed to a pronoun. The strict reading in (49) illustrates this possibility.

(49) Lyndon has managed to praise himself more than any of his aides could (have)

In this case, vehicle change permits the object of elided *praise* to fail to be dependent on *his aides* (though, as explained in section 2.1, the elided object must still be dependent on whatever antecedes *himself*).

The FTIP will play only a supporting role in the main lines of argument for chapters 2 and 3, but the role it plays is part of what distinguishes my approach, as the discussion in those chapters will show. Moreover, it is important to keep in mind that while the FTIP triggers Pragmatic Obviation, the INP does not. In other words, I contend that failure of dependent identity cannot be taken *generally* to establish an expectation of noncoreference, especially once it is clear that the CLP cannot be maintained. As we will see, the distinction between cases where failure of dependent reference results in obviation and cases where it does not has a variety of interesting consequences.

Chapter 2

The Distribution of Dependency

In chapter 1, I sketched what an argument distinguishing the INP from the CLP as a theory of bound readings would look like. According to that sketch, the INP should permit x to depend on y even if y does not c-command x, whereas the CLP is more restrictive in that it permits x to depend on y only if y c-commands x. This difference can be illustrated with the examples in (1). The CLP permits only (1a) and (1d). The INP permits all but (1f).

(1) a. *Everyone* loves *his* mother.

    b. *Everyone's* mother loves *him*. *CLP*

    c. *His* mother loves *Bill*. *CLP

    d. *He* says that Angie loves *him*.

    e. Egil loves *Freya*. Ketil loves *her* too. *CLP

    f. *He* says that Angie loves *him*. *CLP, *INP

In this chapter, I will focus on all the cases where the INP and CLP diverge, as well as (1f), where they appear to coincide. In section 2.1, for example, I argue that we must assume that dependent readings can span sentences, as illustrated in (1e), which the CLP does not allow; and in section 2.2, I argue that a pronoun can depend on an intrasentential non-c-commanding antecedent, as in (1b), which the CLP also rejects. In section 2.5, I argue that the INP should also exclude (1c), as the CLP does, under a plausible extension that plays an important role in chapters 4 and 5.

With respect to intersentential linking, I argue in section 2.1 that it is generally possible, but that its effects are obscured because many standard tests for bound readings are frustrated by independent limitations. For example, many of the arguments supporting one or another theory of the distribution of dependent readings have relied on quantified examples to ensure that the readings involved are in fact dependent. However, quantifier-bound readings are limited by the Scope Condition (see, e.g., Safir 1984, 626).

(2) *Scope Condition*
     A pronoun α dependent on a quantifier β must be in the scope of β.

In light of the Scope Condition, we can distinguish (3a,b).

(3) a. *His mother's statement suggests that Althea might have attacked *every student*.
     b. *His* mother's statement suggests that Althea might have attacked *Carl*.

The fact that *his* cannot depend on *every student* in (3a) plausibly results from the fact that *every student* cannot take scope over the pronoun, a fact we can express as the general clause-boundedness of QR, roughly speaking. We can verify this by considering (4), which does not permit a reading where *every student* takes wide scope (i.e., 'Every student is such that there is a statement suggesting that Althea might have attacked that student', in which case as many statements are involved as there are students, rather than a narrow scope scenario for the universal in which a single statement implicates Althea in all the attacks).

(4) Some statement suggests that Althea might have attacked every student.

Thus, whatever the status of (3b) with respect to dependency of the pronoun, the Scope Condition distinguishes between cases like (3a) and (3b) by requiring that a pronoun fall within the scope of the quantifier that it is dependent on, a condition that does not apply to names insofar as they cannot be construed as bound variables. I will now assume that intrasentential scope is consistently determined by (5). Both the Scope Condition in (2) and the syntactic instantiation of scope in (5) have long been widely assumed in the literature under a variety of names.

(5) *Scope*

The scope of a sentence-bound quantifier includes only what it c-commands at LF.

While (5) states a crucial part of the syntactic contribution to scope interpretation, it is very likely that the Scope Condition is not a principle of syntax, but a consequence of any reasonable theory of compositional semantics, since it is difficult to conceive how a pronoun outside the scope of a quantifier could be interpreted as a bound variable of that quantifier. Given that most quantification scope is limited by sentence grammar, we must expect forms or traces dependent on quantifiers to be limited in the same way. This is true whether one believes in LF movement of quantifiers (feeding (5)) or not.[1]

The most obvious differences between the CLP and the INP are that the INP permits (a) dependency on an extrasentential antecedent and (b) dependency on a non-c-commanding intrasentential antecedent. Sections 2.1 and 2.2 provide evidence for these claims. Section 2.3 explores some cases of codependency, where the choice of c-commanding antecedent, when there is one, plays an important role. The result of the analysis in section 2.3 supports the results of the first two sections. Cases like (1f), where the CLP and the INP overlap in ruling out the dependency, are also commonly understood as involving Principle C effects. Section 2.4 addresses cases where the INP and the FTIP overlap (the context of Principle C effects) and shows that the principles have distinguishable effects. Section 2.5 reevaluates the assumption that the INP would permit the dependency in (1c), arguing that a plausible extension of the INP should block it. The patterns of dependency permitted by the INP, summarized in section 2.6, will then be shown in chapters 3 and 4 to derive crossover effects without further revision.

2.1 Extrasentential Dependency

As just established, even if pronouns can depend on extrasentential antecedents, we cannot generally expect to find cases where the dependent pronoun is in the scope of a quantifier, since quantifier scope is essentially sentence bound. Thus, if we are to make a case that a pronoun can formally depend on an extrasentential antecedent, then we must examine dependency relations that do not involve quantification.

As noted in chapter 1, and as is well known, ellipsis constructions permit strict and sloppy readings. Moreover, sloppy readings do not have be parallel to quantificationally anteceded dependencies. This is illustrated in (6), drawn from section 1.2.

(6) Mara believes Sean loves her and Sheila does too.
    a. Sheila believes that Sean loves her=Sheila.
    b. Sheila believes that Sean loves Mara.

What is also well known, though much less discussed, is that if *Mara* and *her* are coconstrued in the first conjunct, there is no reading of (6) whereby Sean loves someone other than Mara or Sheila. This restriction is just as strong if there is no ellipsis, as in (7).[2]

(7) Mara believes Sean loves her and Sheila believes Sean loves her.

This restriction is characterized in the literature as a parallelism requirement, insofar as the first conjunct is a model that must be mirrored by the second conjunct, both with respect to structure (which I will not discuss) and with respect to interpretation.

Although any discussion of ellipsis assumes some account of parallelism, the way that parallelism of interpretation is enforced is not always explicitly discussed. However, Fiengo and May (1994) do provide a fairly explicit account. They employ their double index system, which, as discussed in chapter 1, involves two sorts of coindexation. Their α coindexation represents symmetric coreference (covaluation), and their β coindexation represents dependent coreference. If one phrase or sentence (x) is parallel to another (y), then x must be parallel with respect to one form of coindexation on the corresponding nominals in y. Then x can achieve parallelism by matching the dependency index in y, hence copying the pattern of dependency for y, or else parallelism is achieved by matching the covaluation index. In this very explicit way, a third party reading is ruled out, since it would involve an indexation that does not satisfy parallelism.

I have argued, however, against the existence of indices and in particular against the existence of the covaluation index as an unnecessary device that predicts the existence of nonexistent forms of anaphora (e.g., covaluation-bound, as opposed to dependent-bound, syntactic anaphors).[3] However, in a theory that has no indices and only represents dependencies, the exact device that represents parallelism of interpretation then becomes mysterious. (The same problem arises for theories

employing indices that do not distinguish bound and coreferent readings.)
Put another way, if coreference, as opposed to dependency, is not marked
in the grammar, how do we ensure coreference for the strict reading
without also allowing some third party reading?

The answer is that the dependency relation is all we need, once we
abandon the CLP and permit dependency relations to hold across sentences. For example, it is possible in my system for *her* in the second
conjunct of (6), whether it is null or overt, to depend on *her* in the first
conjunct even though the dependency arrow between *Mara* and *her* in the
first conjunct is not copied. In other words, what must be required of the
strict reading is that the second conjunct pronoun find an antecedent to
depend on in the first conjunct that is structurally parallel, or find a dependency that is parallel. Thus, (8a) is the reconstructed (filled-in ellipsis)
strict reading for (7), where the second pronoun depends on the first, and
(8b) is the reconstructed sloppy one, where only the dependency arrow is
copied to achieve parallelism.

(8) a. *Mara* believes Sean loves *her* and Sheila believes Sean loves *her*.

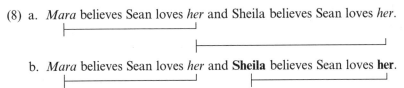

     b. *Mara* believes Sean loves *her* and **Sheila** believes Sean loves **her**.

It does not matter if *her* in conjunct 1 is covalued with *Mara* by virtue of
dependency or not, as long as covaluation of *her* with *Mara* in conjunct 1
is achieved. All that parallelism must say is then familiar: the pronouns in
conjunct 2 must achieve their values by virtue of either (a) copying the
same dependencies as those in conjunct 1, or (b) depending on the same
value as the parallel position in conjunct 1. For the strict reading in
ellipsis cases, depending on an antecedent in a structurally parallel position is not really distinct from dependent identity generally, except for the
structural condition imposed by parallelism, which any indexing theory
would also require.[4]

We can now extend this reasoning as follows. It is not possible for (9)
to mean that for every x, x a boy, x loves x's mother and for every y, y a
husband, y loves x's mother. For such an interpretation to be possible,
the Scope Condition requires that *every* of the first conjunct would have
to take scope over the ellipsis site containing the pronoun, yet no such
scope holds across a sentence conjunction.

(9) Every boy loves his mother and every husband does too.

Thus, (9) has only a sloppy reading. If I did not assume the Scope Condition, nothing would block the reading I have just ruled out, given that my account allows dependency without c-command.

In short, since dependency on an antecedent does not require a c-commanding antecedent in the theory proposed here, there is no need to appeal to coindexation to prevent third party readings in ellipsis contexts; rather, parallelism generally requires dependency on an elided pronoun for the strict reading. This provides support for the view that indices used to represent coconstrual can be eliminated from syntactic representations as too powerful and unnecessary.

The proposal that both strict and sloppy readings in ellipsis contexts arise from dependent identity relations also solves a problem facing accounts that presume, as Grodzinsky and Reinhart's (1993) does, that bound readings are the favored way to express covaluation unless there is some reason to avoid a dependent reading (see also Safir 2004, sec. 2.2, for related discussion). In coindexing accounts of ellipsis, the difference between sloppy and strict readings has often been discussed as a difference between bound and covalued readings, respectively. In cases like (10), where *him* could be coconstrued with *Jens* or not, the covalued reading must be a bound reading, by this reasoning, because there is no semantic difference between the readings in this example.

(10) a. *Jens* thinks that Martha loves *him*.
    b. *Jens* thinks that Martha loves *him* and Nils does too.

Covaluation without the bound coconstrual should be contrary to expectation and marked as such, yet for examples like (10b), both strict and sloppy readings are completely unmarked. The use of *Jens* in the first conjunct in place of *him*, presumably with added stress, would require a strict interpretation of the ellipsis, since the parallel dependent interpretation would be blocked by the FTIP (although stress would overcome the expectation of noncoreference). However, the strict interpretation is optionally available even when a bound interpretation is *required* by the assumption that the bound interpretation is always favored. In other words, it is not obvious how Grodzinsky and Reinhart's account ever permits the strict interpretation for (10b) if *Jens* and *him* are coconstrued.

By contrast, the assumption that ellipsis contexts always require a bound reading, or in my account, a dependent identity one, involves no appeal to covaluation at all. For both the strict and sloppy readings of (10b), the elided pronoun is dependent on its antecedent, whether it be *Nils* for the sloppy reading or *Jens* for the strict one.

2.2   Dependency on an Intrasentential Non-c-commanding Antecedent

In this section, I establish that pronouns can depend on non-c-commanding antecedents to yield bound readings even where quantification is absent. By contrast, Reinhart (1983a,b) and Grodzinsky and Reinhart (1993, 74) have argued that an antecedent must c-command a pronoun dependent on it even if the antecedent is not quantified, appealing to examples like (11) and (12).[5]

(11) Most of *her* friends adore *Lucie* and Zelda too.
    a. Lucie's friends adore Zelda.
    b. *Not:* Zelda's friends adore Zelda. (Zelda (λx (x's friends adore x)))

(12) A party without *Lucie* annoys *her* and a party without Zelda (would) too.
    Only: A party without Zelda annoys Lucie.

What is less generally noted, or at least not as often exploited, is that although ellipsis fails with some almost c-command cases under the bound reading, it succeeds, or nearly so, with others. For example, almost all speakers accept (13a) with a sloppy reading and many find the sloppy reading for (13b) acceptable (whereby many Chicagoans love its weather), though most find it marginal to some degree.[6]

(13) a. *Bob's* mother loves *him* but I doubt that Bill's mother does.
    b. Many people in Miami love its weather, but I doubt that many people in Chicago do.

However, I have not found a speaker who does not accept (14a) (if *him* in the first disjunct is coconstrued with *everyone's*), probably because the quantification introduced by *no one* requires a bound reading (under coconstrual with the first disjunct) if the sentence is to be acceptable at all.

(14) a. *Everyone's* mother loves *him* but no one's lawyer does.
    b. Someone in *every northern city* loves *its* weather, but I doubt anyone in Houston does.

I assume here, as most theorists do, that *no one* takes scope over the second disjunct somehow. Speakers are less consistent about the acceptability of (14b), assigning it perhaps a question mark under the sloppy reading. Thus, I take the data in (11) and (12) to be misleading, concluding instead on the basis of (13) and (14) that a pronoun can be dependent on an antecedent that does not c-command it and that the INP makes better predictions about the contexts where dependent identity is blocked.[7]

Of course, cases like (14) are actually just elaborations of the almost c-command counterexamples to the CLP raised in section 1.1. All of those cases involved quantificational antecedents, and the suggestion advanced then was that QR at LF might put the possessor quantifier in a position to c-command a pronoun in object position. Under the analysis proposed here, the position of the quantifier at LF determines its scope, but the pronoun is dependent on the trace of QR in the possessor position. The reason I assume that the dependency relation is established from the position of the trace is that scopal c-command is not at issue for cases like (13a,b) since there is no scope-taking element, yet a dependent interpretation succeeds just the same.

With these considerations in mind, consider Hardt's (1999) suggestion that the antecedent of a pronoun in an elided VP can sometimes be found outside the VP it is in a parallelism relation with. For example, Hardt argues that the pronoun in the elided VP in (15) can be understood to be *Harry*, even though the referential value for the pronoun in the VP (*help him*) that the elided VP is dependent on is *Tom*.

(15) If Tom was having trouble in school, I would help him. If Harry was having trouble in school, I wouldn't.

Hardt discusses this case in terms of reference to a shifted "discourse center," a notion that still must ensure that no third party reading can arise (someone other than *Tom* or *Harry*), but I believe it is better understood as a form of sloppy identity. A sloppy reading arises here because parallelism includes the conditional, and there is a bound reading relationship between *Tom* and *him*, enabled by the conditional, that is copied onto the elided VP in the *Harry* sentence. To see why (15) is not really about a shift in discourse center, compare (16), where there is no conditional, but there is presumably a shift in discourse center.

(16) Tom is having trouble in school. Elaine will help him.
    a.   Now you say Harry is having trouble in school. #Elaine won't.
    b.   #Now you say Harry is having trouble in school, but in his case, Elaine won't.

Even in (16b), where the relevance of the relevant parallel VP is helped along, the ellipsis fails with *Harry* as the antecedent of the elided pronoun. Thus, it appears that the conditional provides a crucial scopal effect that permits the bound variable (sloppy) reading in (15), even though *Tom* is not a quantifier and does not c-command *him*. The assumption that there is a bound reading between *Tom* and *him* in (15) is only possible, however, in a theory that does not assume that a bound reading requires a c-commanding antecedent. In other words, the CLP theory would not permit this analysis, but the INP theory correctly does.

2.3 Preferred Dependent Interpretations and Rule H

There are certain contexts where more than one way of achieving co-construal is available, yet dependent identity interpretations of one sort or another appear to be the preferred means of capturing them. To show what is at stake, I begin by addressing some nondependent, or at least *codependent*, instances of anaphora.

2.3.1 Codependency
In Safir 2004, sec. 4.1, I point out that LAL enforces a more subtle antecedency restriction than is usually assumed.

(17) *Local Antecedent Licensing (LAL)*
   An anaphor must be c-anteceded in domain D.

(18) x *c-antecedes* y if x covaries with y and x c-commands y.

The notion "c-antecede" will surely seem odd, as it is not stated on dependency relations or even covaluation, though the relation may also be understood as *codependency* of two terms on a third (as will become clear). Let us consider the sorts of cases that motivate this formulation.

   Recall our discussion of instantiation contexts, that is, ones where the expectation of noncoreference is suspended. For instance, in example (13) from chapter 1, Oscar's incompetence is something that even he recognizes, which is to say that even someone who would not be expected to have this belief nonetheless has this belief. The expectation of noncoreference is overcome in the same fashion in the following cases:

(19) a. Everyone expects O.J. to be acquitted.
      Bill expects him to be acquitted.
      Sarah expects him to be acquitted.
      . . .
   b. Even O.J. expects O.J. to be acquitted.

In (19b), we are adding O.J. to the list of those who have this belief about O.J. In the manner of reasoning proposed here, this means that the referential value of the embedded *O.J.* is determined without dependence on *even O.J.* because the FTIP would rule out a dependent interpretation. By this same reasoning, we are forced to consider (20) as a case where *himself* does not depend on *O.J.*[8]

(20) Even O.J. expects himself to be acquitted.

In other words, in (20) *himself* must permit a reading independent of *even O.J.*, adding even O.J. to the list of people who think O.J. will be acquitted. Notice that *himself* cannot be anteceded by something that does not c-command it, and so (20) could not be followed by (21).

(21) *Why, even his wife's sister expects himself to be acquitted.

This, then, is part of my reasoning for stating the restriction on syntactic anaphors, LAL, on c-antecedency rather than on local dependent identity, since the latter relation clearly is too restrictive to permit *himself* to be construed as it is in (20).[9]

There is, of course, a locally dependent interpretation for (20), but it would be deviant following the discourse established by (19a). By contrast, the use of *himself* is required in (22b) given the preceding discourse in (22a), since the locally dependent relationship (expecting it of oneself that one will be acquitted) is the criterion of set membership.

(22) a. Everyone expects himself to be acquitted.
   b. Even O.J. expects himself/*him/*O.J. to be acquitted.

The relationships may be represented with dependency arrows as in (23a,b), where (23a) corresponds to the codependent reading in (20) and (23b) corresponds to the locally dependent reading in (22b).

(23) a. Everyone expects *O.J.* ... *Even O.J.* expects *himself* to be
      acquitted.

```
       |————————|
   |———————————————————|
```

   b. *Even O.J.* expects *himself* to be acquitted.
```
   |———————————————|
```

The representation in (23a) treats *even O.J.* as potentially dependent on an earlier mention of *O.J.* This may seem odd, but I assume that names, like definite descriptions, are potential dependents (when they are familiar), though not potential variables. This claim is not crucial for the line of argument in this case, however, as *even he* in place of *even O.J.* in (19b) and (20) will have the same effect.

It is perhaps now clearer what is at stake in cases of coconstrual that are not cases of direct dependence. Notice that in isolation, (20) would apparently always be understood in the same manner as (22b) (i.e., as in (23b)), not necessarily implicating any previous mention that is somehow missing in the discourse. It appears necessary to say that local dependency is always preferred over the more distant kind, where there is no intervention from quantifiers or markers that adjust expectations in the manner described.

The latter proposal brings to mind that of Reinhart (1999) (a descendant of a view that extends back to Reinhart 1983b, including Grodzinsky and Reinhart 1993) that binding is always the preferred way of representing covaluation unless one has reason to avoid the bound reading. I have objected to this because that system, relying on the CLP, assumes that bound readings are always conditioned by c-command—a false assumption, as my account of the distribution of bound readings under ellipsis helps to establish. In addition, where dependency fails and c-command does not hold, obviation in the manner of Principle B or C effects is not the result.

For the cases we are examining now, where a syntactic anaphor requires a local c-commanding antecedent, preference for a local dependency over a more distant one requires no statement about covaluation that is not already part of LAL, nor does it require any notion of c-command, although it is not clear how the locality preference is computed without c-command. This suggests that the preference for local dependent identity relations may indeed be conditioned by c-command, though the relation in question is probably not conditioned by covaluation at all.

Some evidence that bears on the latter view is presented by Fox (1998, 2000), building on work by Heim (1993). Fox argues that UG contains a rule that favors local dependencies, and hence chained dependency in cases like (24a), over multiple direct dependency, as in (24b), when there is no semantic distinction between (24a,b) for both *he* and *his* dependent on *John*.

(24) *John* said that *he* liked *his* mother.
    a. *John* said that *he* liked *his* mother.

b. *John* said that *he* liked *his* mother.
```
|————————————|
|——————————————————|
```

The preference for the representation in (24a) results from what Fox (1998, 129) calls Rule H, which he states as in (25), where his traditional use of *binding* means c-command and coindexing.

(25) *Rule H*

A variable, x, cannot be bound by an antecedent, α, in cases where a more local antecedent, β, could bind x and yield the same semantic interpretation.

Rule H requires that (24) have the chained dependency interpretation represented by (24a) since direct dependency of *his* on *John* in (24b) would not yield a distinct interpretation.

The pattern of dependency in (24b) can be well formed (for most speakers), as in (26a) (see (23a)), which contrasts with (26b) (these examples based on similar ones discussed by Heim (1993), Reinhart (1997), and Fox (2000, 125)).

(26) a. *Every woman* thought that *only she* voted for *her*.

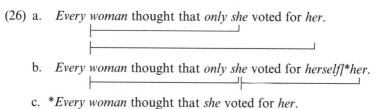

b. *Every woman* thought that *only she* voted for *herself/*her*.

c. *Every woman* thought that *she* voted for *her*.

The result we want is that (26a) should be permitted with obviation between *only she* and *her* that is overcome by the expectation-adjusting marker *only*, such that *her* does not depend on *only she*, but can depend on *every woman*. In (26b), the most dependent form available, *herself*, can be dependent on its coargument subject, and *herself* is not excluded by LAL. Thus, use of *her* for the most local dependent interpretation is obviated in (26b), since nothing semantically distinct from the locally bound interpretation is implicated. All of these relations of expected non-coreference arise from dependencies blocked by the FTIP, and Rule H is not responsible for deriving them. Moreover, Rule H does not apply to exclude (26a), because *only* introduces an element (quantificational in Heim 1993 and Reinhart 1997) that distinguishes the interpretations in (26a), (26b), and (26c).[10]

So far, the only representation that I have claimed Rule H would block is the one in (24b), and this does not appear to have any empirical effect on interpretation. In cases like (26a), the same sort of representation is permitted because the failure of local dependency is signaled by the quantifier. However, one clear empirical effect that Rule H can be recruited to explain is the fact that (20) must be interpreted as in (23b) when it occurs in isolation. Consider (27), where it is possible for *only she* to antecede a SELF form even where the latter is nonlocally dependent.

(27) a. *Every senator* claimed that *only she* expected *herself* to win.
   b. *Every senator* claimed that everyone except *her* thought *she* would lose.
   c. *Every senator* claimed that no other senator expected to win.

It is possible for (27a) to permit either of the entailments in (27b) and (27c) (but not both at once). Insofar as (27b) is a possible entailment of (27a), antecedency by *only she* of *herself* in exceptional Case-marking environments seems to satisfy LAL without forcing the locally bound reading.[11]

In cases like (28), by contrast, where no expectation-modifying marker is included (i.e., where *she* is not focused by stress or intonation), if there is a representational difference between (28a) and (28b), there does not appear to be any empirical difference in interpretation. Rule H predicts that (28b) is not possible, since *she* is a more local c-commander that could be the source of a bound reading.

(28) *Every senator* claimed that *she* expected *herself* to win.
   a. *Every senator* claimed that *she* expected *herself* to win.

   b. *Every senator* claimed that *she* expected *herself* to win.

The argumentation to follow will verify that the interpretation of (28) must arise from the relationships represented in (28a), not those in (28b).

2.3.2 Rule H and Ellipsis

Fox (2000) concludes that (24) and (28) must be represented by (24a) and (28a), respectively, and not by (24b) and (28b), respectively, on the basis of a famous anaphora puzzle, originally discovered by Dahl (1974) (for additional references, see Fox 2000, 113n4). This puzzle is posed by the set of coconstrual interpretations that are allowed for the elided portion of (29) in (29a–d) (from Fox 1998, 130), where *John, he,* and *his* are coconstrued in the first conjunct.

(29) *John* said that *he* liked *his* mother and Bill did too.
    a.   Bill said that John liked John's mother.
    b.   Bill said that Bill liked Bill's mother.
    c.   Bill said that Bill liked John's mother.
    d. *Bill said that John liked Bill's mother.

This pattern is expected if the relation that licenses parallel interpretations for elided VPs is one that recapitulates (a) just the dependency of *he* on *his* (drawing antecedency from the first conjunct for *he*) as in (29a); (b) the chained dependency (but not the antecedency) of *he* on *John* and *his* on *he*, as in (29b); and (c) only the dependency of *he* on *John*, but not that of *his* on *he*, such that only *his* draws its antecedent from the first conjunct, as in (29c). However, what is not possible is for a dependency of *his* on *John* to skip across the dependency of *he* on *John*, allowing for the interpretation in (29d), which appears to be exactly what Rule H prevents by excluding the representation in (24b), repeated here.

(24) a. *John* said that *he* liked *his* mother.

b. *John* said that *he* liked *his* mother.

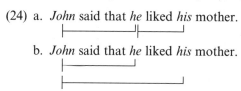

Now if it is correct to exclude the use of indices in syntactic theory, then there is no notion of binding consisting of c-command and coindexation, and so I must restate Fox's Rule H as Rule H′, replacing the word *bind*, which I have rejected, by the language of c-command and dependency (which, as the O.J. examples and those like (27) show, binding does not exactly correspond to).

(30) *Rule H′*
    x cannot be identity dependent on an antecedent, α, in case *x* could be identity dependent on a (more local) c-commanding antecedent, β, and yield the same semantic interpretation.

First, consider the crucial mention of c-command. The puzzle of the missing fourth reading in (29d) only arises where the lowest bound pronoun is c-commanded by a more local antecedent than the one in the matrix clause. If there is no c-command by the first of the two dependent pronouns, as in (31a), the fourth reading is then possible (see, e.g., Fiengo and May 1994, 156; Fox 2000, 131), as illustrated with the reconstructed ellipsis in (31b), where the first *his* depends on *Bill* and the second *his* depends on *John*.

(31) a. *Bill* said that all of *his* friends liked *his* mother and John did too.

     b. ... and **John** [said that all of *his* friends liked **his** mother] too

In other words, the reference to c-command in (30) is necessary, since Rule H does not preclude (31b), where only the first *his* in the second conjunct refers to *Bill*, as an acceptable interpretation.

We must also now determine whether or not stating Rule H without appeal to indices lands us in hot water. Fox assumes coindexation under c-command and parallelism achieves covaluation and dependency for the sloppy reading, but he has no notation for covaluation without dependency. Instead, he relies on the assumption discussed earlier that the strict reading is not a dependent one but is a necessarily coreferent one (with *John*). Fox (2000, 117) characterizes the strict reading as adhering to "referential parallelism" as opposed to "structural parallelism," to which he claims the sloppy reading adheres.[12] He must assume this, since neither *John* nor *his* of the first conjunct in (29) c-commands the reconstructed *his* in the second conjunct, and c-command is necessary in his account for dependency on an antecedent (i.e., he is assuming the CLP).

But since referential parallelism must be enforced for the strict reading, this leaves underdetermined how the covalued readings for (29) or the only reading of (32) (where Maurice must love Anton's mother) are enforced or recognized as identical.

(32) Alphonse loves Anton's mother and Maurice does too.

If the strict reading in (31b) draws on a representation in the first conjunct where *his* does not depend on *John*, but is covalued with it (where boldface notates covaluation without dependency—essentially Fiengo and May's (1994) α index) as in (33a), then Fox needs to rule out two representations that could lead to the reading in (29d).

(33) a. *John* said the *he* liked **his** mother and Bill did too.
        ├──────────────┤

     b. *John* said that **he** liked *his* mother and Bill did too.
        ├──────────────┘

     c. *John* said that *he* liked *his* mother and Bill did too.
        ├──────────┤├──────┘

In addition to the case where *his* and *he* each depend directly on *John* in the first conjunct (and *his* does not depend on *he*), Fox must also rule out a representation where *he* does not depend on *John*, but is covalued with it, where again boldface marks covaluation without dependency. With respect to (33b), Fox could presumably make an additional assumption along the lines proposed by Reinhart (1997), that if there is covaluation of a pronoun with a c-commanding antecedent, then the form of it is dependency unless there is reason to believe otherwise, in which case the dependencies are chained as in (33c), pursuant to Rule H.

But if we take the latter step, it is then not clear what is copied in the second conjunct when *his* can refer to *John* and *he* is dependent on the subject *Bill* as in (29c). In that case, *his* in the first conjunct can be covalued with *John*, but, according to Fox, *his* is not dependent on *John* either in the first conjunct (i.e., in (33a)) or in the elided second one. However, if the representation in (33a) is necessary to get the strict interpretation, then this compromises the claim (for the first conjunct) that dependency is always favored as the expression of covaluation. What then becomes possible is that the first conjunct could have treated *he* as covalued/coindexed with *John* and *his* as dependent on *John* as in (33b); but then (29d) becomes a possible reading and the whole account of Dahl's puzzle collapses. In a nutshell, using covaluation rather than dependency in the first conjunct to generate the class of possible strict readings undercuts the prediction made strictly on the basis of dependency relations as expressed in Rule H.

By contrast, as argued in section 2.2, it is possible in my system for *his* in the second conjunct to be dependent on *his* in the first conjunct and have the value of 'John' in both conjuncts even though the dependency arrow between *John* and *his* in the first conjunct is not copied. In other words, what must be required of the strict reading is that the second conjunct pronoun find an antecedent to depend on in the first conjunct that is structurally parallel, but that is not copied with the arrow that connects it to *John* as in the sloppy interpretation. There is no need to appeal to any covaluation mechanism such as referential parallelism or coindexation. This result is possible precisely because dependency on an antecedent does not require a c-commanding antecedent in the theory proposed here.

We need just one more assumption to permit (30) to derive Dahl's pattern, and it is a revision of Reinhart's (1983b) assumption that dependency is the preferred representation of covaluation. Earlier, I criticized this assumption because in Reinhart's account it is based on the premise that dependency could only arise under c-command by an antecedent (the CLP), and because the failure of dependency does not result in obviation, unless its source is an FTIP violation. If, however, there is some sort of preference for dependency independent of c-command, I would put it as follows:

(34) *Preferred Covaluation*
    Covaluation arises from dependent identity unless dependency is blocked.

If x is not permitted to be dependent on y by the INP, then x can be covalued with y in spite of the absence of dependency; but if dependent identity is not blocked, then covaluation is always a case of dependent identity. If dependent identity is blocked by the FTIP, then Pragmatic Obviation ensures an expectation of noncoreference (noncovaluation). If dependent reference is blocked but covaluation is possible, it is most typically codependency on a third term, as in the O.J. instantiation contexts.[13] Like Pragmatic Obviation, Preferred Covaluation is not stated on structures at all. Indeed, as it is stated in (34), one could think of it as a preference to rely on previous mention, if possible, to establish referential value.

Once we adopt Preferred Covaluation, all the coconstruals in (29) and (31) arise by dependency, including the strict interpretation; hence, neither the representation in (33a) nor the one in (33b) is possible for (29). Moreover, the restriction on parallelism, that the elided pronoun must have an antecedent it depends on, can now be attributed to Preferred Covaluation. Then, thanks to Rule H′ (which I will refer to simply as Rule H, hereafter), the representation of the first conjunct in (29) must be as in (24a) and not (24b). Consequently, Dahl's puzzle is solved in essentially the manner that Fox intended it to be, but not within the c-command-conditioned theory of dependency that he assumed. I will return to Rule H in chapters 3 and 4, where it has a role to play in the distribution of strong as opposed to weak crossover.

Before closing this section, let us return to the representations in (28), repeated here, to confirm that the same results hold for syntactic anaphors as well as coconstrued pronouns. Since LAL only requires codependency, not local dependency, either of the representations in (28a,b) would satisfy LAL.

(28) *Every senator* claimed that *she* expected *herself* to win.

    a. *Every senator* claimed that *she* expected *herself* to win.

       ├────────────────────┤├───────────┘

    b. *Every senator* claimed that *she* expected *herself* to win.

       ├────────────────────┘

       ├────────────────────────────────┘

We have seen that Rule H excludes (28b) as a possible representation, even though both representations would presumably have the same interpretation, and now we can confirm this result with an ellipsis test. First let us adjust the example, choosing an antecedent that is not quantified, so strict coconstruals are possible in this configuration. In the absence of any focus marker, the coconstruals in the first conjunct of (35) correctly permit only the interpretations in (35a,b), not that in (35c).

(35) *Hillary* claimed that *she* expected *herself* to win before Olympia did.

    a.   Olympia claimed that Hillary expected Hillary to win.

    b.   Olympia claimed that Olympia expected Olympia to win.

    c.   *Olympia claimed that Hillary expected Olympia to win.

Thus, the pattern of ellipsis coconstruals permits us to confirm that only chained dependencies are allowed if codependent relations do not provide a different interpretation.

2.4 On the Real and Apparent Overlap of the Form-to-Interpretation Principle and the Independence Principle

At this point, I have introduced three different principles regulating dependent reference: Rule H, the INP, and the FTIP. The INP may appear to overlap suspiciously with the FTIP, especially with respect to names c-commanded by their antecedents (Principle C effects), as in (36).

(36) *He* said she saw *Alex*.

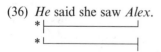

The FTIP rules out dependency of *Alex* on *he* (because a competing form, *him*, could occur in place of *Alex*), and Pragmatic Obviation further renders coreference between *he* and *Alex* unexpected. The INP rules out the possibility that *he* could depend on *Alex*, because *he* c-commands *Alex*. However, there are also cases where the INP rules out interpretations that the FTIP permits (where Principle C effects do not mask the INP effect). Let us consider one sort of case.

There are instances of local anaphora where the structural c-commanding antecedent of a reflexive is not coreferent with it in any sense of co-extension, as pointed out by Jackendoff (1992). For example, suppose Fidel Castro is viewing his statue for the first time in Madame Tussaud's wax museum. We could report this event as in (37).

(37) a. Castro finally saw himself in Mme Tussaud's wax museum.
b. Every celebrity will eventually see himself/herself in Mme Tussaud's wax museum.

Here the SELF form does not agree in animacy with its antecedent since the statue is not animate and Castro is not coextensive with his statue; but it could be said that the identity of the statue is dependent on the reference of *Castro*. Indeed, if the subject is quantified, the issues remain the same, as illustrated in (37b). Now suppose that there is an accident at the museum, such that the statue of Castro falls on a foreign leader visiting the museum, or else a foreign leader is merely dwarfed in the presence of a large statue of Castro.

(38) a. Castro fell over on Mugabe.
b. Castro towered over Mugabe.

A case like (38) shows that there is nothing conceptually difficult or abnormal in linguistic descriptions of statues, denoted by the name of the individual they represent, falling on a person or towering over a person. Yet precisely this interpretation (a statue designated by the name of the individual it represents) is impossible in (39).

(39) a. Castro fell on himself.
b. Castro towered over himself.

The examples in (39) are acceptable to varying degrees for English speakers under the interpretation that the man fell on or towered over the statue, but neither permits an interpretation where the statue of Castro towers over or falls on Castro the man.

Following Safir 2004, where these cases are explored in detail (and where a wider range of references is evaluated), I will use the term *proxy* for names or pronominals designating entities that are representatives or representations of the named individual.[14] Thus, *Castro* designating the statue of Castro is a proxy term, but *the statue of Castro* is not a proxy

term, hence *The statue of Castro fell on Castro* is unsurprisingly acceptable. My theory of proxy terms is simple.

(40) Proxy terms are identity dependent on animate antecedents.

If (40) is true, then the INP predicts that proxy terms can never depend
on any name or individual they c-command. The SELF forms in (39) can
be proxies for statues because they do not c-command the terms on which
they must depend. However, the subjects of these sentences c-command
the SELF forms that they must depend on if the subject is the statue and
the reflexive the man. In other words, LAL (my Principle A) will require
that the SELF form have a local c-antecedent and the FTIP will ensure
that a simple pronoun could not replace the anaphoric one, but only the
INP ensures that the subject cannot depend on the object even where
LAL and the FTIP are otherwise satisfied.

Proxy interpretation is not peculiar to reflexive interpretation. Examples with pronouns that can be interpreted as dependent show the same
sorts of effects. In (41), I expand the range of proxy relations, including
likeness (41a,b), author/work (41c), and player/vehicle (41d,e) (all discussed in more detail and with references in Safir 2004).

(41) a. As they strolled through the wax museum, Fidel could not help
        thinking that he would have looked better in a uniform and
        Marlene could not help thinking that she would have looked
        better without one.
     b. The masquerade ball was a bit disconcerting. It seemed to
        Marlene that everywhere she looked, either her nose was too
        long or her chin too weak.
     c. Grisham claims that he is even more suspenseful in Swahili.
     d. Alice's ball was close to the gate, or it was until the Red Queen
        knocked her into the bushes.
     e. Patton realized that he would be vulnerable to a flanking
        movement.

The INP applies to simple pronouns in the same way it does in the case
of SELF forms, ruling out dependent interpretations for c-commanders
(although it is difficult to construct good examples in part because most
verbs that take a sentential complement favor animate subjects).

(42) a. *David* indicated that *he* must have been very handsome.
     b. The statue of *David* indicated that *he* must have been very
        handsome.

c. *David* indicated that the statue of *him* must have been very handsome.

Although (42b) is a bit awkward, *he* can depend on *David* where both refer to the biblical king; but it is not possible to take (42a) to mean that *David* refers to the statue and *he* to the biblical king. However, if rock star David Bowie were speaking of an effigy of himself that has since been destroyed, in (42a) *David* could easily be taken to refer to the rock star and *he* to his effigy. The latter reading is something like (42c), where both *David* and *him* refer to the rock star. The failure of (42a) is not just a case where an animate interpretation must depend on an inanimate one, but a case where the inanimate statue depends for its value on a pronoun it c-commands, a situation that violates the INP. None of the interpretations discussed for (42a–c) violate the FTIP (or, in binding theory terms, they do not induce Principle C effects).[15]

Thus, the distribution of proxy readings distinguishes the effects of the INP from those of the FTIP, further motivating the INP. In section 2.5 and again in chapters 3 and 4, I explore some further cases where the two principles diverge in empirically detectable ways.

2.5 Extending the Independence Principle?

It is time to reconsider cases like (1c), cases of "backward coreference," which are permitted by the INP as I have formulated it so far, but not by the CLP.

(1) c. *His* mother loves *Bill*. *CLP

In this section, I establish that the INP should exclude a wider range of cases than I have used it for up to now. Extending the INP in this way brings it closer to the FTIP in terms of its syntactic form, but the syntactic similarity also serves to articulate how sharply the two principles differ in their interpretive contribution.

I begin by considering an interesting asymmetry that arises when we look at the range of bound readings that are supported in parallelism structures. Compare (43a) and (43b).

(43) a. Sean insists that *Lucie's* mother means a lot to *her* success and that Sarah's mother does too.
   b. Sean insists that *her* mother means a lot to *Lucie's* success and to Sarah's success too.

While my informants judge the bound reading for the ellipsis in (43a) (Sarah's success) to be marginal to varying degrees, they unanimously find the bound reading to be hopeless in (43b) (Sarah's mother) by comparison. In neither case in (43), however, does the antecedent c-command the dependent (elided) pronoun. This indicates that if there is an asymmetry, it is based not on whether or not the antecedent c-commands, but on whether or not the nominal embedding the pronoun (*her mother* or *her success*) c-commands its antecedent—it does in (43b), but not in (43a). The relevant generalization is provisionally stated in (44).

(44) *Extended INP*
     α cannot depend on β if α is embedded in a nominal γ and γ
     c-commands β.

It follows from the Extended INP that only (45a) could involve a dependency relation (of *her* on *Laura*) and that (45b) must involve a different form of coconstrual, since *her mother* cannot be dependent on *Laura*, which it c-commands.

(45) a. *Laura's* mother loves *her*.
     b. *Her* mother loves *Laura*.

Thus, the role that c-command plays in (43a,b) and (45a,b) is not licensing of the dependent reading, as in Reinhart's account; rather, c-command functions to block dependency according to the Extended INP.

Obviously, the Extended INP bears a striking resemblance to the INP, which is why I have named it as I have. Suppose, then, that the INP is sensitive to an extended sense of the dependency of one argument on another (I will formulate it more precisely later). From this perspective, *her mother* in (46) is dependent on *Laura* because *her* is identity dependent on *Laura*. In this extended sense of dependency, the semantic value for the constituent *her mother* depends on the value for *her*.

(46) *Laura* loves *her* mother.

When we put it this way, if *her* and *Laura* are coconstrued in (45b), the coconstrual cannot involve dependency of *her* on *Laura* because *her mother* cannot depend on any argument it c-commands, by the Extended INP. By the latter reasoning, then, the coconstrual of *her* with *Laura* must be a form of independent coreference, perhaps one where *her* is in fact dependent on a preceding mention of Laura in the discourse. Since the INP does not feed Pragmatic Obviation the way the FTIP does, we might expect backward coreference to be as unmarked as forward coreference is in (46), but this is not the case. Consider the contrast between the paragraphs in (47a) and (47b).

(47) a. His back was to us when we came in. He swiveled in his chair to face us. The penetrating eyes of Count Marzipan were trained upon us.

b. Count Marzipan was brooding. His back was to us when we came in. He swiveled in his chair to face us, his penetrating eyes trained upon us.

The pronouns in (47a) as well as (47b) are permitted to be dependent on *Count Marzipan*, since no quantification is involved that requires sentence-internal dependency and none of the nominals containing pronouns c-command *Count Marzipan*. Clearly, (47a) and (47b) have a different status. Without any context, examples like (47a) are the stuff of mystery stories, where a pronoun is introduced that we have no referent for and we must wait for a plausible candidate to appear that supplies a value for the pronoun. The effect that disfavors backward coreference (and hence backward dependency) in these cases appears to be nothing more than Preferred Covaluation, which forces us to defer the assignment of a dependent reading until we have an appropriate antecedent. Where the antecedent is finally introduced in a position that permits a dependent reading, the tension created by Preferred Covaluation is resolved according to preference, but not in cases where dependency is blocked.

If (44) is on the right track and if it characterizes a way that the INP should be extended, we should be able to find other instances on the model of (45b) where backward coreference is possible but backward dependency fails.

2.5.1 Circular Readings and Backward Anaphora
When Higginbotham (1983, 404–405) introduces the arrow notation, he argues that another advantage is that it can explain what is deviant about circular readings, such as the one represented in (48b).

(48) a. [His$_i$ wife]$_j$ loves [her$_j$ husband]$_i$
b. *[**His** wife] loves [**her** husband]*

In these cases, the interpretation of *his* depends on *her husband*, but the interpretation of *her* depends on *his wife*, with the result that this interpretation is deviant. The indexing notation treats the relations between *his wife* and *her* and between *his* and *her husband* as symmetric and unremarkable, but the arrow notation reveals the asymmetries of dependency that require *his* to depend on an interpretation of *her husband* that cannot be fixed without assigning a value for *his* in *his wife*. Higginbotham (1983, 404) proposes that the value of a linguistic term x cannot depend on itself. He expresses this proposal as a condition on LF representations as in (49), where D^* is the dependency relation.

(49) *Not:* $D^*(X, X)$

The extended notion of dependency described in (44) provides an independently motivated account for circular readings, such as the one illustrated in (48b). Since *his* depends on *her husband*, *his wife* inherits dependency on *her husband*; but *his wife* c-commands *her husband*, hence dependency of *his wife* on *her husband* is blocked by the Extended INP. Such sentences are possible if dependency on *his wife* is not crucial for *her* in *her husband*. In (50), for example, where *Muriel* is appositional (or even parenthetical) to *his wife*, *Muriel* provides an independent antecedent for *her*.

(50) His wife, Muriel, loves her husband.

Examples like (50) show that Higginbotham is right to characterize the ill-formedness of circular readings as a blocked pattern of dependencies; but now the ill-formedness of circular readings like (48) follows from the independently motivated Extended INP, eliminating the need for statements specific to circularity like (49).[16]

2.5.2   The Force of Blocked Dependency

It is important to understand that the FTIP does not employ this extended sense of dependency; if it did, the FTIP algorithm would not function properly. For example, we do not want (51a) to compete with (51b).

(51) a. *Arthur's* mother loves *him*.
     b. *Arthur's* mother loves *Arthur*.

If (51a) and (51b) competed, then (51a) would be a test derivation (an available alternative) for (51b), *him* being a more dependent form than *Arthur*, and the two instances of *Arthur* in (51b) would be in an obviative relation by Pragmatic Obviation, contrary to fact. The INP differs further in that violations of the INP do not feed Pragmatic Obviation; hence,

Pragmatic Obviation does not force us to expect *her* and *Laura* to be expected noncoreferent in (45b). We also do not want the INP to trigger Pragmatic Obviation for the relationship between *he* and *him* in (52).

(52) *Every father* says *he* wants children to love *him*.

In (52), *he* and *him* can be in a dependency relation, but since *he* c-commands *him*, *he* cannot depend on *him*. Pragmatic Obviation, if it applied here, would not allow *he* and *him* to share a value. On the other hand, there is clearly an interpretation of (52) for which we would want to say that *him* depends on *he* and shares the value determined by the quantificational antecedent.

With this extension of the INP in mind (and the distinctions between the FTIP and the INP), let us reconsider cases like (12), repeated here.

(12) A party without *Lucie* annoys *her* and a party without Zelda
     (would) too.
     Only: A party without Zelda annoys Lucie.

Since the key notion for dependency relations of this sort is parallelism, not elision, it is worth considering how much better or worse these examples fare when there is no elision. So, for example, the relevant sloppy reading for (12) is available if there is no elision and there is contrastive stress on the second *her*. But reversal of the pronouns with the proper names on this model does not yield parallel success.

(53) a. A party without *Lucie* annoys *her* and a party without **Zélda**
        annoys **hér**.
     b. A party without *her* annoys *Lucie* and a party without **hér**
        annoys **Zélda**.

While my informants do not unanimously reject a sloppy reading for (53b), even those who accept it find it odd in a way that (53a) is not. I attribute the oddity involved to a failure of parallelism in the following sense. In both (53a) and (53b), we are assuming that unstressed *her* and *Lucie* are coconstrued, but in (53a), stressed **her** seems to strongly favor, if not require, that it refer to Zelda (and not Lucie or any third party). In other words, the parallel stress peaks in (53a) favor a sloppy reading. By contrast, **her** in (53b) could refer to a third party, say, Eileen, as easily as to Zelda (again, assuming coconstrual of *Lucie* and *her* in the first conjunct). The apparent lack of parallelism in the second conjunct of (53b) arises because the Extended INP does not permit the first conjunct in

(53b) to contain a dependency relation between *her* and *Lucie*. Thus, the second conjunct in (53b) has no model for parallelism with the first conjunct based on dependency. Insofar as the stress peaks of the second conjunct in (53b) create a paired relation, coconstrual is thus not crucial to it, any more than it is in the first conjunct, given the absence of dependent identity.

Returning now to cases like (43b), *her mother* c-commands *Lucie*, so it cannot be the case that *her* depends on *Lucie*. In ellipsis contexts, the reconstructed *her* can only depend on its overt parallel argument for its reference, since there is no dependency relation to copy, and as a result, the only value available for the elided portion of (43b) is the one for *her* that corresponds to *Lucie*. The relative success of (43a) seems to result from the availability of a dependent interpretation that can be copied from the first conjunct, allowing elided *her* to have the value of what it depends on in the second conjunct, namely, *Sarah*.

Thus, it appears that (44) not only accounts for circular readings but also distinguishes the pattern of dependencies permitted for both elided and overt clauses when the latter are in a parallelism relation with a previous clause. Moreover, this extension of the INP serves to create a greater wedge between the predictions of the INP and the predictions of the FTIP. It remains now to integrate (44) into the INP in a more specific way; but I leave that task for later, after we have examined the relevance of this generalization for crossover phenomena.

2.6   Conclusion

I have argued that the INP-based approach to the distribution of dependent identity readings is better than any CLP-based approach, and in so doing I have established a system of principles that determine the possible range of bound reading phenomena. The pattern of possible dependencies reported in (1) may now be revised, as in (54), consistent with the (Extended) INP.

(54) a. *Everyone* loves *his* mother.
         |—————————⌐

     b. *Everyone's* mother loves *him*.
         |————————————⌐

     c. *His mother loves *Bill*.
         ⌐_____|

d. *He* says that Angie loves *him*.
     ├─────────────────────────┘

e. Egil loves *Freya*. Ketil loves *her* too.
              ├──────────────┘

f. *He says that Angie loves *him*.
     └─────────────────────────┤

Since the syntax of dependency presented here is scarcely added to in the chapters that follow, any theory that can derive these principles should have all the same consequences that my theory does for the cross-over and reconstruction phenomena that I discuss in the remaining chapters. One such reduction is considered in section 5.1 (a movement theory of coconstrual, which I reject), but I hope to establish that any alternative theory should preserve the explanatory advantages that this one achieves.

I am also assuming that all of the principles and operations I have defended in this chapter are universal and unparameterized. If the pattern of dependencies differs across languages, then it does so because those languages have derivational or lexical properties that interact with the universal principles proposed here to produce a different pattern.[17] I obliquely touch on these matters with respect to resumption in section 4.7, but I otherwise leave them unexplored until the appendix, where I demonstrate how the proposals made here might fare under plausible assumptions about a scrambling language.

Chapter 3

Deriving Crossover

In chapters 1 and 2, I have established that the INP succeeds in characterizing the syntactic restrictions imposed on the fundamental asymmetry embodied in dependency relations, with a focus on those cases where dependency is not a function of quantification. Now it is time to turn to some of the syntactic asymmetries that emerge when dependency relations arise from quantification-bound readings.

Crossover effects are perhaps the most well-studied phenomenon where dependent identity fails. One class of crossover contrasts is illustrated for direct questions in (1) and (2).

(1) a. *Who* said *he* hates Malva?
    b. **Who* does *he* hate?
    c. **Who* does *he* believe Malva hates?

(2) a. *Who* saw *his* mother?
    b. **Who* did *his* mother see?
    c. **Who* did *his* mother say that Malva saw?

Nothing in the original characterization of these effects referred to them as quantifier-dependent phenomena. According to Postal's (1971) classic description, the ungrammatical (b) and (c) examples are cases that arise when a *wh*-phrase has moved from right to left, "crossing" a pronoun that is supposed to depend on that *wh*-phrase. Later, Wasow (1979) distinguished "strong crossover" (SCO), where the crossed pronoun c-commands the extraction site (as in (1b,c)), from "weak crossover" (WCO), where the crossed pronoun does not c-command the extraction site (as in (2b,c)). The typical claim about the force of the distinction between crossover effects is that WCO is not as robust a judgment as SCO, which native speakers reject more firmly, although in the years since, this dividing line has frayed, as a wider range of constructions and configurations has been examined (as we will see).

Over the last thirty years, numerous proposals have been made that either exclude WCO, as opposed to SCO, by means of a principle uniquely formulated for that purpose (e.g., Higginbotham 1983, 410; Koopman and Sportiche 1983; Safir 1984, 1996a, 1999) or try to derive it from general properties of dependency (Reinhart 1983a,b; Williams 1997); these are reviewed in sections 3.1 and 3.4. In what follows, I will argue (beginning in section 3.2) that the second strategy, deriving crossover from the theory of syntactic dependency restrictions, is correct, but that the existing accounts are not empirically successful, either because they rely on the CLP or linear statements or else because they treat WCO and SCO separately. Although taking account of the role of quantification requires a restriction, developed in section 3.3, on the way that extraction sites, as opposed to pronouns, find their antecedents, I otherwise derive all the properties of crossover (as well as some properties of functional interpretations in section 3.5 and the distribution of "weakest crossover" in section 3.6) from the theory of dependency in chapter 1—without any further stipulation specific to crossover.

3.1 Crossover Phenomena and Previous Accounts

Since I am committed to providing an account of all true crossover effects, it is perhaps useful to present the full range of these effects, as they are understood today, and the interesting stages of research from which they emerged, if only to make clear what is at stake for our understanding of the human linguistic capacity. The stakes were dramatically raised when Chomsky (1976) demonstrated that any relevant account of crossover should extend to the distribution of quantifier-bound readings for pronouns. He noted that the surface position of a quantifier does not permit a bound reading for a pronoun to its left, as in (3b).

(3) a. *Every man* saw *his* mother.
    b. *His mother saw *every man.*

The parallel he notes to cases like those in (2a,b) suggests that the universal quantifier in (3a,b) moves at LF (e.g., by May's (1977) QR) to create a structure, or at least a linear order, similar to the one that (2a,b) has at S-Structure (or else that the S-Structure representations in (3a,b) should be, at LF, more like those of (2a,b)—a position no one has

championed). This result was eventually extended to multiple interroga-
tions like those in (4), once again on the assumption that LF movement
applies to the quantifier (*wh*-in-situ), such that only (4b) is excluded, since
only in (4b) is the dependent pronoun to the left of the quantifier it depends on (Chomsky's Leftness Condition).

(4) a. Which man said that the company sent *which woman* to visit *her*
      secretary?
    b. *Which man said that the company sent *her* secretary to visit
      which woman?
    c. *Which man* said that the company sent which woman to visit *his*
      secretary?
    d. *Which man* said that the company sent *his* secretary to visit
      which woman?

Reinhart (1976, 1983a,b) argues that c-command of the pronoun by the
quantifier, not precedence of the quantifier is the crucial factor distinguishing between (3a)/(4a) and (3b)/(4b), respectively. In (4c) and (4d),
the in-situ quantifier *which woman* that presumably migrates to the matrix
Spec,CP at LF can precede or follow the pronoun, since the pronoun only
depends on *which man*. In many constructions, it does not appear possible
to tell whether the constraint is linear or hierarchical, since for almost any
pair of arguments, the one on the left is, or is embedded in, an argument
structurally higher than any argument to the right. Apparent counterexamples to this view are typically countered in turn with movement and
reconstruction analyses (ideally independently motivated) that reproduce
a hierarchical structure that c-command is computed on.

Although the point has occasionally been misunderstood, it is clear
that the debate is not really about which theory, structural or linear, is
more or less abstract. Both theories must appeal to abstract levels where
the relevant relations hold; otherwise, ellipsis examples would not fall
under the same generalization, as it appears they should (bracketed constituents contain the understood ellipsis).

(5) a. *?Mothers have been known to turn in their sons, but I don't
      know a single boy *who his* mother did [turn in *t*]
    b. Mothers have been known to turn in their sons, but I don't
      know a single mother *who t* did [turn in *her* son]

Moreover, Chomsky's extension of the scope of the phenomenon requires
a view that generalizes across the position of the quantifier in situ and the

position of the trace of *wh*-movement (or at least its launching site). Thus, the view that the *wh*-phrase is superficially to the left of the pronoun it crosses cannot be the key generalization.

A strictly linear view calculated from the position of the variable left by the quantifier (presumably at LF), as in Chomsky's leftness account, has the peculiar property of granting a role to precedence that is not important in the rest of syntactic theory. The FTIP (like the binding theory before it) relies crucially on c-command, not precedence. Thus, I take the burden of proof to fall on the theory that crucially employs precedence, not the theory that employs c-command. Nonetheless, I will point out some specific weaknesses of the linear precedence account from time to time.

It was noticed during the era of Chomsky's *LGB* that the SCO/WCO asymmetry corresponding to a difference in c-command also corresponds to different opportunities to derive crossover from other principles. SCO seemed potentially derivable from either of two general tenets of the *LGB* system. One idea, generally adopted at the time, was to treat the trace of *wh*-movement as if it were a name (r-expression). This stipulation would render the trace of *wh*-movement susceptible to Principle C, and SCO would then simply be a type of Principle C violation. For example, the analogy was between cases like these:

(6) a. **He* said that Abbott likes *Costello*.
    b. **Who* did *he* say that Abbott likes *t*

Within the Principle C account, however, it appeared necessary to stipulate that the *wh*-trace would be susceptible to Principle C only within the domain of the *wh*-operator that binds it; otherwise, examples like (7a,b) would be ruled out (where *he* and *Turley* in (7a) and (7b), respectively, are outside the operator that binds the trace).

(7) a. *He* is the guy *who* Mary saw *t*
    b. *Turley* is tough *Op* for her/**him* to count on *t*
    c. **Turley* considers it tough for her to count on *Turley*.

This objection appears weak for (7a) if Principle C effects are really about dependent identity and not coreference, since the relation between *he* and the relative that follows is mediated by the copula, which has the effect of asserting nondependent coreference. However, the need for the patch in the Principle C account is clearer under the analysis of *tough*-movement first introduced by Chomsky (1977) whereby a null operator in the complement Spec,CP (updating slightly), which is controlled by the matrix subject, leaves a trace (gap) in the infinitive complement of *tough* and predicates like it. SCO effects are found within the *for*-clause, as predicted, because *him* c-commands the trace, but the fact that *Turley* c-commands the trace in (7b) has no effect (when *her* is the subject). Notice that *Turley* in the highest subject position induces a Principle C effect on the lower *Turley* in (7c) (a gapless *tough*-construction). Thus, the Principle C account of SCO imposes a less restrictive condition on the distribution of traces than it does on the distribution of names.

Another view that developed at the same time was that the definition of what counts as a syntactic variable depends on the locality of Ā-binding, and if so, an intervening A-binder (*he* in (6b)) would block the interpretation of *t* from being that of a variable. Then conditions on the licensing of empty categories would do the rest of the work, since an empty category that is not a variable is an anaphor (unless it is licensed as PRO or pro, which is not possible in (6b)), and an anaphor must be locally A-bound within its domain. The trace in (6b) is not locally A-bound *within its domain* (*he* is in a higher clause); hence, if it is treated as an anaphor, it is excluded by Principle A of the binding theory.

The approach to SCO based on the definition of syntactic variable (the *DSV approach*, henceforth) would have seemed the lesser option if there were no independent need for such a definition. However, some such notion appears to be required independently for examples like (8a,b), where a pronoun or an epithet can occupy a position that normally would be a trace in a restrictive relative.

(8) a. Do you remember *that nasty little guy who* we never found out why *he/the little twerp* told on us?
   b. *Any smartass employee* that we have to wonder about whether or not *he/the sneaky little jerk* will be a union man is not going to get promoted around here.

The use of pronouns in these contexts is common in the informal variety of speech that is quite generally spoken, but not written (these examples are improved by embedding them in islands, where no *wh*-movement is possible).

(9) a. *Do you remember that nasty little guy who we never found out why Cantwell told on us?
   b. *Any smartass employee that we have to wonder about whether Cantwell will be a union man is not going to get promoted around here.

The examples in (9a,b) show that some sort of variable is required; lacking a variable, the examples in (8a,b) would not be acceptable. However, if the epithet is not functioning as a locally Ā-bound variable, it is excluded by local A-binding under the FTIP (or any Principle C account), as illustrated in (10a).

(10) a. *He* intends to organize *the bastard's* coworkers.

      b. *Any smartass employee* that we have to wonder about whether or not *he* intends to organize *his/*the bastard's* coworkers has no future around here.

What (10b) crucially shows is that the epithet is not licensed as a syntactic variable unless it is *locally* Ā-bound. In (10b), the epithet *the bastard* is locally A-bound by *he* and bound reference fails. Thus, if the relative clause involves some sort of binding, call it X-binding, for which a pronoun or an epithet can, in the right circumstances, count as a bindee, then whatever X-binding is, it is not A-binding, since syntactic A-binding blocks X-binding of an epithet in these contexts. Yet some argument must be locally X-bound in the restrictive relative clause by either the *wh*-operator or the head of the relative. If we assume that X-binding is in fact Ā-binding, then we can say that a restrictive relative must have nonvacuous Ā-binding.

(11) An Ā-operator must bind something.

If we are to give a name to what an Ā-operator must bind, it seems reasonable to refer to it as a syntactic variable—that is, the element that an Ā-operator locally, nonvacuously binds. Epithets can be interpreted semantically as bound variables, as we saw in section 1.4 for cases like *Every kid's teacher complains that his mother thinks the little bastard is smart*, as long as they are not locally A-bound (and hence excluded by the FTIP), and this account of their behavior as Ā-bound variables is consistent with what we know up to this point (assuming that *everyone* takes scope over the whole sentence after being moved at LF to an Ā-position).

Thus, both the DSV and Principle C approaches to SCO have some independent motivation, at least in the context of 1980's principles-and-parameters syntax, although it would seem fair to say that the stipulation that traces are r-expressions for binding theory is simply one of convenience.

These two accounts of SCO do not extend to WCO effects, which are contexts where a pronoun in the scope of an operator fails to allow a bound reading unless the trace of that operator c-commands the pronoun (assuming LF movement of non-*wh*-quantifiers). Thus, the standard schematic WCO configuration is as in (12), where the pronoun embedded in XP does not c-command the trace (of Q-DP) in YP.

(12) [Q-DP [[$_{XP}$ ... [$_{WP}$ ... pronoun ...] ...] [$_{YP}$ ... t ...]]]

Since there is no c-command, neither the *LGB* binding theory nor the FTIP has anything to say about such cases. Moreover, the syntactic definition of variable is also met, not only for the trace, but also for the pronoun.

Koopman and Sportiche (1983) exploited the latter fact to fashion a principle dedicated to explaining WCO effects, their Bijection Principle, reproduced here.

(13) *Bijection Principle*
There is a bijective correspondence between variables and Ā-positions.

The Bijection Principle handles the standard WCO cases quite naturally, in that in all the typical WCO cases we have discussed so far, there are two local Ā-bindees for a single quantifier, as in (2b,c), (3b), and (4b), but where the Ā-variable c-commands the pronoun, as in (2a), (3a), and (4a), the pronoun is not locally Ā-bound by the quantifier and the result is grammatical. Although the Bijection Principle can be formulated without reference to the syntactic definition of variable, it clearly is an analysis along the same lines as the DSV theory of SCO, since it relies on the locality of Ā-binding.

In Safir 1984, 1986, I criticized the Bijection Principle account because it is too restrictive, though the principle I replaced it with had some of the same key properties. Consider the following cases, where resumptive pronouns appear instead of traces:

(14) a. I would never marry any woman *who* I would never know when *her* mother is going to visit *her*.
    b. Do you remember that sad little kid *who his* mother was always complaining about *his* grades?

WCO is thoroughly missing, not only in colloquial English, but also in languages with more robust resumptive pronoun strategies, such as Irish and Hebrew, as pointed out by McCloskey (1990) and Demirdache (1991), respectively (for discussion, see section 4.7). Given what is known about the need for relative clauses to contain variables, it appears that, formally speaking, the Ā-operator (which I will assume is present in Spec,CP; see Safir 1986, 682–684) binds both pronouns locally, such that it is not obvious how to determine that one or the other pronoun should count as the unique variable. In short, two syntactic variables can be bound by the same operator just in case the two variables are resumptive pronouns.[1]

Notice that across-the-board extraction out of conjunctions also allows two gaps to correspond to a single Ā-antecedent.[2]

(15) a. I don't know who each man spoke to and offended.
　　 b. I don't know who each man claimed to know and to have hired.

It appears that more than one variable can be locally bound by a single Ā-operator, but when that happens, a WCO effect arises if the variables are not of the same type.[3] Simplifying earlier formulations, I express the key idea in (16).

(16) *Parallelism Condition on Operator Binding (PCOB)*
　　 If a single quantifier binds more than one variable, then either (a) or (b).
　　 a. They are both pronouns.
　　 b. They are both traces.

The distinction between traces and pronouns in the PCOB has nothing to do with their morphological content or lack thereof. For example, in Spanish, the null subject of a tensed relative also induces WCO, as does its English translation.

(17) *A quién* pro dijiste que [la **mujer** con quién *pro* habló **t**]
　　 to who (you) said that the woman with which (he) spoke
　　 impresiona *t*
　　 impressed
　　 'Who did you say that [the woman with whom *he* spoke]
　　 impressed *t*'

At this point, I am prepared to offer an important moral, one that will bear repeating. It is often argued that WCO is induced by the interaction of scope with the pattern of dependencies that a trace and a pronoun participate in. Some semanticists have taken this to suggest that crossover phenomena, or at least WCO phenomena, are fundamentally semantic. From this point of view, however, the absence of WCO effects in structural configurations where the same quantifier would otherwise produce such effects is unexpected. For example, where quantificational operators bind resumptive pronouns as well as other pronouns in the WCO configuration, the absence of WCO effects is unexpected, since pronouns interpreted as variables are no different from traces interpreted as variables in any semantic theory I am aware of. Yet this syntactic difference is crucial to the distribution of WCO effects, and it is only one factor where the effect crucially relies on syntactic factors. Since the crossover effects are semantic in their consequences, it is not surprising that there is a semantic component to the explanation, but it cannot be the whole explanation. I will return to this matter in section 3.7.[4]

The force of the PCOB is somewhat compromised, however, by the existence of the famous PRO gate cases first discovered by Higginbotham (1980b), which I illustrate in (18a) with the structural analysis in (18b).

(18) a. *Who* did lying to *his* mother disturb *t*
     b. *Who* did [$_{IP}$[$_{DP}$ *PRO* lying to *his* mother] [$_{VP}$ disturb *t*]]

If we were to analyze (18b) strictly on the basis of the assumptions made up to now, we would expect a WCO effect on the pairing, {*his, t*}. Nonetheless, the presence of PRO seems to render *his* available to be a bound variable paired with the trace following *disturb*. This is explicable, translating Higginbotham's observation into binding, if the PRO A-binds the pronoun *his*, rendering it irrelevant to the PCOB. If that is so, however, then *who* must Ā-bind PRO. Thus, these cases appear to pair PRO with a trace, and so we must conclude that a pairing of trace and PRO should be acceptable. It is not clear why this pairing is different from pro/variable pairings.

The PRO gate effects do not fit neatly into any theory of WCO that I am aware of. Apparently, PRO is never a syntactic variable, for reasons that remain mysterious. With the advent of null Case theory (Chomsky and Lasnik 1995), PRO is not Caseless; but nothing explains, for example, why PRO cannot be a resumptive pronoun.

(19) a. *Do you remember dealing with *that mechanic who* it was unclear when *PRO* to fix the car
     b. Do you remember dealing with *that mechanic who* it was unclear when *he* would fix the car
     c. ?I heard about *the guy who* you were wondering when *his/*PRO* meeting Mary could be arranged

Rather, it seems that PRO in these configurations (where it is not obligatorily controlled owing to lexically determined infinitival complementa-
tion) somehow achieves semantic variable status without crucial reference
to Ā-binding. It is clear, for example, that control of PRO (however that
is achieved), rather than Ā-binding, determines its reference in cases like
(20a,b) just as it does for (20c,d), respectively (from Safir 1984, 614).

(20) a.   *Who* did [*PRO* shaving *himself*] convince *t* to grow a beard
     b.   **Who* did [*PRO* shaving *himself*] convince Mary to trust *t*
     c.   *PRO* shaving *himself* convinced *John* to grow a beard
     d.   **PRO* shaving *himself* convinced Mary to trust *John*

This anomalous property of PRO will not be less mysterious in the new
theory I will propose, and I will have to make a different stipulation
about it (than I did when I proposed the PCOB) when I come to it. For
now, all that is crucial is that PRO cannot count as an Ā-bindee, but it
does count as an A-binder. The claim that PRO is an A-binder is crucial
to any number of configurations where it is required to make the right
predictions, as in (21).

(21) *PRO* to scratch her/*her/herself* would upset Olive

If PRO can count as a binder, the reflexive reading of *scratch* is explained; moreover, if the scratcher is Olive, then *her* can't be Olive by
the usual binding theory reasoning (or the FTIP) and *herself* then must
be Olive. I will therefore set PRO gates aside as a phenomenon that, so
far as I understand it, favors no known theory (but see note 32 of this
chapter).

     From this short, selective history, we may conclude that it is not
obvious that crossover is a unified phenomenon insofar as SCO and
WCO effects do not seem to be induced by the same principles. Whether
the DSV approach or the Principle C approach to SCO is chosen, WCO
requires a separate principle, whether it be the Leftness Condition, the
Bijection Principle, the PCOB, or the like. Moreover, with respect to
WCO accounts, it is not sufficient to simply examine the position of the
variable in relation to the position of the dependent pronoun (whether
one c-commands the other), since it matters whether or not both syntactic
variables are dependent pronouns. It is also not sufficient to simply look
at the relation that the syntactic variables bear to their Ā-binders, since a
single Ā-binder can bind one or more variables if the variables are of the
right type (whatever theory of "the right type" one chooses). On the other

hand, the WCO context (setting aside the effect we have discussed for ellipsis contexts) does not arise *unless* more than one variable is in a position to be locally bound by the same Ā-binder (and the scope condition in (7) is partially responsible for ensuring this).

As a history of crossover phenomena, this discussion is far from complete, particularly since it leaves out the accounts that derive crossover from failure of dependency relations. Nonetheless, it serves to provide sufficient perspective for the theory I am about to present. From here on, I only introduce other developments in the established literature at those points where they become immediately relevant to our discussion.

3.2   A Unified Theory of Crossover

The proposal that serves as the principal theme of this chapter is that it is possible to collapse strong and weak crossover into a single phenomenon, such that the INP, as it interacts with other independently motivated properties of linguistic theory, almost completely suffices to derive the existence and distribution of both.

Without appealing to any extension of dependency, it would appear that the INP straightforwardly predicts the existence of SCO. In such cases, the dependent pronoun directly c-commands the variable it is posited to depend on, as illustrated by (1b,c), repeated here.

(1) a. *Who* said *he* hates Malva?
    b. *Who does *he* hate?
    c. *Who does *he* believe Malva hates?

However, as suggested in section 1.4, the INP, perhaps because it is not exclusively about dependent identity, seems to employ an extended notion of dependency, which I state as in (22) (a more precise rendering of the statement in section 2.5).

(22) If α depends on β, then any nominal node γ that dominates α but does not dominate β also depends on β.

The notion of dependency in (22), coupled with the INP, will straightforwardly distinguish (2a) from (2b,c) and (3a) from (3b) (all repeated here), since in the (a) examples, the variable left by *wh*-movement or LF movement will not be c-commanded by the pronoun or any nominal containing the pronoun, but where *his mother* c-commands the variable, the pronoun cannot depend on the variable, and a WCO effect results.

(2) a. *Who* saw *his* mother?

   b. *Who did *his* mother see?

   c. *Who did *his* mother say that Malva saw?

(3) a. Every man saw his mother.

   b. *His mother saw every man.

Since the INP, including the extended notion of dependency in (22), is independently justified where quantifiers are not involved, as argued in section 1.3.3 for ellipsis asymmetries and in section 1.4 for proxy readings, it would appear that the WCO effects are predicted without any appeal to a new principle.

The core of my crossover theory, uniting both phenomena under the INP, is embodied in the analysis I have just presented for (1)–(3). However, matters are not at all so simple once we examine the full range of crossover patterns. Moreover, a variety of ancillary assumptions are necessary before I can nail down exactly what the INP account is committed to, and exactly what must supplement it. Sections 3.3 and 3.4 investigate these commitments and supplements.[5]

3.3 Q-variables and Quantifier Dependency

It is time to explore exactly how the INP is brought to bear on the crossover phenomenon. Above, I suggested that crossover effects arise from the inability of pronouns to have bound readings when they c-command the variables of quantifiers they depend on. However, to ensure this result, we must be precise about what the "variable of a quantifier" is in this theory, and we must require that such pronouns cannot receive a bound variable interpretation in any other way.

In *LGB*, the trace of wh-movement is treated as a syntactic variable, either because it is locally Ā-bound (and is thus contextually defined as a variable) or because the trace is intrinsically marked as a syntactic variable by virtue of wh-movement taking place from that position. In the latter case, the syntactic variable is treated as a name for the purposes of Principle C. From the perspective of the FTIP, if a wh-trace is c-commanded by an element it depends on, then it is well formed as long as it qualifies as the most dependent form available in that environment. Translating the Principle C theory of SCO into the terms of the FTIP, we would have to say that wh-traces count as names and names are less dependent than pronouns; but for this to work, we must add that pronouns could otherwise appear in these positions. However, it is not obvious that pronouns can otherwise appear in the positions of *wh*-traces if the numeration does not introduce them and move them, leaving a copy.

For example, consider what is left behind when a quantificational *wh*-phrase is moved, as in (23).

(23) Who did Didier see [who]

Since *who* is quantificational in this interrogative sentence, it does not seem possible for the lower copy to remain in the representation as a copy; if it does, the higher copy binds no variable (*Didier* is not an appropriate variable). Moreover, when we come to consider some scope reconstruction facts, we will have to assume that for scope to be determined unambiguously, only one quantifier out of a set of quantifier copies (produced by movement) can remain a quantified operator, and the rest must be deleted and replaced with variables. Thus, (23) will have the LF representation in (24), where x is a q-variable.

(24) Who did Didier see x

(25) *Q-variable*
　　　α is a q-variable if α replaces the deleted copy of an operator.

The relationship between a q-variable and its operator antecedent is asymmetric, in the sense that the q-variable is in the scope of the operator and hence depends on the quantifier for its interpretation (for a contrast with pure copies, see below). I assume the process of q-variable insertion to be obligatory whenever more than one copy of an operator with the same numeration index arises.

Notice now that there is no requirement so far that a q-variable must be locally Ā-bound or even locally dependent on the operator that has left the q-variable. Unless we introduce a condition to block it, we might expect that the q-variable could depend on the pronoun (which depends on the operator), as in the representations for (1b) and (2b) with dependency arrows in (26a) and (26b), respectively.

(26) a. *Who* does *he* hate *x*
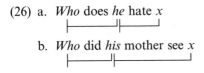

　　　b. *Who* did *his* mother see *x*

Alternatively, both the pronouns and the q-variable may depend directly on the quantificational operator, as in (27a,b).

(27) a. *Who* does *he* hate *x*

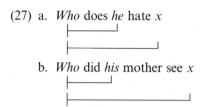

    b. *Who* did *his* mother see *x*

Neither of these representations violates the INP, since no pronoun or variable c-commands a pronoun or variable it depends on. If the INP is to be brought to bear on these cases, it will have to be by forcing pronouns construed as bound variables to depend on the q-variable, as in (28).[6]

(28) *Quantifier Dependency Condition (QDC)*
    x can be interpreted as dependent on a quantified antecedent *y* only if *x* is a q-variable of *y* or *x* is dependent on a q-variable of *y*, or there is no q-variable of *y*.

Given the QDC, the only dependency relations that are possible for the relevant coconstrual are those in (29a,b).

(29) a. *Who* does *he* hate *x*

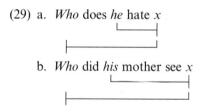

    b. *Who* did *his* mother see *x*

Now the INP will rule out both SCO in (29a) and WCO in (29b) since in both cases, a pronoun is dependent on an element it (or the argument containing it) c-commands.

It is important to keep in mind that for the definition of q-variable in (25), what counts as a q-variable does not follow from any claim about locality of Ā-binders, but rather is an intrinsic property of deleted quantifier copy sites. The definition of q-variable does not induce ill-formedness if a q-variable is c-commanded by something that is purportedly dependent on it. However, the QDC generally ensures that a pronoun must depend on a q-variable to be coconstrued with it, and this induces patterns of dependency that the INP excludes, including those where a pronoun depends on a q-variable it c-commands.[7]

3.4 Earlier Accounts from the Perspective of This One

Most of the principles-and-parameters accounts described in section 2.1 treated SCO and WCO as distinct phenomena, the product of distinct principles, where SCO is purported to follow from the definition of variable or Principle C, while WCO is accounted for by a uniqueness or parallelism condition on syntactic variables. The Leftness Condition accounted for both, but I argue later in this section that leftness, as a restriction on dependency, is not a part of sentence grammar and not the source of crossover effects (and the objection to appealing to linearity raised in section 3.1 also applies). Hornstein (1995) introduces a linking account that bears some affinity to this one, but he too proposes a WCO-specific principle that requires bound variable pronouns to be (almost) c-commanded, sharing with Reinhart's approach the view that dependency requires c-command, a view I have already argued against in chapters 1 and 2.

The only configurational account that distinguishes the two crossover phenomena while still reducing one to the other is that of Stowell (1987), who extends my (1984, 1986) indexing procedure (in turn based on Haïk's (1984)) to embedded pronouns in order to derive WCO from SCO. The heart of Stowell's idea is that the index on the pronoun in (30a) is "handed up" to the phrase containing it (as in (30b)), at which point an illicit binding relation ensues, such that the definition of syntactic variable (or Principle C) rules out the result.

(30) a. *Who$_i$ did his$_i$ mother see t$_i$
      b. *Who$_i$ did [his$_i$ mother]$_{j/i}$ see t$_i$

The indexing algorithm subordinates the index of *his* to that of *his mother*, but the subordinate index is now in a position to c-command the trace. In effect, the trace is "weakly bound" by the *his* of *his mother*, hence a "weak" version of an SCO effect. For reasons I have discussed throughout, I am not assuming that indices play a role in explaining dependency phenomena, and so it would be unfortunate to have to rely on them here. Stowell's proposal is in fact more congenial in the dependency theory setting, and I have adapted the core of his idea to derive the WCO effect from the same mechanism that derives SCO. However, in my account it is the INP, not the DSV or Principle C, that derives SCO.[8]

Moreover, the QDC predicts the absence of WCO effects where there is no q-variable. In examples like those in (31) (see also (14)), more than one pronoun is locally Ā-bound, but neither is the copy-trace of a quantified Ā-operator. Thus, nothing prevents the second of these pronouns from depending on the first, nor must either of these resumptive pronouns depend on the other, as long as both depend on their antecedent (whether that is taken to be *who* or *the sort of woman* or both). There is no INP violation.

(31) a. Jones would never marry any woman *who* he would never be able to guess when *her* mother is going to visit *her*.
   b. Do you remember that sad little kid *who his* mother was always complaining about *his* grades?
   c. Jones would never marry the sort of woman *who* he would have to guess when *she* was going to visit *her* mother.

In (31c), Rule H requires that *her* must depend on *she* (rather than directly on *who*) if they are to be coconstrued, but this requirement does not appear to be testable.

It would appear that the parallelism concerns of the PCOB and its descendants (e.g., Ā-consistency in Safir 1996a, 1999) are met by the formulation of q-variable, including across-the-board extractions like those in (15), repeated here as (32), with q-variables inserted.

(32) a. I don't know *who* each man spoke to x and offended x.
   b. I don't know *who* each man claimed to know x and to have hired x.

Most accounts of these extractions (beginning, e.g., with Williams 1978) assume that in both conjuncts the gaps result from movement, hence that both conjuncts have q-variables in them and both q-variables can depend directly on the quantifier they are bound variables of, namely, *who* in these examples.[9]

This new analysis also resolves a difficulty for the PCOB that is shared by every theory of crossover I am aware of with respect to examples like the following:[10]

(33) a. *Who* will Rochelle make sure she speaks to t before *he* enters the room
   b. *Who*, before *he* enters the room, will Rochelle make sure she speaks to t
   c. *Who will *his* hostess make sure she speaks to t

(34) a. Penelope gave *every suitor* a glass of champagne before *he* was to speak.

    b. ?Before *he* was to speak, Penelope gave *every suitor* a glass of
       wine.
    c. **His* hostess gave *every suitor* a glass of wine.

Under the theory of WCO that relies on locality of Ā-binding, (33a,b)
should both be excluded, since both *him* and the trace of *who* are
locally Ā-bound. Moreover, accounts like Reinhart's (1983a,b), which
rely on licensing of bound variable pronouns based on c-command by
the trace, also predict such cases to be ungrammatical. Finally, examples
like (33b) are not expected to be acceptable from the perspective of any
precedence-/leftness-style account of WCO (e.g., the account proposed by
Williams (1994), who only considers examples like (33a)), though I take
the "?" in (34a) to be the residue of a linear effect not peculiar to crossover.[11] The account proposed here is the only one that makes the right
prediction: no nominal containing *him* c-commands the trace in (33a,b) or
in (34a,b), so nothing blocks the pronoun from depending on the trace.[12]

3.5 Scopal Interaction and Functional Interpretations

The account I have given so far is silent on a very common class of examples, namely, those where a quantified expression in object position
has scope over one in subject position.

(35) a. Someone loves everyone.
     b. Some x (every y (x loves y))
     c. Every y (some x (x loves y))

It is reasonable to ask in this context how *everyone* could have scope
over *someone* where the q-variable of the existential c-commands the
q-variable of the universal. According to the INP, the q-variable of the
existential cannot depend on the q-variable of the universal. However,
the QDC (28) does not require this. All that matters for the relative scope
in this case is the relative quantifier scope, since both q-variables are
already directly dependent on their local Ā-antecedents. For relative
scope, in short, only the positions of quantifiers are evaluated, not the
positions of their q-variables.[13]

    However, if the q-variable of one quantifier were forced to depend di-
rectly on the q-variable of another, the INP would predict an interesting
class of asymmetries. Consider in this light the work of Chierchia (1991),
who extends the force of WCO to the interpretive properties of answers

to questions. Chierchia points out that there is a subject-object asymmetry in the availability of functional answers to questions in examples like (36a,b).

(36) a. Who does *every soldier* write letters to t
          Answer: *His* mother.
      b. Who t writes letters to *every soldier*
          Answer: *?*His* mother.

He argues that this asymmetry would be explicable in terms of WCO if the traces in (36a) and (36b) actually have pronouns embedded in them corresponding to those in the answers, as in (37) (as a representation of (36b)), although he has no independent empirical reason to posit an embedded pronoun supporting a functional dependency in (37a,b).[14]

(37) a. Who$_i$ [$_{IP}$ does every soldier$_j$ write letters to [$_{DP}$ pro$_j$ t$_i$]]
      b. *Who$_i$ [$_{IP}$[$_{DP}$ pro$_j$ t$_i$] writes letters to [every soldier]$_j$]

Then whatever theory of WCO one chooses would presumably rule out the result in the same way it does in (38b) but not (38a).

(38) a. *Every soldier* writes letters to *his* mother.
      b. **His* mother writes letters to *every soldier*.

From the perspective of my proposals, the functional reading is one where the *wh*-trace in examples like (36a,b) depends not only on the *wh*-antecedent, but also on the quantificational trace. The INP predicts that if the trace c-commands *every soldier*, then it cannot depend on *every soldier*. Thus, what is WCO-like in the phenomenon from my perspective is that the INP can be brought to bear on these cases without resorting to the artificial device of building in a pronoun to trigger the effect.

I have thus distinguished cases like (35), where only the relative position of the quantifiers at LF matters to determine the patterns of dependency, from functional interpretations that involve dependency of one q-variable on another. This position is justified by a further distinction. The apparent wide scope for the universal in the functional answer case appears to reside in the necessary dependency of the *wh*-trace on the universal, not dependency of interrogative force on the universal. After all, (36a) is still a question. Instead, I express the wide scope of the universal as the requirement that the *wh*-trace must depend directly on the q-variable of the universal, even though it is also identity dependent on the *wh*-expression it is a copy of. It then follows that whenever the trace of *wh*-movement c-commands a q-variable it is supposed to depend on, it will fail to have a functional reading.[15]

Notice that the WCO effect on functional interpretation is not limited to *wh*-constructions. Consider the contrast in (39a,b). ((39c,d) are controls to show the effect is restricted to quantifier interaction.)

(39) a. *Everyone* loves someone, namely, *his* fairy godmother.
     b. *Someone loves *everyone*, namely, *his* fairy godmother.
     c. *Bill* loves someone, namely, *his* fairy godmother.
     d. Someone loves *Bill*, namely, *his* fairy godmother.

In this context, just in case the functional specification is for an indefinite in subject position, the functional interpretation fails.[16] This is predictable in that the cases that fail to have the functional reading are those where the functionally interpreted q-variable c-commands the q-variable (of the universal) it depends on.[17]

To recapitulate my account of functional interpretation asymmetries, the WCO effect is a consequence of the pattern of dependencies that are required for the functional interpretation, such that the variable corresponding to the answer to the functional question c-commands something it must depend on (e.g., *every soldier* in (40b)).

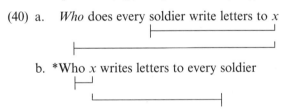

(40) a. *Who* does every soldier write letters to *x*

     b. *Who *x* writes letters to every soldier

I have not complicated the representations by including QR of *every soldier*, which would leave the q-variable in the position of the universal expression, since the pattern of dependencies would be the same (in the relevant respect), by hypothesis. No special index on the trace is required (as in my earlier theories) and no pronoun needs to be inserted (as in Chierchia's account), a stipulation that would be particularly unfortunate since it is not justified by the copy mechanism of movement.

3.6   Weakest Crossover

Work by Lasnik and Stowell (1991) (henceforth, L&S) shifted the empirical ground underneath the purely configurational account of WCO based on the Bijection Principle and the PCOB. L&S point out that WCO is not observed in a variety of structures where, in purely configurational terms, one might expect it.[18] (In (41), coconstruals are represented with indices, as in L&S's theory.)

(41) a. Who$_i$ t$_i$ will it be easy [Op$_i$ for us [to get [his$_i$ mother] to talk to t$_i$]]

   b. Thor$_i$ is too angry [Op$_i$ for [his$_i$ mother] to talk to t$_i$]

   c. Who$_i$ did you stay with t$_i$ [Op$_i$ before [his$_i$ wife] had spoken to t$_i$]

   d. This book$_i$, [I expect [its$_i$ author] to buy t$_i$]

L&S suggest that the range of structures where crossover produces no unacceptability may be characterized by the absence of syntactic operators corresponding to "true quantifiers." They propose distinguishing between operators that correspond to true quantifiers and those that do not in terms of the nature of the syntactic variables they bind. Syntactic operators that are not true quantifiers $\bar{\text{A}}$-bind null epithets, which L&S take to be just like overt epithets, subject to Principle C, but capable of being $\bar{\text{A}}$-bound.

For principled reasons I will explore directly, I do not think that (41a–d) should all have the same analysis, nor do I think that the null epithet analysis is ever right. However, I do take L&S's distinction between quantified and nonquantified operators to have been an important advance. From the point of view of my definition of q-variable and the QDC, if the operator is not a quantifier, it is plausible that its trace is not a q-variable. If there is no q-variable, then the QDC does not apply to require a pronoun to depend on the trace even when they are both ultimately codependent on the same operator antecedent. In other words, if there is no q-variable, then no WCO effect is expected. For some of the weakest crossover cases, I will pursue a strategy of this sort, while for other cases, the view that quantification is not involved is harder to defend, and so a different sort of analysis is required.

First, let us consider the epithet analysis that L&S offer. They argue that the trace of a nonquantificational $\bar{\text{A}}$-operator is to be evaluated as a null epithet, in the sense that the element left by the movement is subject to Principle C, hence susceptible to SCO under the Principle C theory of SCO. Since nonquantificational null operators leave epithets, L&S reason, an A-binder outside the domain of the null operator would still induce a Principle C effect on the epithet. They exploit this analysis to predict that parasitic gaps (pg) will not be supported by c-commanding subject traces, as in (42a), on the parallel with (42b).

(42) a. *Who t [talked to Melba [Op just before the police arrested pg]]
     b. *He [talked to Melba just [before the police arrested Joseph]]

By comparison, in (43a,b), where the trace of movement does not c-command the parasitic gap, the result is acceptable.

(43) a. Who did Joseph [talk to t] [Op just before the police arrested pg]
     b. We [talked to him] [Op just before the police arrested Joseph]

However, if (42a) is excluded because the subject trace A-binds a null epithet in the object position of arrested, then we do not expect real epithets to be acceptable in exactly this environment—but they are, as illustrated in (44) (my thanks to Caroline Heycock for suggesting this line of argument).

(44) He/Joseph talked to Melba just before the police arrested the poor bastard.

As Dubinsky and Hamilton (1998) have pointed out, it is not the case that epithets cannot be A-bound at all; rather, they are not possible when embedded in the complements of logophoric verbs (typically verbs of saying or belief) anteceded by the logophoric subject (i.e., the sayer or believer).[19]

(45) *He/Roland says that the police will arrest the poor bastard.

An alternative analysis that bears a kinship to L&S's approach is to treat the traces of nonquantificational operators as elements that are not q-variables, whatever else they are. If the trace is not a q-variable, then nothing blocks either (a) dependency of both the pronoun and the trace directly on the operator, or (b) dependency of the trace on the intervening pronoun, as illustrated earlier for (26a,b) and (27a,b), presented here with a topicalized name in (46a,b) and (47a,b), respectively. Thus, both (46a) and (46b) are predicted to be grammatical, perhaps even with the co-dependency pattern in (47a) and (47b).

(46) a. Carl he says Barb hates t
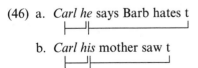

     b. Carl his mother saw t

(47) a. *Carl he* says Barb hates t

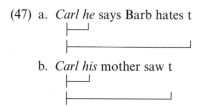

      b. *Carl his* mother saw t

The absence of WCO is now straightforward, since these dependencies are licit (though (47a) is probably blocked by Rule H; see section 2.3) and do not violate the INP.

However, it is also the case that we now expect SCO to be missing, insofar as it is derived by the INP in every Ā-construction where WCO is. Treating (46a) as grammatical seems odd, as for most speakers it is unacceptable; but there is evidence that this is the correct interpretation of the facts, at least as far as the INP is concerned (but I return to it directly with respect to the FTIP).

Consider the topicalization construction, where it is not obvious that what is topicalized is in any way an operator, or even that it involves the intervention of a null operator. I will assume an adjunction-to-IP analysis along the lines proposed by Baltin (1982), or at least fronting to an Ā-position that is not Spec,CP. From the perspective of the copy theory, Ā-traces correspond to whatever they are copies of. If they are not copies of operators converted to q-variables, then they are copies of the fronted constituent, pure and simple. If a name is moved to an Ā-position, then its trace/copy should be a name; but if a pronoun is so moved, then its trace/copy should be a pronoun.

(48) a. *Lyle* I don't like [*Lyle*]
      b. *Him* I don't like [*him*]

If (48a,b) were in FTIP competition, then the pronoun in (48b) would be a competing form with respect to (48a) to determine whether the copy *Lyle* is the most dependent form available. We would expect (48b) to win the competition for the dependent reading, since the copy *him* is more dependent than the copy *Lyle*. Thus, (48a) would never be possible, contrary to fact.

However, (48a,b) are not in competition. The copy relation is one of indistinctness, not dependency (unless an operator copy is converted to a q-variable). Thus, the copy of *Lyle* does not depend on *Lyle* any more than the copy of *him* depends on *him*. Thus, even if the FTIP were to apply between copies and the moved constituents they are copies of, covaluation does not rely on dependency in these cases—indistinct entities cannot help but be covalued. On the other hand, the lowest copy can indeed be evaluated by the FTIP with respect to dependency of that lowest copy on some c-commanding antecedent that it is *not* a copy of. Consider (49) and (50), based on examples originally given by Postal (1971, 1997), where the brackets enclose the unpronounced copies left by movement.[20]

(49) a. *Him, he* knew she thought little of [*him*]
     b. ??*Louis, he* knew she thought little of [*Louis*]
     c. **Louis, he* thought little of [*Louis*]
     d. *?*Him, he* thought little of [*him*]
     e. *Himself, he* thought little of [*himself*]

(50) a. *Him, he* knew she would never work hard for [*him*]
     b. ??*Louis, he* knew she would never work hard for [*Louis*]
     c. **Louis, he* worked hard for [*Louis*]
     d. *?*Him, he* worked hard for [*him*]
     e. *Himself, he* worked hard for [*himself*]

In all of these examples, we can assume that the copy left by movement matches the displaced copy, be it pronominal or an r-expression, and is indistinct from it. The FTIP predicts that (49c,d) and (50c,d) are strongly unacceptable, since neither a pronominal copy nor an r-expression copy results in the most dependent form available (with respect to dependency on the matrix subject) by comparison with a copy of *himself* as in (49e) and (50e). I am assuming, with respect to (49e) and (50e), that since the lower copy of *himself* satisfies LAL, the higher one does not have to, as the two are indistinct. If a SELF form were available in an otherwise identical numeration, then the forms in the (e) examples would be in competition and thereby obviate the forms in the (c) and (d) examples. For (49a) and (50a), a SELF form would violate LAL, so the most dependent form available (with respect to the matrix subject) is a pronoun that leaves a pronominal copy. Thus, (49a) and (50a) are fine because the copy is a pronoun deemed well formed by the FTIP. Moreover, it would appear that (49a) and (50a) should obviate (49b) and (50b), respectively. (The same account applies to (46a), although the effect is not as strong here (and for some speakers is very weak), for reasons that will be explored in section 4.2 (concerning the possibility of vehicle change).)

Cases like (49) and (50) are strong evidence against the view that all
Ā-traces should be treated as names (or epithets, for that matter), since
the copy theory of movement, in conspiracy with the FTIP, makes the
right prediction only if copies are faithful in this environment. If all of
the Ā-movement constructions behaved the way topicalizations like (49)
and (50) do, then the FTIP would predict where SCO is well formed and
where it is not; but in fact topicalizations are atypical, since what is
fronted is not an operator that leaves a q-variable. Here again, we see a
divergence between what the FTIP predicts and what the INP predicts.

However, if we consider topicalizations that include a quantified fronted
constituent, we expect SCO to reappear, since the trace would be (or
would contain) a quantifier copy that is replaced by a q-variable. Normally, it is not felicitous to front a quantifier in a topicalization structure,
but it is possible to do so just in case the topicalization is contrastive.
Consider the contrast between (51a) and (51b).[21] ((51c) is a control to
show that the problem only arises under the appropriate coconstrual.)

(51) a.   For *her*, *she* can never expect that we will work hard *t*, though
          for ***hím***, ***he*** can be sure that we will work hard *t* indeed

     b.   For *her*, *she* can never expect that we will work hard *t*, though
          *for ***any mán***, ***he*** can be sure that we will work hard *t* indeed

     c.   For *her*, *she* can never expect that we will work hard *t*, though
          for ***any mán***, *she* can be sure that we will work hard *t* indeed

The SCO effect in (51b) arises because the QDC requires *he* to depend on
the trace, not because the FTIP is violated.

The latter point deserves explication. Consider some simpler cases first,
such as those in (52a) and (52b).

(52) a.   **He* loves *Rex's* mother.

     b.   **He* loves *everyone's* mother.

While (52a) is clearly excluded by the FTIP, I am contending now that
(52b) is excluded not by the FTIP, but by the INP exclusively (because
the QDC requires *he* to depend on the trace of *everyone* that will arise by
QR). The FTIP can apply to (52b) because a pronoun is more dependent
than a name and a pronoun can converge in place of a name in the numeration for (52a). But notice that I am assuming that a name is *on* the
most dependent scale, meaning that it is a form that *can* be dependent. If
I open a conversation by saying *Rex is late*, then even if you don't know
Rex you will assume that I assume you do. This effect is missing if I
precede *Rex is late* with *That guy is Rex* (pointing to Rex). Thus, under

normal circumstances, names are familiar. As argued in Safir 2004, pronouns are essentially reduced definite descriptions. A pronoun in place of a name or definite description in an FTIP competition does not lose information because an identity-dependent position c-commanded by an antecedent with the same information is already posited as part of the calculation. The FTIP algorithm permits us to replace *Rex* in the numeration of (52a) with a less dependent form, a pronoun; the pronoun converges; and so the failed dependency of *Rex* on its c-commander is fed to Pragmatic Obviation.

By contrast, *everyone*, a quantifier, is not recoverable from a c-commanding antecedent, since the antecedent depends on the quantifier itself.[22] Thus, a quantified expression is not on the most-dependent scale and the algorithm that instantiates the FTIP cannot replace a quantified expression with a name or a pronoun in a test to see if a less dependent competitor could converge. I conclude that the FTIP does not derive SCO (in the manner that Principle C derived it as a c-commanded name within the *LGB* theory) because the trace of the Ā-operator is, in most cases (e.g., not the topicalization of a nonquantifier), a q-variable, and could not be anything else. This is a good result, reducing some potential redundancies, since the SCO effects in quantificational structures like those in (52b) are all now uniquely attributable to the INP, and those in topicalized structures are uniquely attributed to the FTIP.

Of course, we have achieved more than simply reducing redundancy among theory-internal principles. Returning now to the contrast between (51a) and (51b), (51b) falls under the INP since the QDC regulates the q-variable, feeding a dependency relation to the INP that is rejected. By contrast, (51a) does not fall under the QDC, since the trace is a pronominal copy, not a q-variable, and so the INP does not rule it out. Moreover, the pronominal copy trace is the most dependent form available in this environment, so the FTIP doesn't rule out either. The absence of SCO is explained.

Extending this result further, restrictive relatives, free relatives, and embedded questions all leave q-variables and thus all induce crossover effects.

(53) a. *[*The man who* we think *he* bought a picture of *t*] walked out
      b. *Elena will avoid [*whoever he* makes it unlikely that we will like *t*]
      c. *We wondered [*who he* is likely to buy a picture of *t*]

In these instances, there is no competitor that obviates the choice of *who* or *whoever* in these derivations, and so the trace left behind is a q-variable and is not susceptible to the FTIP.

The account of missing SCO just presented for topicalization cases does not, however, extend to some of the null operator constructions (41a–c) that L&S show to be weakest crossover environments. For example, it is not clear what the trace of a null operator should be evaluated to be. If it is not a q-variable, but a copy, it is not obvious what it is a copy of, if operators cannot be vacuous. On the other hand, if we say that null operators of the relevant type bind q-variables, then we would expect these constructions to exhibit both SCO and WCO. In fact, though, they only exhibit SCO. ((54b) is from L&S 1991, 709.)

(54) a. *Terry* is tough [Op PRO to ask *him* to criticize *t*]
  b. *Who* did you talk to *t* [Op after *he* asked you to stay with *t*]
  c. *Sally* is too self-righteous [Op for *her* to ever get Portia to support *t*]

Moreover, if we assume that the traces of these null operators are simply pronominal copies, as proposed in Safir 1996a, then we will neutralize WCO, as desired, but we will also neutralize SCO, given that we do not rely here on the definition of syntactic variable.[23]

The fact that the constructions in (54) involve null operators may be misleading, however. Notice that similar effects hold for nonrestrictive relative clauses.[24]

(55) a. *Rex*, who *his* accountant loves *t*, is a Republican
  b. **Rex*, who *he* loves *t*, is a Republican
  c. **Rex*, who *he* says Mary loves *t*, is a Republican

The absence of the WCO effect in this environment, if it is related to the cases in (54), cannot be attributed to the nullity of the operator. However, as Hornstein (1995, 100–106) has observed, what both cases have in common is that the status of the operator is determined by an antecedent independently established outside the domain of the operator. In other words, the *his* in (55a) could depend directly on *Rex* instead of depending on the operator *who*[25] *or the q-variable of that operator*. Thus, all of these cases will license WCO because they provide an antecedent external to the operator, as in (56a,b), but one that is nonetheless covalued with the operator and its q-variable.[26]

(56) a. *Rex, who his* accountant loves *t* , is a Republican

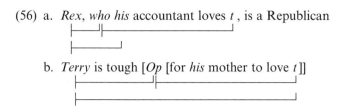

   b. *Terry* is tough [*Op* [for *his* mother to love *t*]]

Now I must explain why the same sort of dependency does not erase SCO effects for (55b) and (55c), since an INP violation can be avoided by permitting dependency on an external antecedent, as in (57a) (corresponding to (55b)) or (57b) (an example similar to (54a)).[27]

(57) a. *Rex, who he* loves *t,* is a Republican

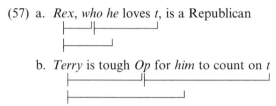

   b. *Terry* is tough *Op* for *him* to count on *t*

The representations in (57a,b) (as opposed to those in (56a,b)) are prohibited by Rule H, however, which requires chained representations when the lowest dependent is c-commanded by all the intervening (A-)dependents, which are in turn anteceded by the ultimate c-commanding antecedent (I do not assume that intervening Ā-positions have to be chained). Rule H will only allow the representations (58a,b) for the sentences in (57a,b), respectively, if the q-variable and the pronoun are both ultimately identity dependent on the external antecedent of the operator.

(58) a. *Rex, who he* loves *t,* is a Republican

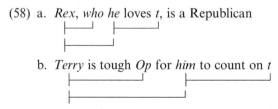

   b. *Terry* is tough *Op* for *him* to count on *t*

Thus, Rule H intervenes to force the q-variable to locally depend on the c-commanding pronoun instead of on the operator in (58a,b), but this violates the QDC, since *him* must depend on the q-variable, which is the trace.

The only remaining possible representation for (55b) is (59a); and for (57b) and (58b), the only representation that is allowed is (59b). In both

(59a) and (59b), the pronoun depends on the q-variable of the operator, violating the INP.[28]

(59) a. *Rex, who he* loves *t*, is a Republican

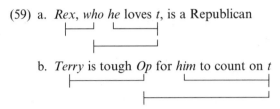

   b. *Terry* is tough *Op* for *him* to count on *t*

Thus, we need only appeal to two independently motivated restrictions, Rule H (see section 2.3) and the QDC, to ensure that where WCO is neutralized by an operator-external antecedent, SCO is not so neutralized as well.[29]

There is independent evidence to support this analysis of those weakest crossover contexts that involve operators. As I have pointed out elsewhere (Safir 1986, 669; 1999, 593), one cannot conclude from the fact that primary WCO is neutralized in nonrestrictive relatives that crossover effects in such relatives are alleviated entirely. They are alleviated when the potentially dependent pronoun corresponds to the external head of the construction, as in (55a), but not when the operator pied-pipes a larger constituent to which the external head of the nonrestrictive relative does not correspond. If crossover is calculated for that larger constituent, primary WCO still holds, as illustrated in the contrasts between (60a,b) and (60c,d).

(60) a. *?Joe, [*a cousin of whom*] *her* child loves *t*, hates kids
   b.   Joe, [*a cousin of whom*] *t* loves *her* child, hates kids
   c. *?Joe, [*whose sister*] *her* child loves *t*, hates kids
   d.   Joe, [*whose sister*] *t* loves *her* child, hates kids

If *her* must depend on the constituent containing the q-variable in the position of the trace (e.g., *a cousin of x* in (60a)), then the INP still applies to rule it out, since in these cases, direct reliance on an antecedent external to the operator is not possible.[30]

An important feature of this account of weakest crossover that distinguishes it from earlier accounts, such as those in L&S 1991, Postal 1993, and Safir 1996a, 1999, is that I do not have to insist that the operators in weakest crossover contexts are not quantificational, nor do I claim that it matters if they are or not. Operators leave copies or q-variables, whether or not they pied-pipe larger constituents. This avoids the problems faced by previous accounts with respect to weakest cross-over contexts that clearly do involve quantification, such as parasitic gap constructions where the licensing Ā-antecedent is quantified.

(61) a. *Who* [did Lydia [interrupt *t*] [*Op* before *his* wife could even speak to *t*]]

   b. *The man* [*who* [Lydia interrupted *t*] [*Op* before *his* wife could even talk to *t*]] is one of her lovers

Under this account, one must only assume that the null operators in these constructions are parasitically quantificational on their antecedents, not that they are not quantificational at all. All that matters for the WCO effect to be overcome in operator constructions such as these is that the antecedent should be external to and independent of the operator. In the parasitic gap construction, the pronoun embedded in the adjunct can be directly dependent on the trace of the main clause (which does not c-command the pronoun). SCO is still induced within the adjunct where the q-variable (parasitic gap) is identity dependent on a c-commanding nominal. Either the (pro) nominal in question must depend on the q-variable, which induces an INP violation, or the pronoun depends on an adjunct-external antecedent, in which case Rule H requires the q-variable to depend on the c-commanding pronoun (instead of the null operator), violating the QDC. In other words, the explanation for the absence of WCO but the presence of SCO in adjuncts containing a parasitic gap is the same explanation given for nonrestrictive relatives.[31]

To summarize, there are two strategies for neutralizing crossover effects in Ā-contexts that account for the weakest crossover cases (neither one dependent on resumption, which is yet another strategy that can neutralize crossover effects).

One strategy involves literal copies, which do not induce crossover blocked by the INP because they do not involve q-variables. For topicalization structures, for example, an effect reminiscent of crossover is induced by the FTIP, which arises because the fronted constituent competes with a more dependent form. If, however, the most dependent form available (with respect to the intervening antecedent) is employed as the fronted constituent, then there is no crossover effect at all (a similar analysis can be extended to clefts).

The other weakest crossover environments are more similar to INP-induced crossover environments in that they involve operators that leave behind not copies, but q-variables (or q-variables embedded in a larger

copied constituent). What makes the weakest crossover operator constructions distinctive, however, is that in all of them, the operator in
question is fully dependent on an otherwise independent external antecedent. It does not matter whether or not the antecedent outside the operator is quantified—only whether or not that antecedent counts as an
independent A-position. In the one context where pied-piping can be used
as a test, crossover effects still hold within the domain of the operator
with respect to the pied-piped constituent, even though the operator
embedded in the pied-piped constituent is one that otherwise appears to
participate in a weakest crossover context.[32]

One way of looking at the theoretical design of this analysis is to regard
the QDC as a means of ensuring that bound variable interpretations for
pronouns are filtered through the INP. Similarly, Rule H ensures that
there are no representations of operator-external antecedency that permit
SCO cases to escape the INP. Thus, all of the true crossover effects are
now derived by the INP.

3.7   The Nature of This Explanation

The nature and distribution of the effects presented here are best understood as the interpretive consequence of a set of syntactic restrictions. For
the INP to do its work, all that the syntax must encode, besides phrase
markers, are asymmetric sentence-internal dependency relations. The INP
only blocks dependency relations; it does not mandate that they should
exist or that they should have any particular content (although I have
focused on identity relations here). Indeed, for the INP, the semantic nature or content of the dependency is essentially irrelevant, which means
that dependencies that do not correspond to dependent identities are also
blocked, as in the case of functional answers to questions.

If this approach is correct, it has consequences for any theory of the
syntax/semantics interface. For instance, it does not appear possible that
the detailed patterning of crossover effects will follow directly from some
nuanced principle of semantic composition that subsumes the INP. To see
why, let us consider one plausible version of how such a semantic approach might proceed.

Insofar as c-command relies on sisterhood, the possibility arises that
the function composition of two nodes in a combinatory semantics may
be sensitive to the dependency relations between the two nodes. For ex-

ample, where dependency relations are well formed, a combination between YP and Z' (assuming that the basic asymmetry of structure would
combine a specifier with a Z' constituent to make a ZP) is one where an
open variable β in Z' is bound by virtue of combination with YP. The
c-commanding YP is the antecedent or contains the antecedent. Where
dependency goes wrong, the c-commander has an open variable that depends on a subconstituent of the Z' it combines with, and perhaps it does
not have access to that relation within Z'.[33]

(62) a. $[_{ZP}[_{YP} \ldots \alpha \ldots] [_{Z'} \ldots \beta \ldots]]$

b. *$[_{ZP}[_{YP} \ldots \alpha \ldots] [_{Z'} \ldots \beta \ldots]]$

On this approach, a version of one suggested by Bittner (1998), the INP is
never stated as a syntactic restriction; instead, it is strictly a restriction on
composing Z' with YP, if YP depends on anything in Z' (the relationships
represented by dependency arrows have to be assumed, of course).

Any semantic approach, however, would still have to assume the QDC,
which is crucial to determining what depends on what (what the arrows
connect). In particular, there is nothing straightforward about the semantics of pronominal forms interpreted as bound variables that predicts
why a resumptive pronoun would not trigger WCO, as mentioned earlier
(see also the discussion of late adjunction in sections 4.3–4.4). Only the
result of the syntactic derivation as regulated by the QDC ensures this
outcome. Thus, the dependency relations encoded in arrow representations crucially depend on syntactic factors. If the pattern of dependency
relations depends on syntactic factors that the principle of composition
does not regulate, then no theory of crossover effects will follow directly
from semantic composition.

The semantic proposal introduced above is not a straw man, however.
I suspect attributing the INP to a restriction on semantic composition, a
restriction that stops a specifier from depending in any way on what is
predicated of it, is the right idea once the syntactic origin of the pattern of
dependencies is acknowledged. In other words, the relevant principle of
semantic composition must only apply to the patterns of dependency that
do not violate the QDC, Rule H, or the FTIP. On this account, crossover
effects are ultimately enforced by a semantic principle, but the distribution of the effect is essentially determined by the patterns of dependency
that the syntax allows. Reducing the INP to a semantic principle would,

moreover, lend force to my contention that the INP should not be reduced to a newly crafted version of movement or to some wider application of the FTIP (as discussed in chapter 5), both of which would clutter a
semantic constraint with a variety of extraneous syntactic properties. I
take the semantic alternative to the INP as I have described it here to
be both plausible and intriguing, but I will not explore it further in this
book.

Chapter 4

Reconstruction and Dependent Readings

Reconstruction has become a loosely used empirical term that character-izes syntactic contexts where a displaced constituent or a portion of its contents acts as if it had never been displaced. There was a time when linguists used the term to refer to a process by means of which displaced constituents were actually returned to their places of origin, but with the reemergence of the copy theory in the 1990s, reconstruction effects have been increasingly seen as instances where copies left by movement play a special role in interpretation. My main goal in this chapter is to show that the account of crossover developed in chapter 3 does not have to be com-plicated in any way to extend to reconstruction effects, given the copy theory of movement. In this regard, this chapter serves as an argument for the copy theory and the assumptions supporting it, insofar as the distribution of copies plays a key role in the explanations I develop for the persistence or disappearance of dependent readings in reconstruction contexts.

4.1 Secondary Crossover

The empirical force of the crossover generalizations was extended in Safir 1984 (where I built on earlier observations by Higginbotham (1980b)) to what Postal (1993) has since called secondary crossover effects. Secondary crossover arises most obviously when an overt *wh*-operator pied-pipes a larger constituent, such that the trace, in an indexing theory, would not match that of the pronoun that is crossed over by the operator. For ex-ample, secondary SCO arises in cases like (1a–c) and secondary WCO in ones like (2a–c).

(1) a. **Whose* mother did *he* see?
    b. *any boy *whose* mother the policeman thought *he* saw
    c. **Not one student's* teacher did *he* speak to.

(2) a. *_Whose_ mother did _his_ teacher see?

    b. *any boy _whose_ mother the policewoman thought _his_ teacher saw

    c. *_Not one student's_ mother did _his_ teacher speak to.

In (1), it does not appear on the surface as if the _wh_ or negative quantifier will be c-commanded by the subject; hence, no Principle C effect is expected unless some sort of reconstruction device is invoked to restore the quantifier to the c-command domain of the subject. The same is true of (2), in that the subject containing the pronoun does not c-command the quantifier trace in (2), since the quantifier has been pied-piped away, leaving behind a trace whose index does not correspond to that of the pronoun (_his_) presumably inducing the effect.

As pointed out in Safir 1996a, however (and in a slightly different form in Safir 1984), the relevant relations can be expressed in this theory if a special algorithm manipulating the indices of pied-piped constituents is introduced. That algorithm, the Q-Chain Convention (see Safir 1996a for details), essentially restores to the trace of the pied-piped constituent a subordinate index corresponding to the quantifier contained in the overtly extracted phrase, as illustrated in (3a,b) for secondary SCO.

(3) a. *$[\text{Whose}_i \text{ mother}]_{k/i}$ did he_i see $t_{k/i}$

    b. $[\text{Whose}_i \text{ mother}]_{k/i}$ $t_{k/i}$ saw him_i

In (3a), the subordinate index (the one to the right of the slash) in the complex index of the object trace is still bound by the index of the subject, violating the definition of variable (i.e., the index i is not locally $\bar{\text{A}}$-bound). By contrast, extraction of the subject containing a quantifier would leave a complex index on the subject trace in (3b) that could c-command a pronoun in the object position, preventing the index of the pronominal object from being locally $\bar{\text{A}}$-bound by the subordinate index of the operator. The complex indices thus function to restore the DSV account of SCO.

Under this theory of complex indices, the representation of secondary WCO is as follows:

(4) a. *$[\text{Whose}_i \text{ mother}]_{k/i}$ did $[\text{his}_i \text{ teacher}]$ see $t_{k/i}$

    b. $[\text{Whose}_i \text{ mother}]_{k/i}$ $t_{k/i}$ saw his_i teacher

Since the PCOB is only sensitive to parallel locally $\bar{\text{A}}$-bound elements, it applies to rule out (4a) but not (4b). The fronted operators in (4a) and (4b) have the same subordinate and superordinate indices (by part of the algorithm I won't review). What is different is the position of their traces.

In (4b), the subordinate index i of the trace c-commands *his* and the result is well formed. In (4a), by contrast, *his* and the subordinate i index of the trace are both locally bound by the subordinate i index of *whose mother*. Thus, the PCOB applies to rule out the nonparallelism in (4a), but not (4b) (and the Ā-consistency account in Safir 1996a would make the same distinction).

Besides the fact that the indexing theory proposed in Safir 1984, 1996a, is embedded in a nonunitary account of crossover, the indexing theory itself is a very powerful extension of indexing unmotivated outside of crossover phenomena. From the present perspective, however, the more fundamental issue is that no appeal to indices is permitted because indices (other than numeration indices) do not exist in the minimalist-based theory I have developed here. Clearly, we require an alternative account of these facts.

Fortunately, the INP account of crossover in chapter 3 extends to secondary crossover without any further stipulation. Consider the representation of secondary SCO in (5), where we are now assuming the copy theory.

(5) a. *[*Whose* mother] [did *he* see [x mother]]
    b. *anyone* [[*whose* mother] [*he* saw [x mother]]]

The q-variable in these cases is the deleted copy of the quantifier in the Ā-antecedent and *he* c-commands this q-variable—hence, *he* cannot depend on the q-variable by the INP. If the pronoun does not c-command the q-variable, then the INP does not block *him* from depending on the q-variable, as in (6a,b).

(6) a. [*Whose* mother] [[x's mother] saw *him*]
    b. *anyone* [[*whose* mother] [[x's mother] saw *him*]]

The representations for secondary WCO in (7a,b) receive exactly the same explanation.

(7) a. *[*Whose* mother] [did [*his* teacher] see [x's mother]]
    b. [*Whose* mother] [[x's mother] saw [*his* teacher]]

Once again, where *his* can depend on the q-variable, as in (7b), no crossover effect is induced, but the INP blocks dependency of *his* on the q-variable in (7a), since *his teacher* c-commands the q-variable.

The fact that WCO and SCO both induce secondary effects is suggestive evidence that they are the same phenomenon and should be treated by the same principle (which appears to be the intuition behind Postal's (1993) discussion). In the present account, the unification of these effects is achieved by the INP, which is independently required for the ellipsis cases (and proxy and circular readings) where quantification is not crucial, as it interacts with the independently motivated copy theory (to which I return in section 4.3). Thus, no special indexing device is required to unify these two cases as in my earlier proposals or in Stowell's (1987) approach, or for that matter, Demirdache's (1991) approach.[1]

4.2 Secondary Weakest Crossover

Postal (1993) points to additional evidence that WCO and SCO are the same phenomenon, namely, that both forms of secondary crossover fail to induce violations in weakest crossover contexts. Compare (8) with (9) ((8a,b) and (9a,b) are from Postal 1993, 543–544, and (8c) and (9c) are from Safir 1996a, 324).

(8) a. It was *Jerome's* sister that I informed *him* that you were waiting for *t*
    b. *Jack's* wife I had told *him* that I had called *t*
    c. ?*Abe's* mom is too poor to get *him* to ask for money from *t*
    d. ?*Milton's* mom is easy for *him* to praise *t*

(9) a. *It was *somebody else's* sister that I informed *him* that you were waiting for *t*
    b. **Everybody else's* wife I had told *him* that I had called *t*
    c. ?*Nobody else's* mom is too poor to get *him* to ask for money from *t*
    d. ?*Everyone's* mom is easy for *him* to praise *t*

In Safir 1996a, the absence of such effects was derived by the assumption that the forms left by movement in (8a–d) could count as pronominal, not as variables, in contrast to the movements in (9a–d), which could not leave traces that count as pronouns. However, the contrast between (9a,b), on the one hand, and (9c,d), on the other, remained unexplained.

No independent motivation was offered in Safir 1996a about why syntactic variables of nontrue quantifiers could be replaced with pronouns. However, the proposal that the absence of crossover effects was due to a pronominal trace was supported by analogy with resumptive pronoun examples, which yield contrasts like those in (10a,b) for secondary SCO and (11a,b) for secondary WCO. ((10a,b) and (11a,b) are from Safir 1996a, 327–328, where further discussion of how the examples are constructed is to be found. Some who are generally uncomfortable with the register that permits resumptive pronouns in English may find the (b) examples degraded.)

(10) a. *I can think of [no one else's$_i$ mother]$_j$ who we would have to keep begging him$_i$ to tell us about t$_j$

   b. ?I can think of [no one else's$_i$ mother]$_j$ who we would have to keep begging him$_i$ to tell us about what she$_j$ was like

(11) a. *I can think of [no one else's$_i$ mother]$_j$ who we would have to keep begging his$_i$ brother to tell us about t$_j$

   b. I can think of [no one else's$_i$ mother]$_j$ who we would have to keep begging his$_i$ brother to tell us about what she$_j$ was like

If there is a resumptive pronoun instead of a q-variable in (10b) and (11b), then no crossover violation is expected, because, according to the QDC, either the second pronoun (*she*) can depend on the first, or else both pronouns can depend directly on the operator (if Rule H does not intervene). If there is a q-variable, however, then crossover is in force because the pronoun c-commands the q-variable (10a) or else an argument containing that pronoun c-commands the q-variable (11a). The absence of crossover effects for primary overt resumptives thus extends to these cases.

If we were to accept the proposition that the disarming of crossover in (8) is due to the presence of a null pronoun in the trace position in lieu of a q-variable, then it might appear that the same account I have provided for overt resumption in (10b) and (11b) can be exploited for (8a–d), at least for WCO. However, there is a difference between (8a,b) and (8c,d), such that the second two involve a null operator and a q-variable and the first two do not. If pronominals are never permitted to substitute for a q-variable, as I will argue below, then at least (8c,d) cannot be accounted for that way. Let us consider the latter cases first.

For (8c,d), our assumption that an operator mediates the relation between the antecedent embedding a quantifier and the trace means for (9c,d) that *no one else's mom* and *everyone's mom* are not in the same copy set as the trace of the operator. The notion of copy set is a straightforward consequence of our assumptions about how numeration indices are propagated.

(12) *Copy set*

The copy set for a string x includes x and every other string that has the identical forms bearing identical numeration indices as those in x.

The copy set for a single form is all the identical forms that bear the same numeration index. If we assume that the operator in null operator constructions is a single form selected from the lexicon and included in a numeration, then that form bears a numeration index distinct from that of its antecedent or any forms embedded in its antecedent. In (8c,d), replacement of the in-situ operator copy with a q-variable leaves nothing in that position that corresponds to any embedded property of its ultimate antecedent (the antecedent of the null operator); that is, the q-variable has no internal structure. In (9d), for example, there is no q-variable in the domain of the null operator that corresponds to or depends directly on *everyone*; hence, there is no crossover effect, even though the ultimate antecedent (the antecedent of the null operator—for example, *everyone's mom* in (9d)) embeds a quantified expression. The representation of (9d) is illustrated in (13).

(13) ?*Everyone's mom* is easy [*Op* for **him** to praise *t*]

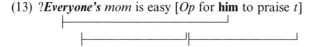

While *him* depends directly on *everyone*, the q-variable trace of the operator depends directly on the operator, since in these cases, Rule H does not intervene (*him* does not correspond to the trace, since the latter corresponds to *mom*). Thus, both secondary SCO and secondary WCO (replacing *him* in (13) with *his relatives*) are predicted to be neutralized.[2]

For (8a,b), however, we have a different expectation. In these cases, where no operator mediates the relation between the ultimate antecedent and the trace, the representations leave behind copies.

(14) a. It was [*Jerome's* sister] that I informed *him* that you were waiting for [*Jerome's* sister]
b. *Jack's* wife I had told *him* that I had called [*Jack's* wife]

In these cases, the copy in the position of the trace should induce an FTIP effect, in that *him* c-commands the lower copy *Jerome/Jack*. Here the strategy of replacing names with pronouns within the lowest copy—that is, replacing *Jack's* or *Jerome's* with *his*—would make the right prediction. We do have a model for this sort of substitution, namely, the vehicle change operation of Fiengo and May (1994) that we employed in elision environments to account for strict readings of positions corresponding to elided SELF forms (see section 1.4, example (46)).

Let us now suppose that vehicle change is generalized to apply to any unpronounced nominal identical in form to its copy or elision counterpart.[3] If so, *Jack's* and *Jerome's* can undergo vehicle change in (14a,b) and no FTIP effect is induced, since an overt pronoun would tie with a vehicle-changed one as the most dependent form available. More must be said to avoid undercutting the account of (49a–e) in section 3.6 (to be repeated below as (20a–e)), but on the assumption that the right distinction can be made, we can now account for the absence of a secondary SCO-like effect for (8a,b) (we are actually neutralizing an FTIP effect).

When we turn to (9a,b), however, we find that the fronted constituent embeds a quantifier; hence, the lower copy of the quantifier has to be replaced by a q-variable, as in (15a,b).

(15) a. *It was *somebody else's* sister [that I informed *him* that you were waiting for [x's sister]]
     b. **Everybody else's* wife I had told *him* that I had called [x's wife]

If the q-variable can undergo vehicle change, then we incorrectly predict that SCO is erased, since the conspiracy between the QDC and the INP is triggered only by the presence of a q-variable.

It seems we must ban vehicle change of a q-variable. Fortunately, exactly the same restriction holds on the ellipsis context as well. Recall that Fiengo and May (1994) justify vehicle change for cases where an elided constituent is parallel to one that contains a name that ought to trigger a Principle C effect in the second conjunct, yet no such effect is found. Instead, it appears that (16a) behaves like the overt (16c) rather than the overt (16b).

(16) a. Hal hates *Ann's* accountant and *she* does too.
     b. *Hal hates *Ann's* accountant and *she* does [hates *Ann's* accountant] too
     c. Hal hates *Ann's* accountant and *she* does [hates *her* accountant] too

If the bracketed portion corresponds to the ellipsis site, then vehicle change to a pronoun defuses the FTIP effect, since a pronoun in genitive position is then the most dependent form available in that position. Now notice that it cannot be the case that an elided q-variable can undergo vehicle change; if it could, (17a) would not show crossover effects, contrary to fact.

(17) a. *I don't know who Sheena saw, but I know *who his* mother did
         [see *t*]
     b. I don't know for sure *who* hasn't seen *his* mother, but I know
         who t has [seen ***his*** mother]

The parallels between the alleviation of FTIP (Principle C) effects in ellipsis contexts and their alleviation in unpronounced copy contexts thus justify treating vehicle change as the operation that applies in both environments. I formulate vehicle change as in (18).[4]

(18) *Vehicle change*
     If an unpronounced nominal is not a q-variable, it may be
     converted to a pronoun.

Since vehicle change does not apply to q-variables, it only alleviates FTIP violations with r-expressions, not INP effects, which in my account are the true cases of crossover.[5]

It is important to note in this context that the restriction on vehicle change is not simply a case where the requirements of a bound variable interpretation are not met for any semantic reason. In ellipsis environments, vehicle change is not prohibited from changing copies to pronouns when the copy has a quantifier-dependent pronoun embedded in it (i.e., a pronoun as bound variable). For example, compare (19a) and (19b).

(19) a. **Every comedian** says ***his*** *mother* wants **him** to visit ***his*** *mother*.
     b. **Every comedian** visits ***his*** *mother* less than ***his*** *mother* wants him
         to [visit *her/***his** mother*]

There is a typical Principle C effect derived by the FTIP in (19a), since the second italicized *his mother* is not a pronoun (even though it contains one). However, (19b) (with the elided portion in brackets) is not ruled out because vehicle change replaces *his mother* with *her* in the superficially elided constituent; hence, the most dependent form available has been used and the dependent interpretation is supported. Thus, vehicle change is not sensitive to bound variable interpretation, just to the presence of a q-variable.

There do seem to be some additional minor restrictions on vehicle change (see also section 4.5). Recall the discussion of the contrast between (49a) and (49b) in section 3.6, repeated here as (20a,b).

(20) a.   *Him, he* knew she thought little of [*him*]

   b.   ??*Louis, he* knew she thought little of [*Louis*]

   c.   **Louis, he* thought little of [*Louis*]

   d.   *?*Him, he* thought little of [*him*]

   e.   *Himself, he* thought little of [*himself*]

If vehicle change can change *Louis* to a pronoun in (20b), then (20a) and (20b) ought not to contrast at all, and for some speakers the contrast is small. It would appear that there is some minor effect on FTIP calculations such that if a pronoun is the most dependent form available without appealing to vehicle change, it is preferable not to appeal to it.[6] Of course, I am not assuming that vehicle change can save the more local cases where a SELF form is a competitor (20c–e), since, as argued in section 2.2 (and note 2 of chapter 2), vehicle change only transforms nominals to pronouns, not to any other sort of form.

It has now been demonstrated that all crossover phenomena—SCO, WCO, and secondary versions of each (where they exist)—are derived by independently motivated properties of grammar, including the INP, the copy theory of movement, general assumptions about scope assignment, and vehicle change. The QDC, while specific to dependency on a quantifier, does not directly impose any structural condition on the distribution of variables. Appeal to the copy theory eliminates any need to record the history of dependency relations by means of the Q-Chain Convention or anything like it.[7] There is no principle of grammar that must be appealed to (such as the Leftness Condition, the Bijection Principle, or the PCOB) to specifically rule out crossover configurations; rather, all crossover effects now derive from conspiracies of independently motivated principles.

4.3   Copy Sets, Reconstruction, and Late Adjunction

Part of the original justification for the copy theory in Chomsky 1995 was based on the view that phenomena that had been discussed as reconstruction or "antireconstruction" effects could be elegantly captured within a framework where movement leaves a copy and trees are constructed by generalized transformations applying to the contents of the numeration. In earlier research within the principles-and-parameters framework, it was assumed that all structure not derived by movement is in the tree before movement operations begin. Part of the reason for positing the operation of generalized transformations in derivations is the claim that adjunction to a constituent after it has been moved is possible. I argue in this section that this mechanism must indeed be invoked to account for reconstruction effects, but not for most of the cases for which it was originally motivated. I then demonstrate that the mode of explanation I have developed for crossover effects, when integrated with the operation of late adjunction, extends to predict an additional range of subtle empirical patterns.

At least some of the secondary crossover phenomena discussed so far have also occasionally been regarded as reconstruction effects. However, most linguists have more typically used the term *antireconstruction* to characterize cases where an embedded pronoun, anaphor, or r-expression in a displaced constituent behaves as if it is not subject to the c-command relations that hold of the position it originated in—as in the cases where secondary SCO is neutralized, for example.

To get the flavor of the data that have been used to support reconstruction or antireconstruction, consider the SELF-form examples in (21a,b) and compare them with the examples in (21c,d) where no relevant movement is involved. Next, consider the purported reconstruction-inducing Principle C effects in (22a,b) (marked with "%" because the interpretation of the facts is disputed). Finally, compare (22a,b) with (23a,b), where the fronted constituent contains an adjunct clause for which no Principle C effect is observed, but where one would be expected if reconstruction occurred, as in the unmoved examples (23c,d).

(21) a. Which pictures of *himself* did Marty think that *Ralph* would buy?

b. *Woody* wondered which pictures of *himself* Wanda would buy.

c. Marty thought that *Ralph* would buy several pictures of *himself*.

d. %*Woody* wondered when Wanda would buy pictures of *himself*.

(22) a. %Which allegation that *Clarence* had harassed her did *he* later deny she had made?

b. %Which picture of *Bill* was *he* afraid that Hillary would be thinking of?

c. **He* later admitted *he* had made a/the claim that *Rick* would defeat Hillary.

d. **He* was sure that Hillary was thinking of a picture of *Bill*.

(23) a. Which claim that inflated *Al's* importance did *he* later admit
       was untrue?

   b. Which picture in *Bill's* wallet did *he* expect that the press would
      use?

   c. *He later admitted that the claim that inflated *Al's* importance
      was untrue.

   d. *He expected that the press would use the picture in *Bill's*
      wallet.

Examples (21a,b) do not make much of a case for reconstruction, since
even their (rough) unmoved counterparts do not appear to strongly contrast. The contrast between (22a,b), for those who reject them, and (22c,d),
which no one accepts, appears to favor reconstruction. The contrast between (23a,b) and (23c,d), which is fairly robust, appears to argue for
antireconstruction.

   The general line I will take about almost all of the constructions in
(21a,b), (22a,b), and (23a,b) is that they provide no clear evidence for or
against reconstruction, but that other sorts of examples do. Since much of
the literature on these issues has assumed that (21a,b) and (22a,b) are true
cases of reconstruction, I must first make clear why I reject this interpretation of such data. I then turn to the examples that really do make a case
for what has been called reconstruction.

   Let us begin with (21a,b). Notice that these examples are based on
SELF forms that are embedded in picture contexts where they have
no possible thematically distinct antecedent in their thematic complex.
In Safir 1997, 2004, I argue that such SELF forms are promoted to
discourse-sensitive forms, with the same dependency rating as pronouns,
such that they are not in complementary distribution with pronouns,
modulo discourse saliency factors of emphasis and conversational context. If so, whether or not their purported antecedents c-command these
forms is not even directly relevant in (21c,d). There is also evidence that
phrases like *which pictures of himself* permit coconstrual in contexts that
do not involve any possible derivation that would bring them close enough
to their antecedents to satisfy anyone's version of Principle A, as in (24)
(see Safir 1999, 594–596, for further discussion and references).

(24) *The rock star* said that *his* wife would not identify which pictures of
     himself she had defiantly sent t to the tabloids

As I concluded in Safir 1999, it does not appear that reconstruction is either a necessary or a sufficient condition for the interpretation of pronoun-SELF complements to nominal heads.

More interesting, for our purposes, are the reported Principle C effects embodied in the purported contrast between (22a,b) and (23a,b), originally pointed out by Freidin (1986) and Lebeaux (1990). Lebeaux's suggestion about how to account for these distinctions is that complements cannot be added late in a derivation, but must instead be in the tree prior to the movement that pied-pipes them along with the operator. That means, if they leave copies as traces, or if the rules of anaphora apply to representations prior to movement, that the r-expressions embedded in the moved constituent will be evaluated in their base positions. Adjuncts containing dependent pronouns, since they are adjoined "late" and higher in the tree, do not have traces lower in the tree where they could be reconstructed.

Chomsky (1995) attempts to derive the difference between complements and adjuncts from his extension requirement, according to which tree-building operations (Merge and overt Move α) always extend a constituent "K to K^*, which includes K as a proper part" (p. 190). Merging an adjunct to a moved phrase is possible as long as the proviso that "nothing can join to a nonprojecting category" (p. 234) is satisfied (e.g., X adjoined to a projection of Y forms another constituent that is a projection of Y). If complements enter the derivation by merging with X^0 to form X^1 and the Merge operation "applies at the root only" (p. 248), then there is no way that a complement can be added to the X^0 of a formed XP and satisfy the extension requirement.

Chomsky's execution of Lebeaux's late adjunction analysis of reconstruction asymmetries depends on the notion that copies are left by movement in an example like (22a) with a CP clause complement to N (i.e., the complement to *allegation*), as represented in (25a), but that no copy is left behind for the clause portion of (23a), which has a gap relative, as illustrated in (25b).

(25) a. [Which allegation [that *Clarence* had harassed her]] did *he* later deny she had made [x allegation [that *Clarence* had harassed her]]

   b. [Which claim [that inflated *Al's* importance]] did *he* later admit [x claim] was untrue

Chomsky further assumes that restrictions on quantifiers in the highest position are deleted under the pressure of his Preference Principle, which requires that restrictions are minimized at the head of a chain. On the assumption that one copy, but only one, needs to be maintained, the Preference Principle always favors preservation of the lowest copy (the one after *made* in (25a)) and not the highest one (the one following *which allegation* in (25a)) when there is a choice between the two. Notice, however, that in the absence of any motivation for it, deletion of the highest copy here is not crucial (once the x-SELF cases have been set aside), but preservation of the lowest copy is crucial for these predictions whenever a portion of that lowest copy is in an anaphoric relation. For example, if the lowest copy remains, *he* c-commands *Clarence* in (25), and Principle C should be violated. By contrast, when the relative clause is not lexically licensed (the way the complement to *allegation* is), it is assumed to be possible that the relative clause is an adjunct, perhaps to DP. The adjunct relative is optionally added to the moved constituent *which claim* rather than to *which claim* in its base position where it is the subject of *was untrue*. If adjunction is late, then there is no point in the derivation where *Al* is c-commanded by *he*; hence, coconstrual is possible.

The central problem with the Freidin-Lebeaux generalization (FLG) distinguishing adjuncts from complements, embodied here in the purported contrast between (22a,b) and (23a,b), is that this contrast is at best not very sharp and at worst undetectable across a wide range of cases.[8] Bianchi (1995), Postal (1997), and Kuno (1997) have all questioned whether the FLG correctly interprets the facts. For example, Bianchi (1995, 129) reminds us of Higginbotham's (1983, 411) judgment for (26a), Kuno (1997) reports that most speakers accept (26b–e), and Postal reports (26f–i) as acceptable (Postal draws (26h) from Ross 1973, 198, and (26i) from Culicover 1997, 333). Finally, (26j) is reported by Heycock (1995, 557n13), who finds it acceptable unless *best* is omitted. See also Van Riemsdijk and Williams (1981, 203) for additional cases inconsistent with the FLG.

(26) a. Which biography of *Picasso* do you think *he* wants to read?
   b. Which witness's attack on *Lee* did *he* try to get expunged from the trial records?
   c. Which criticism of *Lee* did *he* choose to ignore?
   d. Which evaluation of *Lee's* physical fitness did *he* use when *he* applied to NASA for space training?

    e. Whose allegation that *Lee* was less than truthful did *he* refute
       vehemently?
    f. Most articles about *Mary* I am sure *she* hates.
    g. That *the director* was corrupt everyone knew that *he* would
       always be able to deny with a straight face.
    h. That *Ed* was under surveillance *he* never realized.
    i. That *John* had seen the movie *he* never admitted.
    j. Which picture of *John* does *he* like ??(best)?

Though I don't find all of these examples equally acceptable, most do
seem acceptable under favorable discourse conditions. As we will see,
these judgments are muddy by comparison with judgments for other
arguments merged before Ā-movement, so there is still some effect specific to complements, perhaps to be understood as further subtle restrictions on vehicle change in complement positions.[9]

The reason I contest the validity of the FLG (with respect to r-
expressions) is that my view of vehicle change does not predict any distinction between (22a,b) and (23a,b). Both should be acceptable, but for
different reasons. I accept the Lebeaux-Chomsky view that late adjuncts
in (23a,b) do not leave copies that could induce binding theory violations,
but I also expect (22a,b) to be acceptable because the names of the copies
in the lowest position should all permit vehicle change, in which case the
c-commanded pronoun is the most dependent form available. If this line
of analysis is right, the distinction between the two cases is structurally
correct, but it does not correspond to a robust empirical contrast if indeed
there is any empirical contrast at all.[10]

On the other hand, where vehicle change is not possible, we may expect
the optional late merger of adjuncts to be distinguishable from the obligatory early merger of complements. Section 4.4 examines cases where the
distinction between late and early merger actually does play a role in explaining possible coconstruals.

4.4   Late Adjunction and Bound Variable Pronouns

In this section, I examine a class of cases where vehicle change is blocked
by the role of quantification in bound variable interpretation (as stated in
(18)), with the result that the contrast between late-adjoined constituents
and complements emerges more robustly. Consider the contrasts in (27)
and (28).[11]

(27) a. *Which reviews of *every poet's* book does *he* try to ignore t
     b. ?Which reviews of *every poet's* book t give *him* the most
         satisfaction
     c. ??Which analysis of *every poet's* book does *his* mother try to
         ignore t
     d. Which analysis of *every poet's* book t gives *his* mother the
         most satisfaction
     e. *He* tries to ignore certain reviews of *every poet's* book.

(28) a. Which book on *every poet's* shelf is *he* particularly proud of t
     b. Which book on *every poet's* shelf t gives *him* lasting satisfaction
     c. Which book on *every poet's* shelf is *his* mother most proud of t
     d. Which book on *every poet's* shelf t gives *his* mother lasting
         satisfaction
     e. *He* is particularly proud of a certain book on *every poet's* shelf.

These distinctions, discussed in greater detail in Safir 1999, show that
pied-piped complements of nominals, those arguments thematically related to the nominal head, act as though they leave copies of themselves
in the extraction site (marked with *t* in the examples above), but adjuncts
forming a constituent with a fronted nominal do not act as though they
leave copies at the bottom of the tree. Thus, *he* and *his mother* will c-
command the lowest q-variable of *every poet* in (27a) and (27c), respectively, as illustrated for (27a) with the partial derivation in (29) (y is the
q-variable of *every poet*).

(29) a. *Which reviews of *every poet's* book does *he* try to ignore
         [which reviews of *every poet's* book]
     b. *Which reviews of *every poet's* book does *he* try to ignore
         [x reviews of *every poet's* book]
     c. *Which reviews of *every poet's* book does *he* try to ignore
         [x reviews of *y's* book]

By contrast, the optional late adjunction hypothesis permits adjunction of
on every poet's shelf to *which reviews* after *which reviews* has been fronted,
hence the derivation of (28a) in (30).

(30) a. Which book is *he* particularly proud of [which book]
     b. Which book on *every poet's* shelf is *he* particularly proud of
         [which book]
     c. Which book on *every poet's* shelf is *he* particularly proud of
         [x book]

Where there is no movement, as in (28e), late adjunction makes no difference in the outcome, since the pronoun will c-command the q-variable.

There is a potential formal flaw in this account that requires a small elaboration. If the quantifiers in (29c) and (30c) are raised, then the final representations are actually more like (31a) and (31b), respectively.

(31) a. *Every (*poet*) *y* [which x [x reviews of *y's* book]] [does *he* try to ignore [x reviews of *y's* book]]

    b. Every (*poet*) *y* [[which x [x book on *y's* shelf]] [is *he* particularly proud of [x book]]]

These representations have two q-variables for the quantified expression *every poet* that *he* might depend on. Without clarification, it would appear that *he* in (31a) could depend on the first q-variable, rather than the second, without violating the INP. Such a result would erase all the relevant distinctions. However, it is natural to suppose that two q-variables of the same quantifier, being identical in form and substance, are indistinct, such that dependency on one is equivalent to dependency on the other (whereas quantifiers, q-variables, and pronouns are distinct from one another). If so, the creation of new q-variables in the fronted constituent has no consequence for relations that hold between pronouns and the lowest q-variable of the same quantifier.

As pointed out in Safir 1999, the pied-piped prenominal genitive position in English leaves a copy subject to vehicle change, in that Principle C effects do not seem to hold of pied-piped possessor names, as illustrated by the lack of contrast between (32a) and (32b). Nonetheless, as illustrated in (33a,b), the pied-piped possessor, when it is a quantifier, acts as though it is adjoined prior to movement, insofar as speakers detect a contrast between (33a) and (33b) (which are similar to examples provided by Van Riemsdijk and Williams (1981, 203)).

(32) a. Max, Janet's description of whom she varies according to her audience . . .

    b. Max, Janet's description of whom varies according to her audience . . .

(33) a. *Max, *every woman's* description of whom *she* varies according to *her* audience . . .

    b. Max, *every woman's* description of whom varies according to *her* audience . . .

In Safir 1999, 599–600, I argue on independent grounds that possessors must merge before *wh*-pied-piping; hence, they leave copies that will induce crossover effects. This additional effect provides the opportunity to extend the pattern and test for additional effects in constructions where some points of the analysis would otherwise remain unclear (see especially section 4.6).

4.5 Scope Reconstruction

As I have just demonstrated, adjunction after movement can introduce quantifiers that do not leave q-variables in the position from which the operator phrase originates. In such a case, no crossover effects are expected, if the q-variable embedded in the adjunct is outside the c-command domain of a pronoun that must depend on it. By this logic, if there are reasons why an adjunct must be merged with an operator before that operator has reached its highest landing site, then the adjunct will be subject to c-command by any intervening structure between the final landing site and the position where it is first merged.

There are interesting facts that test this prediction, first introduced into the literature by Heycock (1995) and elaborated with additional types of cases in a copy theory account by Fox (1999). In the relevant contexts, the scope of a quantifier must be interpreted in a position that is lower than its final landing site. Pied-piped material appears to be sensitive to the c-command relations that hold in the position where the "reconstructed" scope must be interpreted. Fox examines three sorts of paradigms, of which I will briefly review two.

The first paradigm, adapted from Lebeaux 1990, introduces a pronoun that must be bound in a copy position by a quantifier that has that copy in its scope. In these cases, the pronoun embedded in the surface position is not within the scope of the quantifier.

(34) [Which of the papers that *he* gave to Ms. Brown] did *every student*
       hope that she would read t

The pronoun *he* can only be interpreted as bound if it is within the scope of the quantifier *every* in (34), and it is only in the scope of that quantifier if the adjunct that contains the pronoun *that he gave to Ms. Brown* is merged with the operator phrase *which of the papers* before that operator phrase reaches its highest landing site. In other words, the latest point at which the adjunct could be merged is in the Spec,CP below *every student* (i.e., the one after *hope*), as illustrated in (35).

(35) [Which of the papers [that he gave to Ms. Brown]] did every
      student hope [x of the papers [that he gave to Ms. Brown]] that she
      would read [x of the papers]

Notice that I do not delete any of the higher copies. I leave them because I see no reason to delete them, insofar as they have numeration indices identical to those of the lower copies and hence make no further crucial contribution to interpretation.[12]

In short, the bound pronoun paradigm just described does not require adjusting the proposed theory in any way, insofar as the effect described is predicted by the interaction of the late adjunction theory with the copy theory and the dependency theory account of variable binding and crossover.

The second paradigm involves the force of the FTIP for r-expressions ("Principle C effects"). When a name is contained in an adjunct that enters the derivation in a position where scope reconstruction will force it to be interpreted, Principle C effects might be expected with respect to any c-commanding constituent above the point where the phrase containing the name is interpreted. In other words, scope reconstruction can feed the FTIP. Consider the following paradigm, originally discussed by Heycock (1995) and taken up by Fox (1999, 165–172).

(36) a. How many stories is Diana likely to invent?
     b. How many stories is Diana likely to reinvent?

Fox notes that (36b) is ambiguous in that it could be asking for the number of stories that Diana makes a decision about (she decides about this story but not that story) or for the number of stories, whichever ones they are, that will be reinvented. In the former case, *many* has higher scope than *likely* (*many* > *likely*), while in the latter, *likely* has higher scope than *many* (*likely* > *many*). The following scenario, modeled after one provided by Fox for a different example, illustrates the difference in interpretation:

(37) After reviewing the stories included among the royal anecdotes,
     Diana finds seven that make for bad public relations and she
     decides she will reinvent those seven. None of the other stories seem
     to need work, but for the royal myth to seem coherent, she would
     have to reinvent perhaps as many as twenty others, selected at

random, so that the initial seven do not seem out of character. She
ends up reinventing twenty-seven stories.

"Seven" is the answer to the *many > likely* question, while "Twenty-
seven" is the answer to the *likely > many* question. Heycock and Fox
point out that the ambiguity disappears when the lower verb is a verb of
creation, since there are no preexisting stories to make a decision about,
hence only the *likely > many* interpretation is possible (36a).

Now here is what is at stake in the way this scope distinction is represented: If *many stories* is interpreted above *likely*, then we have a representation for (36b) like (38a); but if *many stories* is interpreted below
likely, then we have a representation like (38b), which also represents the
only interpretation for (36a).

(38) a. [How-x many-y stories] is Diana likely [[x y stories] [to invent
       [x y stories]]]
    b. [How-x ∅ stories] is Diana likely [[x many-y stories] [to invent
       [x y stories]]]

In (38a), the lower copies of *many* are replaced with variables and *many* is
interpreted for scope above *likely*, whereas in (38b), the highest copy of
the quantifier is deleted, leaving empty structure (a variable would not be
scoped) and *many* is interpreted at the intermediate position, binding the
variable y in the lowest copy position. The highest copy [∅ *stories*] is not
interpretable, but since a given numeration index can only be interpreted
once, this higher restriction can be safely ignored (since a different member of the copy set is interpreted).

One of the consequences of this analysis, as Fox and Heycock point
out, is that a name embedded in a pied-piped *how many* phrase should be
sensitive to these distinctions in scopal interpretation. Fox (2000, 155–
156) offers the following contrast:

(39) a. *How many stories about *Diana's* brother is *she* likely to invent?
    b. How many stories about *Diana's* brother is *she* likely to
       reinvent?

Under the scopal interpretation I am positing, *many stories about Diana's
brother* must be interpreted below *likely*, so *about Diana's brother*, even
though it is an adjunct, not a complement, must enter the derivation below *likely*. If *about Diana's brother* is below *likely*, then *she* c-commands
Diana.

(40) a. *[How-x $\emptyset$ stories about Diana's brother] is she likely [x many-
y stories [about Diana's brother]] [to invent [x y stories]]

   b. [How-x many-y stories [about Diana's brother]] is she likely
[x y stories] [to invent [x y stories]]

The result is an FTIP effect, as long as *Diana* (the lower one) cannot undergo vehicle change in (40a). If the lower copy of *Diana* can be vehicle-
changed to a pronoun, then no violation would be expected and the effect
of the scopal distinction could not be accounted for.

A plausible way to exploit the distinction in (40) is to assume that the
highest copy of the whole operator phrase where scope is interpreted is
somehow forbidden to undergo vehicle change. This would mean that
no vehicle change is possible for the highest copy in (40a) (a ban with no
practical effect) or for the intermediate copy in (40b). Thus, (40b) is predicted to evidence the obviation effect.

There is reason to believe this solution is on the right track. After all,
we never assume that vehicle change takes place in the highest copy when
the highest copy is phonologically overt.

(41) *_He_ was completely unaware of the man whose pictures of *Jeb*
Mary admired.

Normally, vehicle change cannot apply to the highest copy simply because it is pronounced, as *Jeb* is here; but the fact that *Jeb* is pronounced
may be accidental if the relevant restriction on vehicle change at LF is
that it cannot apply to any r-expression that is embedded in the restriction of a scope marker (rather than the restriction of one of its variables).
There is a way to determine whether or not this is a special restriction on
vehicle change within copy sets but not generally for other vehicle change
contexts, namely, ellipsis. We need only construct an example where the
highest phrase of the Ā-chain (i.e., the highest phrase of the copy set) contains an r-expression that is c-commanded outside that phrase. Then we
need to complicate the example by creating a parallel clause that licenses
elision of the whole Ā-chain, leaving only the parallel c-commanding
pronoun, as in (42a), represented without the elision in (42b) (where the
bracket labeled α marks the ellipsis). The lowest instance of *Clinton* can
be vehicle-changed, but not the intermediate one.

(42) a. *Gore wondered which pictures of *Clinton* Hillary should
display and *he* did too.

   b. *Gore wondered which pictures of *Clinton* Hillary should
display [which pictures of *Clinton*] and *he* did [$_\alpha$ wonder [which

pictures of *Clinton*] Hillary should display [which pictures of
him/Clinton]] too

The ungrammaticality of (41) and (42a) is unexplained unless we assume,
as above, that the r-expression in the highest copy cannot be vehicle-
changed. The *Diana* paradigm appears to produce the same result, suggesting that vehicle change is restricted in the following way:

(43) An r-expression embedded in the restriction to a scopal marker
      cannot undergo vehicle change.

By contrast, r-expressions embedded in restrictions on the variables of
scopal markers can indeed be vehicle-changed. The reader can confirm
that there is no case of vehicle change I discuss in this book that violates
(43).

I now conclude that the reconstruction effects pointed out by Heycock
(1995) and Fox (1999) require greater precision in my assumptions concerning the relation between scopal markers and the Ā-constituents they
are fronted with, but that the fundamentals of my account do not need
revision, as they make the correct predictions for these cases.

4.6 The Logic of Promotion Analyses

The notion "copy set," as I have employed it here, is the key determinant
of the domain of reconstruction and part of the domain of vehicle change.
If reconstruction effects are only possible where copy sets exist, then we
must examine very closely every context where reconstruction effects are
found to see if they plausibly admit a copy set account—which is to say a
movement account, in that copy sets are generated by movement.

From this perspective, we may ask whether there is any reason to
evaluate the head of a relative clause as part of the same copy set as the
trace of the relative operator it is associated with, or whether the relative
pronoun of the modifying clause is merely in some sort of matching or
agreement relation with the head of the clause. I believe, on the basis of
reconstruction evidence, that the head of a restrictive relative clause may
well be the highest extent of the copy set that includes the relative gap,
but that the same case cannot be made for nonrestrictive relatives (for a
similar conclusion and extensive argumentation, see Bianchi 1995).

Consider the contrasts in (44) and (46) for quantifiers contained in
complements and prenominal genitives, respectively, and the lack of
contrasts in (45) for quantifiers contained in adjuncts. Italics relate the

relative clause head and the trace, and boldface relates the quantifier and the pronoun it should be understood to bind.

(44) a. *[*Pictures of anyone*] which **he** displays *t* prominently are likely to be attractive ones

　　 b. [*Pictures of anyone*] which *t* put **him** in a good light are likely to be attractive ones

　　 c. *?[*Pictures of anyone*] that **his** agent likes *t* are likely to be attractive

　　 d. [*Pictures of anyone*] that *t* please **his** agent are likely to be attractive

(45) a. [*Pictures on anyone's shelf*] which **he** displays *t* prominently are likely to be attractive ones

　　 b. [*Pictures on anyone's shelf*] which *t* put **him** in a good light are likely to be attractive ones

　　 c. [*Pictures on anyone's shelf*] that **his** agent likes *t* are likely to be attractive

　　 d. [*Pictures on anyone's shelf*] that *t* please **his** agent are likely to be attractive

(46) a. *[*Anyone's pictures*] which **he** displays prominently *t* are likely to be attractive ones

　　 b. [*Anyone's pictures*] which *t* put **him** in a good light are likely to be attractive ones

　　 c. *?[*Anyone's pictures*] that **his** agent likes *t* are likely to be attractive ones

　　 d. [*Anyone's pictures*] that *t* please **his** agent are likely to be attractive ones

These effects appear identical to those for topicalizations containing quantifiers and for non-*wh* quantifiers in the operator phrases of relative clauses. In every example above (perhaps slightly more awkwardly for (45a–d)), the quantifier embedded in the relative clause head has scope over the relative clause coda, so pronouns in it can be bound successfully as long as a q-variable is not preserved in the lower copy. Thus, in (47), which represents the position of the lowest copy in (46c), if the trace is in the same copy set as the relative clause head, then a q-variable is preserved in the position of the trace at LF.

(47) *?[[*Anyone's pictures*] [that **his** agent likes [*x's pictures*]]] are likely to be attractive ones

In all the excluded cases, the pronoun or the argument containing it must depend on a q-variable embedded in the trace position it c-commands, violating the INP; but where the adjunct containing the quantifier could be adjoined late to the relative clause head, as in (45), it appears that the copy set in the position of the relative clause trace does not contain a q-variable of the quantifier in the adjunct, and no crossover effects arise.

If we only consider the reconstruction evidence, then, given the logic of copy sets, late adjunction, and the dependency theory, we are led to the conclusion that the heads of restrictive relative clauses arise by movement in a promotion analysis like the one proposed by Kayne (1994) (which harks back to the earlier analyses of Schachter (1973) and Vergnaud (1974)). Both Bianchi (1995) and Åfarli (1994, 89–90) draw this conclusion from observing bound variable effects found with pronouns embedded in relative clause heads (among other arguments), as in examples like (48a–c) (though some speakers do not find the contrast between (48b) and (48c) to be sharp).

(48) a.   [The *picture of **his** mother* that **every soldier** kept *t* wrapped in a sock] was not much use to us in the identification process

   b.   Wilson generally has [an *opinion of **his** book* that **every novelist** respects *t*]

   c.   ??Wilson generally has [an *opinion of **his** book*] that *t* is useful to **every novelist**

Kayne's promotion proposal treats restrictive relatives as being CPs introduced by a D head—for example, *an* in (48b), where *opinion of his book* is fronted from the position of the trace to the Spec,CP position to the left of the C, *that*.

(49) [$_{DP}$ an [$_{CP}$[$_{NP}$ *opinion of **his** book*] [$_{C'}$ that **every novelist** respects [$_{NP}$ *opinion of **his** book*]]]]

Quite a few issues of analysis and empirical prediction arise under the promotion-to-relative-clause-head approach, but the details extend beyond my immediate concerns. I will have to be content here to have laid out the logic that drives my reconstruction account as it applies to these cases and move on, assuming that such a promotion analysis is feasible for restrictive relatives, in spite of all the complications it faces.[13]

The key result of this section is that at least some restrictive relative clause structures are derived by the promotion analysis, since I am assuming that only movement leaves copies and the relevant reconstruction effects arise only where copies are left. If some other operation were to result in copy sets, then I would expect the copy sets to exhibit the same range of reconstruction effects. Assuming movement is crucial to the distribution of copy sets, a rather strong position, predicts that all reconstruction effects respect islands.

To recap, I have so far examined the relationship between copy sets and reconstruction and the consequences this relationship has for the distribution of crossover effects of the type discussed in chapter 3. Emerging from this discussion is another of the ways in which crossover effects may be neutralized in an Ā-binding context. Late adjunction to an Ā-operator of a constituent containing a quantifier will not induce crossover for a quantifier-bound pronoun in the scope of the adjoined-to operator. This is so because the pronoun will not c-command (or be contained in an argument that c-commands) a q-variable of the quantifier. There is no c-commanded copy of the quantifier to form an INP-offending q-variable. This result is consistent with the scope reconstruction phenomena discussed in section 4.5 and extends to the relative clause promotion analysis discussed in this section.

4.7   Some Remarks on Resumption

The QDC does not treat resumptive pronouns as it does q-variables, and because resumptive pronouns are not q-variables, they do not trigger the pattern of dependency relations that results in INP violations. A resumptive pronoun is just a type of bound variable pronoun that happens to be locally Ā-dependent in the absence of any other bindee for an operator that would otherwise be vacuous (as discussed in section 3.1). Thus, relative clauses are not licensed unless they are lexically selected (as is the case for *the allegation/statement/fact that* ..., etc.), or they count as open sentences where an Ā-operator binds a gap, or, failing a gap, a resumptive pronoun.

In many of the world's languages, resumptive pronouns do not have the marginal status that they do in English or Italian, but instead provide the only means of forming garden-variety relative clauses. In these languages, most typically the three properties in (50) hold of them.

(50) a. The resumptive pronoun has the same form as that of a pronoun not associated with resumption environments.

   b. The resumptive pronoun does not induce crossover effects.

c. Nominals embedded in the antecedents of resumptive pronouns do not normally behave as if they are c-commanded by the nodes that c-command the resumptive pronoun; that is, they are not sites for reconstruction effects.

All of these properties are expected if traces are copies of their antecedents and resumptive pronouns are not. This would mean, in the normal case, that resumptive restrictive relatives, unlike restrictive relatives with gaps, are not derived by the promotion analysis. I will assume this is so initially, though this conclusion (particularly (50c)) is contingent on the posited internal structure of the resumptive element.

Setting aside reconstruction, the fact that resumptive pronouns do not induce WCO is robust, as noted earlier in the formulation of the PCOB and its descendants. The Hebrew examples (51a,b) from Demirdache 1991, 51–52 (based on Sells 1984, 76–77) illustrate the contrast in the distribution of WCO (see McCloskey 1990, 236, for the same contrast in Irish).[14]

(51) a. *ha-ʔiš*   še   ʔim-*o*   ʔohevet *oto*
      the-man that mother-his loves   him
      '*the man* that *his* mother loves'
  b. *ha-ʔiš   še   ʔim-*o*   ʔohevet *t*
      the-man that mother-his loves
      '*the man* that *his* mother loves'

The QDC does not require a pronoun dependent on the same Ā-antecedent as the resumptive to depend on the pronoun that is resumptive, and so the pattern of dependencies that induces INP violations is missing. Alternatively, it could be argued that when two pronouns are both locally dependent on a single Ā-antecedent, it is not obvious which counts as the resumptive one.

This last suggested analysis is in the spirit of the account by Demirdache (1991), who treats Hebrew resumptive pronouns as operators that move at LF. She points out that if there are two potential operators, the one that leads to a successful derivation will be the one that extracts the pronoun from a constituent that c-commands (and, in her account, precedes) whatever constituent contains the other pronoun. In terms of the QDC, nothing prevents a pronoun from depending directly on a quantificational Ā-antecedent if there is no q-variable. If there is no LF movement of resumptive pronouns, there is no q-variable (and I assume there is not because of the island violations), but if there is such movement, then Demirdache's account is still consistent with the position I have defended here.

On the other hand, one of the motivations for Demirdache's LF movement analysis is that the same morphological form, *oto*, that can remain in situ as a resumptive in Hebrew can also move overtly in syntax, in which case a WCO effect is observed.

(52) **ha-iš*   še   *ʔoto* xana *ʔamra* še   *ʔim-o*   *ʔohevet t*
     the-man that him Xana said   that mother-his loves
     '*the man* that Xana says that *his* mother loves'

If *oto* is just a pronoun, then when it moves it leaves a pronominal copy behind rather than a q-variable, and WCO is not expected, contrary to fact. However, contrasts such as that in (51) independently suggest an optional movement, which is problematic in most economy approaches to syntax, since movement is expensive. The usual means of reducing optionality is to include a triggering feature or morpheme in the numeration that renders the movement account more economical where it applies.[15]

If the feature in question is a *wh*-feature in the restrictive relative context, then it is reasonable to assume this feature renders the moved relative pronoun quantificational in the same sense that *who* in a restrictive clause in English is. In other words, the logic reducing optionality in economy accounts of movement supplies an independent reason not to regard *oto* as functioning identically as a resumptive and as an operator. The result for my account is that when *oto* moves, it leaves a q-variable because it is acting as an operator, but when it does not move, it is a pronoun locally dependent on a null restrictive operator (or on the promoted relative clause head). In the latter case, *oto* functions as a pronoun, not a q-variable.[16]

Turning now to the question of reconstruction, it does not appear that resumption permits reconstruction of bound variable interpretations and the like. There are some cases where it is argued that anaphors reconstruct into positions where they would be c-commanded by their antecedents; but as we have seen for English, one must be careful to determine whether or not the anaphor in question is still acting as a true anaphor, rather than as an anaphor licensed to act as a pronoun, when it is interpreted as if dependent on a position it could be reconstructed into. For example, in English, resumption does not permit (53a), where a bound variable interpretation needs to be reconstructed, but it does permit (53b), probably because reconstruction is not necessary for *himself* to find an antecedent, as indicated by the relatively acceptable (53c).

(53) a. Do you remember **any of *his* doctors** that we had a single reason
     to ask why *Harry/*each client* was missing appointments with
     her?

   b. Speaking of *Mapplethorpe*, do you remember **those racy pictures
      of *himself*** that we couldn't think of a single reason why *he*
      would send **them** to us?

   c. Speaking of *Mapplethorpe*, do you remember **those pictures of
      *himself*** which we couldn't figure out whether or not **they** would
      be appropriate for the exhibition?

Citing unpublished work by Shlonsky, Demirdache (1991, 98) provides
(54a) as evidence for reconstruction into the positions of resumptive pronouns where a full picture nominal is resumed by the feminine pronoun
hi. Notice, however, that *ʔacmo* in (54a) would not be in a position to be
bound by *Dani* in its position of origin, and so it seems plausible that
these are not true cases of reconstruction.[17]

(54) a. zo-hi ha-tmuna ha-yexida šel ʔacmo še   dani lo
        this-is the-picture the-only   of himself that Dani not
        zaxar   ʔim   hi mudbeket heitev ba-ʔalbom
        remembered whether she glued   well in-the-album
        'This is the picture of himself that Dani did not remember if it is
        glued well in the album.'

   b. lefi   dani, zo-hi ha-tmuna ha-yexida šel ʔacmo
      according.to Dani, this-is the-picture the-only   of himself
      še-mucaʔat   le-mxira
      that-offered(F.SG.PRES.PASS) for-sale
      'According to Dani, this is the only picture of himself that is
      offered for sale.'

In fact, as (54b) shows (due to Ron Artstein, personal communication),
ʔacmo, like English *himself*, can appear in picture nominals even when it
does not have a c-commanding antecedent. Thus, (54a) is not evidence
that true reconstruction takes place in these cases.

   There are further reasons, besides the weak crossover facts, to believe
that pronouns and traces cannot be treated alike as bound variables. As
Doron (1982) originally pointed out, resumptive pronouns in restrictive
relatives lack certain readings that are permissible for restrictive relatives
with gaps, as illustrated in this example from Demirdache 1991, 99.

(55) a. ha-ʔiša   še   kol   gever baxar *t* tišlax   lo tmuna
        the-woman that every man   chose   will-send him a-picture

b. ha-ʔiša   še   kol   gever baxar *ota* tišlax   lo   tmuna
the-woman that every man chose her will-send him a-picture
'The woman that every man chose will send him a picture.'

(55a) is ambiguous, permitting a reading where *him* is bound by *every man* as well as one where *him* is some third party; but (55b) only permits the third party reading, not the one where the universal binds the pronoun.

In Hebrew, moreover, even questions can be formed with resumptive pronouns, and Sharvit (1999b, 594–595) shows that the use of a resumptive pronoun precludes certain functional readings as evidenced in the possible answers to questions. She notes the following contrast, where the question is well formed with either a resumptive pronoun or a gap:

(56) a. ezyo iša   kol   gever hizmin ____/ota
         which woman every man   invited ____/her
         'Which woman did every man invite?'

     b. et   Gila
         ACC Gila
         'Gila.'

     c. et   imo
         ACC mother-his
         'His mother.'

     d. Yosi et   Gila: Rami et   Rina
         Yosi ACC Gila Rami ACC Rina
         'Yosi, Gila; Rami, Rina.'

Both (56a) (an individual answer, a woman named Gila) and (56b) (a "natural function" answer, in Sharvit's terminology, "his mother") are possible answers whether the resumptive is present or not. Pair list answers that are not natural functions, such as (56c), are not possible answers to (56a) when a resumptive pronoun (*ota*) is used, whereas the trace permits them. The difference between trace and pronoun is absolute rather than dependent on relative availability, insofar as the nonnatural functional interpretation is not available with a resumptive pronoun even when there is no potentially competing derivation that allows a trace, as there is in (57), provided by Sharvit (1999b, 595).

(57) ezyo iša   kol   gever rakad ita
      which woman every man   danced with-her
      'Which woman did every man dance with?'

The use of the pronoun in the prepositional phrase is obligatory, but the pair list answer is still not permitted for (57).

Sharvit describes a further difference between traces and resumptive pronouns for the distribution of functional interpretations for relative clauses in Hebrew (relative clause versions of the functional questions discussed in section 3.5). Use of a resumptive pronoun does not allow a natural functional reading, whereas use of the trace does.

(58) ha-iša   še   kol   gever hizmin _____/ota hodeta lo
      the-woman that every man invited _____/her thanked him
      'The woman that every man invited thanked him.'

In other words, the pattern pointed out by Doron for (55) may be thought of as the result of restrictions on the distribution of functional readings that reside in some difference between pronouns and traces.

It is fair to say that my account does not predict the difference between pronouns and traces with respect to functional readings: I see no reason why a resumptive pronoun also dependent on a universal q-variable should not allow a functional reading as long as the INP is satisfied.[18] Nonetheless, this difference is enough to show, as Sharvit points out, that the available bound variable interpretations of pronouns are not always identical to those of traces. From the perspective of my proposal, these contrasts show that pronouns are not identical to q-variables.

It is instructive, given Demirdache's account of fronted resumptive pronouns, that the availability of functional readings patterns with the availabity of gap pronouns when the resumptive pronoun is overtly fronted. Sharvit (1999b, 608) provides the following examples, both of which may receive functional interpretations:

(59) a. ha-iša   *ota* kol   gever hizmin higia   it-o
       the-woman she every man invited arrived with-him
       'The woman every man invited arrived with him.'
    b. ha-iša   *ota* kol   gever hizmin hayta im-o
       the-woman she every man invited was   mother-his
       'The woman every man invited was his mother.'

Thus, whatever the pronoun/q-variable distinction is, it is consistent with the view that the fronted pronoun is more than simply resumptive, in that its trace behaves like a q-variable.

At least one more analytic possibility deserves mention in any discussion of resumption. As discussed in Safir 2004 and literature cited there, it cannot be taken for granted that the internal structure of pronouns is uniform; it is therefore possible that resumptive pronouns, like other pronouns, may have a richer phrasal structure than their morphology

indicates. If this is correct, it is possible that the morphological pronoun
could be embedded in a phrase that contains the trace of Ā-movement as
in (60a,b) (assuming XP to be in an Ā-position).[19]

(60) a. XP [... [$_{DP}$ pronoun [t]]]

     b. XP [... $CL+V$ ... [$_{DP}$ **t** [t]]]

Pronouns in an apparent resumptive relation with an Ā-operator might
be expected to be found uniquely where island conditions are met, since
only in these cases would movement be licensed reconstruction effects be
expected to be found, though not necessarily WCO effects, depending on
whether or not the antecedent is quantificational.

    There is some evidence that the clitic left-dislocation construction may
be a model for (60b), insofar as it typically respects islands and shows
reconstruction effects, but no WCO effect. The literature on clitic left-
dislocation is too rich to review here (e.g., for Romance, see Cinque 1990,
Dobrovie-Sorin 1990, and references cited there; and for references on
Slavic and Balkan, see Franks and King 2000, chap. 7). Nonetheless, the
outline of an analysis consistent with my approach would be (a) to introduce the clitic and the dislocated phrase together as a single constituent
into the derivation, (b) to move the clitic independently pre-Spell-Out to
the clitic position, and (c) to treat the left-dislocated phrase (not necessarily including the trace of the clitic) in Ā-position as also arising from
movement, just as schematically represented in (60b). The Ā-movement
of the left-dislocated phrase would then respect island constraints and
leave a copy inducing reconstruction effects, much as in the case of English
topicalization.[20] As in English topicalization, which typically involves a
nonquantificational antecedent, one would not expect the copy-trace to
contain a q-variable, hence the absence of WCO effects (as Demirdache
(1991, 191–194) points out, also appealing to the nonquantificational
nature of these cases).[21]

    To reiterate, resumptive pronouns are not q-variables in general, and
are not merely phonological spell-outs of what are otherwise copies at
LF, as Pesetsky (1998, 2000) assumes (see also Toman 1998; Shlonsky
1992). This means that resumptive pronouns do not trigger crossover
effects and they do not license reconstruction, unless there is evidence that
the resumptive in question must be analyzed as phrasally complex, containing, in addition to the pronoun, a silent copy of the moved constituent. This analysis permits us to maintain the standard generalization that
movement is restricted by islands at all times, as evidenced in the clitic
left-dislocation cases, which are island sensitive.

I hope these brief remarks on resumptive pronouns provide a sufficient guide to what is at stake for my approach so that it can be evaluated in the light of more comprehensive analyses of other languages and constructions.

4.8 Conclusion

The central goal of this book has been to demonstrate that the pattern of dependent readings permitted by formal grammar can be explained by appeal to the interaction of just a few explanatory principles. The principle in the foreground of this demonstration has been the INP, which, unlike the licensing approaches based on c-command, more accurately and elegantly captures the core array of possible dependencies. Moreover, my approach is crafted around the view that dependency is possible wherever it is not ruled out and that only the INP, the FTIP, and, in a limited class of cases, Rule H, ever rule it out. Failure of a dependent reading induced by the INP does not feed Pragmatic Obviation in the way that the FTIP does.

Extending the notion of dependency, particularly through the QDC, I have derived the existence and distribution of crossover effects, appealing to the FTIP only for a small subset of cases. These mechanisms interact crucially with my assumptions about copy theory and vehicle change to derive reconstruction effects and antireconstruction effects, but there is no principle of grammar that refers to crossover or that is uniquely crafted to rule out crossover effects.

The approach I have outlined here does not resolve all the mysteries and puzzles that the distribution of dependent interpretations present, as a close reading of the notes will show. Nonetheless, a wide range of systematic and subtle empirical patterns that have not received a unified treatment has been shown to arise from the interaction of a very limited set of principles.

Chapter 5

The Independence Principle in the Architecture of Universal Grammar

It is often said in concluding books like this that the theory offered confirms one theoretical framework and no other. I do not believe my results permit so strong an inference. Rather, I think it possible that these principles could be implemented in ways that would make them compatible with a variety of frameworks—though I also believe that frameworks that effectively implement these principles will have to be quite similar to one another. To put it another way, I do not offer these results as confirmation of any particular version of principles-and-parameters syntax; but any framework that cannot represent in a natural way the relations and restrictions I have shown to exist is not likely to be the correct model of innate human linguistic potential.

It is now time to clarify how the principles I have proposed might fit into the architecture of UG. The main principle I have focused on is the INP, which can only be understood if dependency relations determine the class of possible semantic interpretations a sentence can have in terms of its referential values. The general perspective taken throughout has been that any dependency relation is possible that is not explicitly ruled out, either by the FTIP, by Rule H, or by the INP. Two questions must be answered: At what level do these restrictions, particularly the INP, apply? and What must we assume about the vocabulary of formal relations that the INP applies to at that level? Partial answers to both questions have been presented, although there are a number of points that can now be made more explicit.

First of all, the INP applies to LF, the level that results from the complete formation of a convergent derivation, such that no further structure-building operations occur. I assume that if a pronoun is to be introduced by vehicle change, then it is introduced before dependency interpretation, since vehicle change can affect the distribution of crossover effects. I also assume that q-variables must be introduced by LF. Otherwise, the QDC will fail to ensure that certain unacceptable configurations are analyzed in a way that violates the INP. The effects of Rule H must also be in force at the point where the INP applies, since certain dependency relations that do not lead to acceptable interpretations would not otherwise emerge as INP violations. However, the QDC, the INP, and Rule H could apply simultaneously at the point of interpretation, and any conflicts between them also result in ungrammaticality. In other words, these dependency restrictions can apply in a block to LF structures that include q-variables and vehicle-changed pronouns.

It appears that the same may be said of the FTIP, which is not affected by what is required for the QDC or the INP, but is affected by vehicle change. There is evidence also that the FTIP is sensitive to the restrictive effects of Rule H insofar as Rule H permits the FTIP to be a more efficient algorithm. The FTIP requires that a given nominal form (the target) must be evaluated with respect to each c-commanding antecedent to determine whether or not, with respect to that antecedent, the nominal in question can support a dependent identity reading. If two or more c-commanding antecedents of the target are coconstrued, then Rule H ensures that only the lower one has to be evaluated by the FTIP, a point examined in Safir 2004, sec. 7.1, which I will not review here. However, there is no case where the FTIP influences the pattern of dependencies in a way that the INP must have access to in order to apply properly, and vice versa.

As argued in Safir 2004, taken together, the constraints on dependency have the general property that they all apply to convergent derivations, and hence to sentences that, under at least some interpretation (i.e., assignments of referential value) are grammatical. If we conceive of these constraints as participating in a component, then this interpretive component functions to narrow the field of possible coconstruals for otherwise grammatical sentences. In Safir 2004, the competitive constraints, the FTIP, Scope Economy, Rule H, and weak pronoun competition (which is not discussed here, but is related to Preferred Covaluation discussed in section 2.3) are evaluated with respect to their common properties; I will not cover that ground again here.

LF, then, is a level enriched by a pattern of dependency restrictions that apply simultaneously to convergent derivations and cannot conflict. The result of these dependency restrictions is an LF that constitutes the contribution of formal grammar to the interpretation of coconstrual relations. Pragmatic Obviation provides instructions to the pragmatic component, perhaps to be characterized as presuppositions, that covaluation of certain pairs of nominals is unexpected.

Once we group the dependency restrictions as a component, the next natural move is to look for commonalities that might allow us to streamline that component. For example, in addition to their identical point of application, Rule H, the INP, and the FTIP all refer to c-command. These similarities would appear to suggest an opportunity for reduction, yet such attempts face certain notable pitfalls.

Consider, for example, Bianchi's (2001) account of WCO, which is also based on a version of the INP drawn from Higginbotham 1983. Bianchi's (p. 15) formulation of the central constraint, which she embeds in Kayne's (1994) antisymmetry approach, is stated in (1).

(1) *Anti-c-command Condition*
     If x asymmetrically c-commands y, then x cannot (a) denotationally depend on y (directly or indirectly), or (b) be denotationally equal to y.

By assuming (1a), Bianchi extends the condition to cases of indirect dependency in the same way I have extended it here to derive WCO (and see note 5 to chapter 3).

However, Bianchi's theory differs from mine in certain very important respects. She takes (1b) to be sufficient to characterize Principle C effects. Besides the fact that (1b) misses the relation between Principle C effects and Principle B effects, the manner in which (1b) is stated would rule out very simple cases of coreference, such as (2).

(2) *Saul* says that Mary loves *him*.

This problem arises because (1b) does not distinguish between forms of the directly c-commanded prospective dependent, but including such a distinction in the statement of (1b) would return it to a statement virtually identical to Principle C (i.e., x cannot share denotational equality with a name it c-commands). Bianchi sees this problem and introduces a referential hierarchy statement into (1b) (1991, 17) such that the c-commandee must be lower on the referential hierarchy than its antecedent (e.g., name > epithet > pronoun). This runs afoul of cases like (3), however, where *her* is predicted to be noncoreferent with *herself* because anaphors are lower on the hierarchy than pronouns, yet even a bound reading is possible here (and *herself* must antecede *her* by Rule H).

(3) *Sarah/Every woman* considers *herself* capable of achieving *her* goals.

Many other examples of this kind could be constructed.

The FTIP captures much more intuitively (and correctly) what is going on here. The pronoun in the lowest position is the most dependent form available with respect to its antecedent *herself*, and *herself* is the most dependent form available with respect to its antecedent, *Sarah/every woman*. Moreover, combining (1a), a principle blocking dependency, and (1b), a principle inducing obviation, into a single principle captures no more than the obvious similarity between them (namely, that they both rely on c-command), while distinguishing them in every other respect. From my perspective, the conceptual problem with Bianchi's approach is that it attempts to combine a noncompetitive constraint, the INP, with one that involves a competition, the FTIP, and these are different in character.

Bianchi's approach is similar to mine because hers attempts to limit coconstruals by principles that block their distribution, leaving them free otherwise. However, there is another purportedly reductive approach that seeks to account for the pattern of coconstruals based on the limits of the condition that licenses them, as in the CLP theories evaluated in chapters 1 and 2. I turn to this proposal next, and I end with some remarks concerning reduction and theoretical design in section 5.2.

5.1   Against Movement as an Account of Coconstrual

Both Hornstein (2001) and Kayne (2002) propose that coconstrual is achieved by movement. The fact that c-command plays a central role in the regulation of bound readings then becomes a property derived from the movement relation (in Hornstein's account most explicitly (pp. 220–221)), which most typically requires c-command. Hornstein's and Kayne's approaches differ in that movement in Hornstein's approach leaves a copy spelled out as a (bound) pronoun whereas movement in Kayne's approach leaves behind a doubled pronoun.

For example, Hornstein's account derives (4a) in two steps, first a movement leaving a trace, as in (4b), followed by the insertion of a pronoun that yields (4a), whereas in Kayne's account *everyone* enters the derivation in the specifier of [*everyone he*] as illustrated in (4c), and movement of *everyone* to subject position derives (4d).

(4) a. *Everyone* thinks *he* is smart.
    b. *Everyone* thinks *t* is smart

c. [e] thinks [*everyone* [*he*]] is smart
d. *Everyone* thinks [*t* [*he*]] is smart

Kayne suggests that all coconstruals can be derived by movement in this way, but unlike Hornstein, he does not distinguish dependencies from covaluations. However, both seem to imply that all unmarked covaluations arise in this way.

The purported advantage of this way of looking at things is that the c-command condition on movement, where it applies, and the c-command conditioning observed for anaphoric relations, can have their common source in the properties of the movement relation. The intuition behind the idea appears partially inspired by Epstein's (1999) observation that the c-command relation is a natural consequence of minimalist derivation construction by Merge and Move. The latter operations are crucially restricted by Chomsky's (1995, 327–328) notion of extension, which requires Merge and Move to extend the phrase marker by adjoining to its highest node, hence always creating a new highest node (at least before LF). Epstein notes that the consequence is that whatever is merged or moved naturally bears what we can call a c-command relation to everything it is adjoined to. In such a theory, there is no substitution movement to a preexisting position, nor any adjunction or merger to a position lower than the highest point on the tree (but see Safir 1999, 599–600). Hornstein, and those he cites who have championed sideward movement, suggest that in addition to building a tree by movement in (5a,b), it is possible to extend some other subtree that is being built simultaneously by the same numeration, as in (6a–d) to derive (7). In the structures in (5) and (6), the α bracket is the one eligible for extension (and other structure is only specified where necessary for illustrative purposes).[1]

(5) a. [$_\alpha$ did [Erika [see [who]]]]
    b. [$_\alpha$ *who* [did [Erika [see [*t*]]]]]

(6) a. [$_\alpha$ mother] [$_\alpha$ saw [who]]
    b. [$_\alpha$ *whose* [mother]] [$_\alpha$ saw [*t*]]
    c. [$_\alpha$[*whose* [mother]] [[saw [*t*]]]
    d. [$_\alpha$ ... [[*whose* mother [saw *t*]]]]
    e. [$_\alpha$[*whose* mother] [did [Jesse [claim [t saw *him*]]]]]

(7) *Whose* mother did Jesse claim saw *him*?

In Hornstein's account, for example, the trace after *see* would spell out as *him* where it has to (let us suppose for the moment we know when it must), as it does in (6e). The point here is that the movement from the second constituent in (6b) does not extend the second constituent, but it does extend the first. Thus, movement can span unconnected constituents, as long as the extension requirement is satisfied, and the expressive advantage this is purported to have is that coconstrual in (7), for example, can be derived by movement relations. Moreover, the c-command relation, which, strictly speaking, does not characterize the relation between *whose* and *him* in (7), is nonetheless the natural consequence of a point in the derivation, namely, (6b), where the extension of *mother* is formed by Move.

The appeal of this way of thinking, then, is that the distribution of the movement relation can provide a better guide to the possible relations between coconstrued nominals than c-command because it derives exactly those cases where c-command fails to license a bound reading, yet bound readings exist. In other words, sentences like (8a) are derived exactly like (6) up to (6c), and similarly (8b) where the movement out of the constituent *said Elvira saw t* is still an extension of *mother* with subsequent merging of *everyone's mother* to *said Elvira saw him*.

(8) a. *Everyone's* mother saw *him.*

   b. *Everyone's* mother said Elvira saw *him.*

What is not possible either in Hornstein's system or in Kayne's is downward movement, such that (9b) could not possibly be derived from (9a), since the movement does not result in extension, which means that (9a) is excluded.

(9) a. [$_\alpha$ Mort says Elvira [saw]]

   b. [$_\alpha$ *t* says Elvira [saw [*Mort*]]]

   c. *He says Elvira saw *Mort.*

Only (10b) can be derived to relate these two positions with this numeration, with the pronoun inserted (Hornstein) or left behind (Kayne) to yield (10c).

(10) a. [$_\alpha$ says Elvira [saw [*Mort*]]]

   b. [$_\alpha$ *Mort* says Elvira [saw *t*]]

   c. *Mort* says that Elvira saw *him.*

In other words, Principle C is derived in this theory by the prohibition on downward movement, explicitly by the extension requirement as employed in Hornstein's theory.

It is crucial to the derivation of Principle C within the *movement-as-coconstrual theory* (hereafter, MAC) that there be no other way for coconstrual to arise between *he* and *Mort* in (9c)—in other words, there is no coconstrual without movement. This is a large bullet to bite, and the consequence is that movement must now be presumed to relate positions not only where c-command does not hold, but also across islands of all sorts, such as *wh*-islands (11a), relative clause islands (11b), and asymmetric across-the-board extractions (11c), all in instances of movement to what have been regarded as A-positions.

(11) a. *Gabriela* wondered who was asking who wanted to visit *her*.
     b. *Katya* knows the man who pays the woman who phoned *her*.
     c. *Luca* admitted that Chelsea loves *him* and *he* loves Miranda.

This newly powerful variety of Move, which I will refer to as *MAC-Move*, requires that the theory of islands be recast as an inquiry into when it is necessary to insert (or strand) a pronoun rather than leave a trace.[2] Presumably, the decision to leave a trace or pronoun must be folded into the movement operation, rendering it much more complex, or else some subsequent operation will have to evaluate the locality relations that hold between an extraction site and its antecedent (by contrast, note that vehicle change and the insertion of q-variables are insensitive to locality). Thus, MAC-Move must be a more complex operation than the one that simply leaves copies.

Consider further that movement to non-c-commanding positions is possible because Move allows adjunction to α brackets that do not dominate the moved constituent. Thus, it is not surprising that MAC also allows movement to positions in other sentences.[3]

(12) *Zack* is here. *He* is smart.

This means that *he* in the second sentence gets its reference from the first because *Zack*, originating in the second sentence, moves to extend *is here* in the first to form *Zack is here*, leaving behind *He is smart*. A rather weird anticipatory relation must be presumed, such that one lines up in advance all of the sentences one is going to say in order to be sure that all the pronouns have the same source. One could imagine, though not too plausibly, that with each mention of the pronoun the whole preceding monologue is recomputed and left null. This provides a derivational source for the pronoun and allows that each sentence can be uttered without including the first in the same derivation.

Now it may appear that what I am asking of the MAC theory is unreasonable and unnecessary to its logic, but, once again, Principle C is not derived unless movement is the only device that ensures coconstrual. This issue looms larger as we consider what is necessary when speaker A mentions a name that speaker B then refers to.

(13) A: I like Flo.
     B: I think she loves Joe.

Surely speaker B is not MAC-moving *she* into speaker A's sentence, and so the recomputed monologue hypothesized for (12) is in fact a fully recomputed discourse, so speaker B can derive the necessary syntactic relations to use the pronoun *she*. If one is not troubled by all that is required so far, then it will not seem disconcerting that many pronouns do not have linguistic antecedents, as Postal (1971) pointed out. If A and B, previously unacquainted, are watching some farmer (also unknown to them) beating his donkey, and the donkey does not start walking, A and B can remark:

(14) A: He should use a bigger stick.
     B: No, he should give it a carrot.

The only way we can derive these sentences with pronouns in them is by positing a linguistic antecedent, perhaps a null proposition with *the farmer* and *the donkey* represented in it, and MAC-moving the pronouns in recomputed discourse to positions in this abstract sentence. Unless such a proposal is adopted in the MAC theory, it is necessary to allow pronouns to be generated without antecedents in (14), and then it is always possible that these pronouns could accidentally corefer with other pronouns in the discourse, along the lines of Lasnik's (1976) accidental coreference discussed in section 1.2.[4]

Unfortunately, there are also cases where the MAC theory is unable to generate a coconstrual relation where one is clearly possible. Consider examples like (15).

(15) A picture of *Martin* fell right on top of *him*.

Now in this case, movement from the object position of *of* must land in a position where it extends a constituent. However, the object of *of*, before *of* is merged to it, is not an α projection that could be extended. This is a movement into undefined space. The best that might be said is that *Martin* merges to *of*, but this is backward in terms of what is supposed to be derived, especially in theories that are supposed to distinguish right from left. If one is not daunted by the level of abstractness the theory already requires, then one will not flinch at assuming that *Martin* MAC-moves left and merges to an abstract α constituent, and that *of* then merges with that. Without these adjustments, the coconstrual in (15) is not permitted to arise.

All of this seems dire, but if one allows that it is possible, then the MAC theory can be said to nearly deliver on its claim that it derives Principle C (but only if it is also amended as in note 4 to this chapter). It is striking, however, that the MAC theory derives none of the other conditions on dependency that I have discussed here.

For example, Hornstein (p. 140) adopts a version of the INP (also adapted from Higginbotham 1983) to rule out crossover.

(16) A pronoun cannot be linked to a variable to its right.

Something like this is necessary for both Kayne's and Hornstein's theories, since they permit the derivation in (17a–e) to derive (17f).

(17) a. $[_\alpha$ mother$]$ $[_\alpha$ love who$]$
     b. $[_\alpha$ *who* [mother]] $[_\alpha$ love $t]$
     c. $[_\alpha[$*who* [mother]] $[_\alpha$ love $t]]$
     d. $[_\alpha$ does $[$*who* [mother]] $[_\alpha$ love $t]]$
     e. $[_\alpha$ who $[$does $[$*his* [mother]] $[_\alpha$ love $t]]]$
     f. **Who* does *his* mother love?

However, (16) is not enough in the MAC theory, since something must ensure that *his* depends on the trace and not vice versa. In my theory, the QDC performs this function, and it would appear then that the MAC theory requires both the QDC and at least a version of the INP to rule out weak crossover where it applies.[5]

For the Dahl puzzles discussed in section 2.3.2, as well as for the weakest crossover cases discussed in section 3.6, it would also appear that these accounts will require reference to c-command in the form of Rule H. Indeed, Hornstein (p. 224n33) notes that for the determination of locality required for the Minimal Link Condition, a restriction on movement, locality is only computable if competing c-commanders are considered (as illustrated below for MAC-Move), and the same issue applies for Rule H. Thus, traditional c-command, no longer a natural consequence of the range of movement possibilities, is still required in Hornstein's theory, and would appear to be necessary in Kayne's as well.

In addition to the QDC, Rule H, and the INP, which are still necessary in the MAC theory, Kayne also stipulates Principles A and B.[6] Recall that in the theory proposed here, Principle B is derived along with Principle C from the FTIP, and so the commitment to the MAC theory renders this reduction impossible.

Hornstein makes the more ambitious claim that his MAC theory dissolves the binding theory altogether. He argues that Principle A reduces to movement and the movement in question blocks a pronoun where the reflexive is possible, though the presentation appears incomplete. For example, Hornstein derives (18c) by movement of *John* out of [*John - SELF*].

(18) a. [$_\alpha$ loves [*John* - self]]
      b. [$_\alpha$ *John* [loves [*t*-self]]]
      c. *John* loves *him*self.

Spell-out of the lower copy as *him* is only morphologically required by SELF (see Hornstein's p. 161). Considerations of Case assignment block some unwanted derivations, and appeal is made to the existence of derivation (18) involving the insertion of a reflexive, as a preferred option, which obviates an option that would leave a pronoun. What is not explained is that it is necessary to limit the distribution of forms like *Fred-self*, which do not exist even where reflexives without antecedents are permitted (as mentioned in section 4.3 and references noted there), and that examples like (19a), derived from (19b) by MAC-Move in (19c), must also be ruled out.

(19) a. *Fred thinks Helga loves *him*self.
      b. [$_\alpha$ thinks [Helga loves [Fred-self]]]
      c. [$_\alpha$ Fred [thinks [Helga loves [Fred-self]]]]

For (19), some locality restriction on movement originating in SELF forms is still required, or else some restriction stating when it is not possible to insert a SELF form; the latter restriction would have to refer to whether the movement is local or not. This locally restricted movement is unlike movement that permits covaluation in all the cases in (11) (and similarly for (20)), since SELF cannot be inserted in those cases. In other words, a version of movement specific to Principle A, or some new version of Principle A that limits SELF insertion, will then be required, along with reference to traditional c-command as well as locality, since locality is only computable if c-command plays a role.

To see why this is so, consider (20).

(20) a. *Thor's mother loves himself.
 b. [α mother] [α loves [Thor-self]]
 c. [α Thor's [mother]] [α loves [Thor-self]]

Hornstein views the successful convergence of (20a) as an advantage for his theory,[7] despite its clear unacceptability. But even if one wanted to treat (20a) as grammatical (at least with respect to MAC-Move—in which case, something else must be devised to explain its ill-formedness), it is worth pointing out that there is no way to measure the locality of MAC-Move in cases like (20). For example, MAC-Move would apply in exactly the same way, no more or less locally, in (21c), yet the first α constituent of (21c) does not have to be merged with the rest until all of the intervening material has expanded the second α constituent in (21c) as in (21d) (internal brackets omitted for illustration).[8]

(21) a. *Thor's mother told Helga that Marike believes that Smila loves himself.
 b. [α mother] [α loves [Thor-self]]
 c. [α Thor's [mother]] [α loves [Thor-self]]
 d. [α Thor's [mother]] [α told Helga that Marike believes that Smila [loves [Thor-self]]]
 e. [α[Thor's [mother]] [told Helga that Marike believes that Smila [loves [Thor-self]]]]

The constituent Thor's mother does not have to be finally merged with the second α constituent to become the subject of the latter until the last step. Thus, there is no way to calculate the locality of a sideward movement. In fact, unless traditional c-command is added to the theory, virtually no theory of movement can define locality, even with respect to proposals like feature movement (see, e.g., Pesetsky 2000, 55).

What, then, has MAC bought us? Move is now a much less restricted relation, no longer deriving c-command the way Epstein envisioned, but capable of extending any constituent, not just the one it originates in. To capture all the possible coconstrual relations allowed, MAC-Move is now permitted to extract out of islands, span discourses, and eviscerate locality. But what evidence is there, besides coconstrual, that the movement relation must be expanded in all these ways? The reason it was restricted in all these ways, going at least as far back as Chomsky 1977, is that a large class of constructions show all the same familiar limitations, and coconstrual is not one of them. Rather, in order to achieve a (flawed) derivation of Principle C effects, the ban on downward movement is taken as the one crucial property of movement. Why is this more appealing than assuming that the one true property of movement is locality or sentence bounding or both? My point is that the parallel between movement and Principle C effects is very shallow.

It would appear that the MAC theory has only managed to turn an otherwise unmotivated form of movement into a new notation for coconstruals, a notation I do not believe is a necessary part of formal grammar to begin with for all the reasons discussed in chapters 1 and 2. Since the movement relation required for coconstrual lacks independent motivation, it only weakens our more restrictive notion of Move. Nor does the MAC theory effectively reduce any of the central principles proposed here to any other, since it still requires all the restrictions that have been established in this book to provide LF with just the information it needs, including Rule H, the QDC, the INP, a version of Principle A, and a version of Principle B.

It is striking that insofar as coconstrual is possible across sentences, it is a necessary consequence of the MAC theory that Move cannot be restricted to sentence grammar. The approach presented here (and Bianchi's), by contrast, does not explicitly license dependent identity relations; rather, it blocks certain relations in configurations that crucially appeal to the distribution of c-command relations. Traditional c-command (as it emerges in Epstein's account of it before the extension requirement was extended) has the advantage that it only holds within sentence grammar. Thus, relations that are not ruled out within sentence grammar are always possible across sentences, as dependencies generally are. I take it to be an important restrictive advantage of the theory proposed here that it respects the Insularity Principle on human grammars, a principle so long assumed that it has only now, in the face of MAC-Move, become necessary to state (but see also Epstein's (1999, 334) First Law, which addresses the same point).[9]

(22) *Insularity Principle*
  No rule, operation, or principle of syntax ever applies to relate
  structures α and β unless α and β are dominated by some γ
  immediately after the rule, operation, or principle has applied.

It would be appropriate to think of the Insularity Principle as a boundary condition on what syntax actually is.

In summary, I do not believe that the appeal to movement relations as the single source for the distribution of coconstruals provides any explanatory advantage over the proposals made here; rather, several notable disadvantages emerge from the MAC theory that are more likely to obscure the interesting issues rather than resolve them.

5.2 Closing Remarks

My assessment of the movement theory of coconstrual is negative not because it is reductive in character, but because nothing is effectively reduced. Versions of the INP, the FTIP, Rule H, and the QDC are all required if the MAC theory is to compete with the one I propose, and the MAC theory is not consistent with the Insularity Principle, which would appear to be a reasonable and highly restrictive condition on possible human grammars. However, showing that other theories fail to reduce the central principles does not excuse us from searching for ways to render a more elegant account of the human language faculty.

I have proposed that the INP may reduce to a semantic restriction, once the other principles that restrict dependency are taken to guide semantic interpretation at LF. I have suggested that neither covaluation nor dependency relations need to be notationally coded in syntactic structures at all, since these are relations that are required independently of our language faculty, and it is not obvious that the principles need to produce concrete markers that crucially figure in syntactic rules. I have proposed that factors that adjust our expectations about covaluation do not refer to syntactic structure directly, although there are indirect effects (based on the pattern of prohibited dependencies), as in the case of Pragmatic Obviation and Preferred Covaluation. I have also suggested that the interpretive principles form a unified component, which characterizes them as having certain commonalities of effect and composition. Perhaps these commonalities will prove reducible to a more axiomatized system.

What has been achieved, however, is that the full range of crossover effects—primary and secondary, strong, weak, and weakest—are straightforwardly derived from the same principles that are invoked to account for the general distribution of structurally conditioned dependency relations in chapters 1 and 2: There is no weak crossover constraint. Moreover, the copy theory of movement is supported by a detailed examination of the pattern of anaphora, both reconstruction and antireconstruction, that results from displacements. Perhaps some other theoretical architecture can recover the anaphoric relations perturbed by displacement in the same way, and perhaps the dependency restrictions can be formulated and simplified in some other architecture, but any theory that does not derive the complete distribution of crossover from independently required dependency principles cannot seriously compete with the theory proposed here.

Appendix

Scrambling and Reconstruction

As noted at the end of chapter 2, I am claiming that the FTIP, Rule H, and the INP are universal and unparameterized, and thus should compute any natural language input in the same fashion. Insofar as English does not provide an easy way to observe certain phenomena that are widely attested in other languages, it is necessary, if only to illustrate what is at issue for the principles I propose, to show how the theory might plausibly be extended to classes of languages that evidence displacement phenomena different from those we have examined for English.

In many languages, word order can be very flexible, so much so that it is difficult to settle upon any unmarked order of the major constituents— subject, object, tensed verb, untensed verb, and indirect object. Nonetheless, however a relatively neutral or unmarked word order is characterized (perhaps in terms of its less forceful pragmatic presuppositions), various displacements from the neutral order are accorded some sort of focusing or backgrounding effect. Languages that more freely admit displacements from the neutral order, or for which the neutral order is not at all obvious, are generally called scrambling languages. Many scrambling displacements have been claimed to induce crossover effects and/or yield reconstruction effects (as first pointed out by Saito and Hoji (1983), who use crossover effects as evidence for VP in Japanese), while other scrambling displacements have been argued to produce no such effects. For reasons like these, most researchers who treat scrambling effects as arising from movement do not assume that all scrambling movements are alike.[1] In fact, some researchers (see, e.g., Webelhuth 1992) contend that scrambling movements are not really characterizable by the standard Government-Binding era division between A-movement and Ā-movement.

I am certainly committed to the existence of movements that leave copies, and any variety of movement that leaves a copy that can be converted into a q-variable should have the potential to induce crossover effects. Displacements analyzed as Ā-movements are those that leave copies, and members of this class include movement to Spec,CP and topicalization. QR at LF may be an Ā-movement, but what is important for the present account is that it establishes scope and permits the insertion of a q-variable (see note 7 of chapter 4).

Up to this point, I have not examined A-movements with respect to reconstruction, except in passing, but I assume that A-movements are like Ā-movements in that they leave copies that show some reconstruction effects (see, e.g., Lebeaux 1998) and are subject to vehicle change (see Safir 2004, sec. 5.1). The issue that arises in this appendix is whether or not reconstruction can save anaphors contained in A-moved constituents, a less commonly made assumption. The matter is not readily testable for English because A-movement does not raise past c-commanding arguments, but since A-movement should, in principle, be able to leave copies, we should see detectable effects in scrambling languages where scrambling is A-movement that overcomes minimality.

What is more typically at issue in discussions of scrambling is whether or not the output of scrambling creates new A-binders for anaphors and bound pronouns. If so, the landing site must be an A-position and the displacement is A-movement by definition. Thus, an issue arises for A-movement that does not arise for Ā-movement, since Ā-movement does not provide potential binders for anaphors.

If A-movement and Ā-movement both can leave copies to which the FTIP and the INP are always sensitive, then the fundamental generalization one might expect is the following:

(1) Reconstructed crossover effects should be found where there are reconstructed FTIP effects and vice versa.

Given the conclusions of the preceding chapters, however, (1) will often fail to hold, as there are a wide variety of factors that can intervene to either neutralize reconstruction altogether, or just neutralize one effect without neutralizing the other. As we have seen, FTIP effects for names can be neutralized by vehicle change, WCO can be neutralized by an operator-external antecedent (as in the case of appositives and parasitic gaps) or by an Ā-antecedent that is not an operator (as in the case of topicalization), and crossover is also neutralized when the quantifier antecedent enters the derivation by late adjunction. To know whether or not these factors play a role is to know a great deal about the structural analysis of a language, and it requires detailed study.

The literature on scrambling is pertinent, rich, and complex, but for reasons of space and energy, I cannot enter into it in any comprehensive way. Rather, I confine myself, in this short appendix, to showing how the tools of analysis developed up to this point might permit us to account for some apparent deviations from the expected pattern. To do this, I briefly examine scrambling and reconstruction facts in just one language with a challenging pattern (Hindi), at the same time sketching some alternatives for analysis that my account up to this point makes available. In other words, my account of Hindi is relatively superficial, but I hope it will open up lines of inquiry by providing a model for how, in the context of scrambling, crossover and reconstruction can be investigated within my assumptions.

A.1   Hindi Scrambling: Reconstruction and Crossover

Scrambling and its relation to reconstruction and crossover have been a central topic in the study of Hindi-Urdu for some time (see Gurtu 1985; Mahajan 1989; Dayal 1993; Kidwai 2000; and references cited in these works). Some of these studies address the heart of this phenomenon cross-linguistically, but I will largely confine my remarks to a few small sets of Hindi examples, and set aside even cases of rightward scrambling (if indeed rightward scrambling as rightward movement exists; see Mahajan 1997 for discussion).[2]

Hindi-Urdu is generally considered to be an SOV language but one that requires a focused constituent to appear in the preverbal position. The movements associated with scrambling seem to be motivated, in a discourse-functional sense, as a strategy or conspiracy that attempts to situate the focused constituent next to the verb. I will assume that the reorderings in question are nonetheless syntactic movements that contribute in a formal way to interpretation at LF; otherwise, we would not expect these reorderings of constituents to have any effect on dependent identity interpretations. I am not assuming that sentences are necessarily shaped for discourse usages, however. Just as the good skipping stones one finds on the beach are those that happen to have the right properties for skipping (palm-sized, round, and flat), so the sentences made available by the grammar that happen to have the right shape will be used for purposes their shape suits them for (e.g., ones that have the right constituent in the focus slot are useful or not in a given discourse).[3]

These preliminaries aside, now consider the contrasts in (2a,b) (from Kidwai 2000, 31, though this contrast is first discussed in Gurtu 1985) and (3a,b) (from Kidwai 2000, 29) where the pronoun *uski* is understood as bound to the interrogative nominal.[4]

(2) a. **uski* behen   *kisko*   pyar kərti hɛ
       his sister-SU who-DO love does is
       '*Who* does *his* sister love?'

    b. *kisko*   *uski* behen   pyar kərti hɛ
       who-DO his sister-SU love does is
       '*Who* does *his* sister love?'

(3) a. **raja-ne *uske* pita-ko   *konsi dasi* lota di
       king-SU her father-DO which maid returned
       '*Which maid* did the king return to *her* father?'

    b. raja-ne *konsi dasi* *uske* pita-ko   lota di
       king-SU which maid her father-DO returned
       '*Which maid* did the king return to *her* father?'

These contrasts suggest that overt movement does not induce WCO but covert movement does.[5] If a universal is substituted into the position of the *wh*-phrase, then WCO also is (correctly) expected, as illustrated in (4a,b) (from Kidwai 2000, 7).

(4) a. **uski* behen-ne *har   larke-ko* dekha
       his sister-SU each boy-DO saw
       '*His* sister saw *each boy*.'

    b. *har   larke-ko* *uski* gehen-ne t dekha
       each boy-DO his sister-SU   saw
       '*His* sister saw *each boy*.'

From this perspective, it would appear that clause-internal scrambling to the left of the subject patterns with A-movement in that it creates (in Government-Binding parlance) new A-binders.

Another way in which scrambling has been claimed to pattern with A-movement is illustrated in (5) (from Kidwai 2000, 31), where the direct object can, when scrambled, antecede a possessive anaphor inside the subject, at least for some speakers (not Dayal (1993)). The anaphor in question, *apne*, is not well formed unless it has a locality-restricted c-commanding antecedent that is the subject of the sentence (see Safir 2004 for discussion and references).

(5) a. *apne* baccõ-ne   *mohan-ko* gar-se   nikal diya
       APNE's children-SU Mohan-DO house-from threw gave
       '*His* children threw *Mohan* out of the house.'
   b. ?*mohan-ko apne* baccõ-ne   t gar-se   nikul diya
       Mohan-DO APNE children-SU   house-from threw gave
       '*His* children threw *Mohan* out of the house.'

However, the evidence in (5b) is not really evidence that the anaphor *apne* depends on the scrambled antecedent, since if it were, subject orientation would be violated; *mohan-ko* is not a subject. In Safir 2004 (and references cited there), it is argued that subject orientation of *apne* arises from LF movement to a tense position uniquely locally c-commanded by the subject. In that position, subject orientation is expected of not just any c-commanding A-antecedent, but uniquely of the subject A-antecedent, as is the case for the majority dialect (and perhaps also the minority dialect; see appendix note 6).

Kidwai, essentially following a line of argument offered by Dayal (1993), argues that cases like (5b) are really a kind of "referential" use of *apne*, which is merely coreferent with *mohan-ko*.[6] In support of a referential use of *apne*, Kidwai shows that *apne* can appear without an antecedent, in which case it typically refers to the conversational participants together, apparently as 'we'; but that does not appear to be the intended reading of (5b). In any case, the acceptability of (5b) is not evidence for the A-movement analysis because it is not consistent with subject orientation.

Kidwai goes a step further, claiming that the apparent disrespect for the subject orientation requirement in (5b) argues against Mahajan's proposal that scrambling is potentially an A-movement operation. However, if Kidwai is right to treat the use of *apne* in (5b) as referential (in her sense) or at least exceptionally bound, then it still only follows that (5b) is not evidence *for* an A-movement analysis—it does not rule such an analysis out, since whatever is required for subject orientation is enough to rule it out independently.

By contrast, (2b) and (3b), where the bindees are pronouns, provide better evidence in favor of the view that the scrambled constituent is an A-binder. If the fronted quantified antecedents in these examples arose from Ā-movement, we would expect crossover effects to arise, contrary to fact. Thus, scrambling in (2b) and (3b) must be A-movement, by this reasoning.

On the other hand, some have argued that leftward scrambling must be an Ā-movement, insofar as Ā-movement consistently shows reconstruction effects. The following contrast is originally from Mahajan 1989:[7]

(6) a. *ram-ne* mohan-ko *apni* kitab lɔtai
       Ram-su Mohan-io APNI book returned
       '*Ram* returned *his* book to Mohan.'
    b. *apni* kitab *ram-ne* mohan-ko lɔtai
       APNI book Ram-su Mohan-io returned
       '*Ram* returned *his* book to Mohan.'

If the fronted position of *apni kitab* in (6b) arises by Ā-movement, then it would be expected to leave a copy that can be interpreted in situ, predicting the acceptability of (6b). However, Ā-movement is only necessary for (6b) if it is assumed that an A-movement analysis would not leave a copy, preventing the anaphor from being anteceded, contrary to fact (but see the discussion of (8)).[8]

The essence of Mahajan's view of these relations is that scrambling can arise by A-movement or Ā-movement in Hindi, but the resulting word order may mask which movement is involved in a given case. This view predicts that scrambling within a clause should permit the union of all those outcomes permitted by either A-movement or Ā-movement, but not those outcomes licensed by neither movement. Dayal argues that Hindi scrambling provides no evidence for A-movement, but then must resort to the expanded typologies of Déprez (1989) and Webelhuth (1992), who argue that an additional form of phrasal movement besides Ā-movement and A-movement must be posited. I believe the right interpretation of the anaphor and crossover evidence in Hindi does not require us to abandon Mahajan's more limited approach to the A/Ā distinction, although his position is ultimately better supported by the interpretation of the facts proposed by Kidwai and Dayal.

We have just seen that if the possessive anaphor evidence is not relevant (because leftward A-movement does not create new binders for the possessive anaphor for an independent reason), then there is no argument *against* the possibility that scrambling is sometimes A-movement. The absence of crossover effects in cases like (2b), (3b), and (4b) is evidence *for* scrambling as A-movement, as opposed to QR, which induces WCO in (2a), (3a), and (4a).

Now let us consider the relation of scrambled direct objects to coargument anaphors. In (7a,b), we see that an object anaphor anteceded by the subject can still be so anteceded when the object anaphor is scrambled leftward.

(7) a. nur   əpne-ap-ko pyar kərti hɛ
       Noor-(SU) APNE-(DO) love does is
       'Noor loves himself.'
    b. əpne-ap-ko nur   _____ pyar kərti hɛ
       APNE-(DO) Noor-(SU)   love does is
       'Himself Noor loves.'

This is possible according to what is permitted by either movement, since a copy is left behind in the position of the dash, which can satisfy LAL and the FTIP in the object position. Here I assume (8), as I did for English (for cases such as *Himself, Lyle likes*), though (8) is really just a restatement of the assertion that copies are indistinct.

(8) If one member of a copy set satisfies a condition, then all members do.

On the other hand, to ensure that the leftward-scrambled anaphor does not c-command the subject in a way that would invoke the FTIP, we may assume that the higher copy deletes. After all, the higher copy is not crucially needed as an antecedent for anything else in (7b) and does not fulfill any thematic requirement.

Kidwai, however, who also argues against the view that the A/Ā distinction makes the right cut, employs Dayal's observation that a direct object scrambled to a purported A-position ought to be able to antecede a subject coargument anaphor; yet (9b) does not contrast with (9a) (from Kidwai 2000, 7).

(9) a. *apne(ap)-ne mohən-ko mara
       APNE-AP-SU Mohan-DO hit
       '*Himself* hit *Mohan*.' (i.e., '*Mohan* hit *himself*.')
    b. *mohən-ko apne(ap)-ne mara
       Mohan-DO APNE-AP-SU hit
       '*Himself* hit *Mohan*.' (i.e., '*Mohan* hit *himself*.')

However, (9a) fails not only because *apne-ap* is not anteceded, but also because it is subject oriented, a separate matter. Once again, then, the question of whether or not the scrambled position of the direct object *Mohan* is an A- or Ā-position is not relevant for (9b); all that matters is that the scrambled position is not a subject, hence not a potential antecedent for *apne-ap*.[9]

On the other hand, this leaves us with the now unexplained fact that these cases are rejected even by those who accept (5b) with what Kidwai calls the referential interpretation (which ought to be possible where the A-antecedent is not required to be a subject). Rather than appealing to the referential interpretation, I suspect that (5b) is (perhaps) not as bad as (9b) for the anaphoric interpretation because in (9b) the anaphor c-commands the trace of its antecedent (here rendered as a copy), as illustrated schematically in (10a), but the anaphor does not directly c-command its trace in (5b). This is illustrated schematically in (10b), where γ labels the left edge of the clause before scrambling and Vx labels some projection of the verb that contains the object but not the subject.

(10) a. *[Mohan-DO [$_\gamma$ APNE(-AP)-SU [$_{Vx}$[Mohan-DO] V]]]
     b. ?[Mohan-DO [$_\gamma$[[APNE's] children-SU] [$_{Vx}$[Mohan-DO] PP V]]]

First let us consider how the distinction in (10a) could serve an Ā-analysis of (9b). If scrambling in (9b)/(10b) is Ā-movement of a non-quantified antecedent, then the movement should leave a copy (i.e., *mohan-ko*) that the subject *apne-ap* would c-command. The INP is not violated because *apne-ap* could uniquely depend on c-commanding *mohan-ko* in its scrambled position, since the trace is not a q-variable (it is not a copy of a quantifier). Moreover, the relation between copies is not dependency, so the intervention of the subject between copies of *mohan* would not be a problem. Nonetheless, the FTIP algorithm will exclude (9b), since the name copy in its position of origin is not the least dependent form with respect to the c-commanding subject, *apne-ap*, and vehicle change of the lower copy to a pronoun is still not more dependent than an anaphor in that position. Therefore, *mohan-ko* not only fails to depend on the subject by the FTIP, but must be obviative, by Pragmatic Obviation. Thus, there is no successful derivation for (9b) if the leftward scrambling is Ā-movement.

We can now also ask whether or not (9b) and (10b) are expected to be grammatical as an instance of A-movement, again setting aside the subject orientation question. If A-movement leaves a copy, then the FTIP will rule it out as in the Ā-movement case because a name in object position would be obviative with respect to the subject. If, on the other hand, the trace of *mohan-ko* undergoes vehicle change to a pronoun, then it must be interpreted as dependent. The vehicle-changed pronoun could then depend on the subject anaphor, which could in turn depend on the fronted *mohan-ko*. This too would violate the FTIP because an alternative numeration containing an anaphor in place of *mohan-ko* could satisfy LAL and converge in object position.

In appealing to the FTIP to rule out A-movement and Ā-movement analyses of (9b), however, the blocking numeration I appealed to is one where both the subject and the object are anaphors; that is, the blocking, convergent numeration is would one where *apne-ap-ne* antecedes *apne-ap-ko* (for English, this would amount to <u>*Himself, himself loves*</u>). In that circumstance, the object *apne-ap* could successfully depend on the subject *apne-ap* and the subject *apne-ap* could successfully depend on the fronted one, satisfying the FTIP (and Rule H). Then the fronted *apne-ap* would be well formed with respect to LAL by (8), but it could not be deleted, since it is needed to antecede the subject *apne-ap* (permitting the subject to satisfy LAL and hence be available for the FTIP). However, such a configuration would entail a form of referential circularity that violates the INP, given that we have assumed (8). Since the topicalized object anaphor c-commands the subject, but a copy of the object anaphor depends on the subject, the topicalized object depends on the subject as well, with the result that the topicalized anaphor c-commands a position that it depends on. Vehicle change of the trace of the topicalized anaphor to a pronoun would avoid the INP violation, since the pronoun could depend on the subject anaphor, which in turn depends on the topicalized anaphor (Rule H would not allow anything else). However, the result of that would be a violation of the FTIP, since a vehicle-changed pronoun is not the most dependent form available—rather, the anaphor copy would be.

This reasoning illustrates an important fact about the interaction of the FTIP and the INP. The INP does not figure in availability calculations for the FTIP. This is because the INP only bans interpretations based on c-command between nodes, not any relation between forms, and availability calculations for the FTIP evaluate syntactic conditions on forms, given an interpretation held constant (recall the critique of Bianchi's (2001) approach in chapter 5).[10] The form that according to the FTIP is the most dependent one available for a given dependent interpretation may still fail to represent that interpretation if dependent interpretation in that configuration is independently banned by the INP. Thus, it is consistent with the FTIP for a derivation that converges, but violates the INP, to block a derivation that also converges, but with a less dependent form in the position the FTIP tests for.

If this analysis of leftward scrambling as A-movement can be upheld as an option, then, contrary to Kidwai and to Dayal, the contrast in

(9a,b) does not create any special problem for an analysis of clause-bound scrambling as ambiguously A/Ā-movement to the left (indeed, A-movement analyses would suffice to generate the clause-bound pattern just discussed, as the reader can confirm). This ultimately upholds Mahajan's position on the basis of a somewhat different interpretation of the relevant facts than the one he offers.

Notice, however, that I have not defined the difference between A-movement and Ā-movement in any principled way. Rather, I have grouped movement to Spec,CP, topicalization, and QR as Ā-movement and I have grouped Case-driven movement and some cases of scrambling as A-movement, and then distinguished what is expected of each kind of movement. I make no proposal about how the distinction between these empirically grouped movement types might be independently defined as A- or Ā-movements (e.g., I do not assume all A-movement is Case driven). At least for the data I consider, it appears that it is not necessary to propose any additional form of phrasal movement relation that differs from, or cuts across, the A/Ā distinction. Despite attempts by Déprez (1989) and Kidwai (2000) to render the distinctions more principled in three-valued or two-valued systems, I still consider the matter an open question.[11]

Before I conclude this appendix, it is worth noting that non-clause-bound scrambling, which is not limited by tense domains, would, under normal expectations, count as Ā-movement. As Mahajan (1989, 41) points out (see also Déprez 1989, 134–135), long-distance scrambling does indeed induce a WCO effect in the higher clause (11a,b), but not the lower one (11c), as would be expected if scrambled elements in the lower clause could first move to an A-position and then move interclausally to an Ā-position (either to the immediate left of the matrix verb and dative, as in (11a), or to left-peripheral position, as in (11b)). (Examples are from Mahajan 1989.)

(11) a. *raam-ne *sab*   *uskii* bahin se kahaa [(ki)   *t*
         Ram-su everyone-DO his   sister to told   that
         aaye   the]
         come-PERF-PL-M be-PST-PL-M
         'It's *everyone* that *his* sister told (that) had come.'
     b. **sab-ko*   *uskii* bahin-ne socaa   ki   raam-ne *t* dekhaa
         everyone-DO his   sister-su thought that Ram-su   saw
         'It's *everyone* that *his* sister thought that Ram saw.'

c. *sab-ko*   raam-ne socaa   ki   *uskii* bahin-ne *t* dekhaa
   everyone-DO Ram-SU thought that his   sister-SU   seen
   thaa
   be-past
   'It's *everyone* that Ram thought that *his* sister had seen.'

It remains for future research to determine whether or not this thumb-nail sketch of the scrambling phenomenon in Hindi is on the right track when examined either in greater detail or in comparison to similar phenomena in other languages. The upshot of this discussion, however, is that if clause-internal scrambling can be achieved in some languages by A-movement to the left of the subject as well as by Ā-movement, then we expect to see phenomena licensed by either construction type. If some scrambling is A-movement, then we do not expect to find WCO effects, though we do expect SCO effects. Where scrambling is clause bound, we will see reconstruction effects, as we do in (5b), but WCO effects will be masked, as long as an A-movement analysis exists for the same word order. Once again, we have appealed to Rule H, the FTIP, and the INP, and we have not had to extend our account by adding any new assumptions.

Notes

Chapter 1

1. Higginbotham (1983, 402) puts it this way: "If X c-commands Y, then Y is not an antecedent of X." See also Evans 1980, 355.

2. In Safir 2004, I propose that c-command can be defined more simply as in (i).

(i) *C-command*
   A c-commands B if the sister of A dominates B.

On this account, no c-command relation holds between sister nodes. Nothing in this book hinges on this suggestion.

3. In an early work, Lasnik (1976, app.) cites quantifier judgments now considered nonstandard. For example, he stars *No one's mother loves him* under the bound reading, though almost all native English speakers accept this.

4. For discussion of the ellipsis issues, see Sag 1976, Williams 1977, 1997, Kitagawa 1991, Fiengo and May 1994, Merchant 1999, and Fox 2000 and references cited there.

5. Reinhart's (1999) revision of Reinhart 1997 explicitly moves to a view that covaluation is blocked only where a bound variable reading under c-command is blocked, a view more similar to the one argued for here. However, then c-command is tacitly admitted to be insufficient as a means of accounting for the distribution of bound variable readings—that is, the CLP is effectively abandoned, although Reinhart does not appear to see it this way. My view that the expectation of noncoreference arises where the dependent identity reading under c-command is blocked was developed around the same time (and presented in lectures in Lund in January 1999 and at the City University of New York in April 1999). Though I have been very much influenced by the competitive approach the original Rule I implied, my account has no Principle B nor any c-command licensing condition for bound variable readings.

6. In a later version of this theory, Reinhart (1997) rejects the use of indices altogether (under the influence of Chomsky and Lasnik 1995), replacing them with the λ-notation conditioned by c-command (consistent with the CLP). Given the c-command condition, this version of the theory is not significantly different from the one addressed in the text.

7. The latter possibility is also raised in G&R's footnote 9 (p. 78), where the answer to a *who* question with a pronoun (e.g., *Who left?*; answer, *He left*) might involve a coindexing that is not on the sentence level. In other words, there may be a form of discourse indexing, since there is certainly some sort of discourse representation that tracks referents and the information about them (see, e.g., Kamp and Reyle 1993). However, there is no reason to believe that this indexing is regulated by syntax. For an argument to the contrary, see Berman and Hestvik 1997 and a brief response in Safir 2004, sec. 3.3.1.

8. Ueyama (1998) proposes an additional indexing and dependency relationship in addition to formal dependency and distinct from coreference based on coindexing, to account for a wide (and interesting) range of E-type cases in Japanese. On E-type cases, see note 1 of chapter 2.

9. F&M argue (1994, 210–216) that the α and β indices also represent the difference between certain thematically restricted readings and thematically unrestricted ones. The former are available only when SELF forms are employed, such as *Aaron Burr defended himself* in the sense that Aaron Burr fought back, as opposed to readings that are thematically unrestricted, such as *Aaron Burr defended himself* in the sense that Aaron Burr mounted a defense of Aaron Burr, perhaps in the legal sense. F&M argue that the thematically unrestricted reading is an α-indexed reading, available to predicates that are not falsified when the object is something that does not necessarily exist, as in *John defended Satan* versus *John hit Satan*. However, this seems to be the wrong generalization, insofar as *Each celebrity positioned himself next to the president* could be a description of the various celebrities placing their statues at the wax museum next to that of the president (and perhaps moving the others aside), but *Patton positioned Satan next to Bradley* could only be true if Satan is real or Patton is placing the statue of Satan next to Bradley—in other words, there is a presupposition of existence for that which is positioned. Such a predicate would not be expected to have an α-reflexive reading. Nonetheless, *Patton positioned himself strategically* is ambiguous between the thematically unrestricted reading and the thematically restricted one, suggesting that whatever the distinction is, it is not one between α and β indices. For further discussion of "proxy" readings in relation to strict readings (from which they are distinguished), see Safir 2004, sec. 4.2.1.

10. Higginbotham (1989) argues that anaphoric coreference must also be captured by grammar in addition to anaphoric dependency. Much of his argumentation depends on the representation of control, which seems to me to involve issues that have more to do with the properties of PRO than they do with the class of possible relations of coreference versus covariance generally.

11. This objection against the crucial use of indices as part of binding also applies to Pollard and Sag's (1994) use of indices, which crucially treats them as part of linguistic representation enforcing covariation (see their discussion, p. 249).

12. Evans (1980, 361) claims that there is never a case where indices on dependents match and the two indexed elements are not c-commanded by a common antecedent. He is assuming that *The woman he hates loves John* is not a case of dependency of the pronoun on *John*, but one of independent reference. Evans

then suggests that Lasnik's (1976) transitivity problem does not arise if the non-c-commanding pronoun in *The woman he loved told him that John was a jerk* is referentially independent (although F&M (1994), Higginbotham (1985), and Williams (1997) assume it is dependent). I argue in section 2.5, however, that it is right to conclude that *he* is not dependent on *John*, but wrong to require forms dependent on the same antecedent to be c-commanded by that antecedent.

13. This raises the question of how obviativity relations are to be kept track of. I return to this in section 1.4.

14. The apparent counterexamples to the derived complementarity theory I propose (and to any other) are cases where either more than one form will do to represent a dependent with respect to some antecedent, or where no form will do as a dependent to some antecedent. In Safir 2004, all of the apparent counterexamples of the first type are argued to involve either (a) distinct interpretations, (b) distinct (licensing of) forms, or (c) distinct structures that have the same linear output. The primary example of the first type (where no form will do), first raised by Lasnik (1976), *John and Mary love her/*herself*, does not allow a dependent interpretation of *her* on *Mary*, at least not under a distributed interpretation for the conjunction (see Reinhart and Reuland 1993, 676–677). This residue of Principle B is argued to be an artifact of a separate principle, nonspecific to pronouns, that also excludes some anaphoric interpretations that are otherwise possible. Interested readers should consult the reference cited. Arguments of forms (a)–(c) that explain why more than one form is available are discussed as cited, but claims along the lines of (a) are necessary to explain the difference between reflexives and reciprocals, at least in English, and many arguments of form (b) are found (e.g., Safir 1992, 1997; Reinhart and Reuland 1991).

15. More concretely, the FTIP can be thought of as an algorithm that applies as described in (i).

(i) *FTIP algorithm*

The input is a given numeration and the resulting LF that contains a nominal A potentially dependent on and c-commanded by a nominal B. Substitute the next most dependent element for A (the target) in the given numeration. If the new test numeration permits an LF structure to be derived that permits the same dependency relation without crashing, then a dependent reading for the target form is unavailable; but if the test derivation crashes, then repeat the process with an even more dependent element substituting for the target until there is no more dependent element to be tested. If there is no substitution of a more dependent referent for the target that permits the derivation to converge, then the dependent reading is indeed available for the target.

Thus, alternative convergent derivations are compared based on alternative numerations differing only with respect to the choice of dependent form for A (in practice, rarely are more than one or two substitutions possible in any given case, so the computation is not complex). The dependency relationship is held constant in the comparison. See Safir 2004 for details. Another process that makes a comparison of derivations with respect to a given interpretation is the theory of

Quantifier Raising (QR) in Fox 2000, where QR is argued to apply only if it can change scope relations. An algorithm that expresses this must involve a comparison of meaning outputs, such that if the same meaning is achieved by both outputs, only the one that does not include QR is grammatical. For other algorithms that involve interpretive competitions, including Rule H, see Safir 2004, chap. 7, and section 2.3 below.

16. See, for example, Kamp and Reyle's (1993) approach. See also note 7 of this chapter.

17. There is a conceptual reason to limit vehicle change as well. I have assumed that anaphors are marked forms (hence subject to LAL) and that pronouns are just reduced definite descriptions (see Safir 2004). Thus, introducing an anaphor in reconstruction would add information to the derivation, but vehicle change to a pronoun always introduces a form the descriptive content of which can be recovered by antecedency.

There are cases that appear to counterexemplify the prediction that vehicle change cannot introduce a reflexive. F&M (1994, 272) consider cases like (ii), pointed out to them by Ivan Sag, to be acceptable for the same reason that (iii) is.

(ii) Mary introduced me to everyone that I did.

(iii) Mary introduced me to everyone that I introduced me to.

Here, first person coreference is overcoming the failure of dependent reference, to put it in my terms, such that the relevant interpretation is available (though to my ear, both are barely acceptable, (ii) perhaps being worse). Similarly, we may expect predicates that permit "Principle B violations" marginally to be similarly marginal. Predicates like *represent* that distinguish identities as proxies or guises (see also Safir 2004 for discussion of these cases) fare better (e.g., *John wanted to represent me more than I did*), especially in instantiation contexts (*John voted for me, Bill voted for me, and I did too*), and this even extends, in a less robust fashion, to cases like *Barbara voted for him, but Bush didn't*, which F&M (p. 213) accept as marked with a reading that Bush didn't vote for himself. Williams (1995), who points out some of the differences between predicates I have discussed here in a slightly different way, suggests that cases like the Bush example should lead us to abandon not only any restriction on vehicle change, but vehicle change itself, along with computations on syntactically active parallel structure in ellipsis sites. If, however, we abandon the restriction on vehicle change that it only convert to pronouns to accommodate these cases, then the robustly excluded cases like *The senators criticized Bill before Bill did* are unaccounted for with respect to the contrast between these cases and the more embedded ones like *Hillary knew that the senators would criticize Bill before Bill did*.

The following contrast, however, noted by Lasnik (1999, 11), where only (v) permits a dependent reading, is not predicted either by my approach or by Reinhart and Reuland's (1993).

(iv) ?Mary believes *him* to be a genius and *Bob* does too.

(v) *Bob* believes *him* to be a genius.

The reason (iv) should not be possible is that *him* reconstructed in the second conjunct is not the most dependent form available here, since vehicle change does not create SELF forms and the preceding clause could not have contained one. Yet the FTIP will put a numeration with a SELF form in place of the pronoun in the second conjunct and determine that use of anything but a SELF form there dependent on *Bob* should be obviative. Reinhart and Reuland's approach would have the same problem with (iv), since it relies on the Chain Condition to rule out (v) and the same account should apply to the ellipsis site in (iv). It is possible, however, that cases like (iv) may simply be instantiation contexts, if we understand that the conjuncts are part of a list of people who consider Bob a genius. This would explain the marginal acceptability of (vi) under this slightly ironic interpretation (i.e., the opposite of what one would expect for coreference) where Bob is also among those who love Bob.

(vi) ?Mary loves Bob and of course Bob does too.

On the other hand, if (iv) is not an instantiation reading, then this example is problematic for most current approaches.

Chapter 2

1. Evans (1980) distinguishes a class of pronouns that are coconstrued with a quantified nominal, but are not bound pronouns dependent on their antecedents. He notes the following difference:

(i) Socrates owns *a dog* and *it* bit Socrates.

(ii) Socrates owns *a dog* which bites *its* tail.

In (i), *it* refers to the unique dog that Socrates owns and that bit Socrates, whereas (ii) is true if, out of any number of dogs that Socrates owns, one of them bites its tail. True bound variable dependence is regulated by c-command, according to Evans, whereas cases like (i) involve what he calls E-type pronouns. E-type pronouns are not in the scope of the quantified nominals to which they are related, he reasons; if they were, *it* in (i) would not have the uniqueness interpretation that shows it lies outside the scope of the existential (Evans 1980, 342–343). E-type pronouns are incompatible with a number of quantifiers, such as negation.

(iii) *Many senators* admire Kennedy, but *they* are very junior.

(iv) *No/Every senator* admires Kennedy, but *he/they* is/are very junior.

Evans and nearly every researcher since have treated E-type pronouns as ruled by scopal generalizations separate from those that determine the success or failure of quantified bound anaphora sentence-internally, and I concur with this division. My account permits dependencies like the one that exists between *many senators* and *they* in (iii). It is perhaps worth considering, however, that the uniqueness or existence presuppositions that accompany E-type readings do not follow from the claim that E-type pronouns are not dependent; rather, these restrictions have been given an analysis that does not treat them like other (intrasentential) bound variable (dependent) pronouns. These readings could also be consistent with the claim that E-type pronouns are restricted in a way that does not bear on whether or not they are variables (e.g., presuppositions of existence or group or exhaustive interpretations). If so, we can say that certain quantifiers or quantifications restricted in certain ways have scope over discourses, and those that do have such scope license dependencies across sentential boundaries. For a recent semantic account arguing that E-type pronouns are stranded determiners of dependent definite descriptions, see Elbourne 2001 (and references cited there).

2. Chomsky and Lasnik (1995) note that parallelism holds even where elision is absent.

(i) *John* saw *his* mother and Bill saw his mother too.

Given the coconstrual in the first conjunct of (i), *his* in the second conjunct must be coconstrued with either *John* or *Bill*, but not with some third party. As pointed out in Safir 2004, however, for discourses like that in (iiA) followed by (iiB), the condition on parallelism for elision cannot reduce to a form without elision (even one mediated by a deletion operation), since there is no overt form that a strict reading of the elision in (iiB) could possibly correspond to, given the meaning that (iiB) is required to have (as indicated by the portion in brackets).

(ii) A: If I were you, I would hate me.
    B: I do [hate you].

In other words, *would hate me* gives the wrong referential value if copied in (iiB), and *would hate you* is not available. Notice also that this is evidence that vehicle change cannot introduce a reflexive form, *x-self*; if it could, (iiB) would incorrectly be allowed to mean 'I would hate myself'.

3. Higginbotham (1989) argues that anaphoric coreference must be captured by grammar in addition to anaphoric dependency. Much of his argumentation depends on the representation of control, which seems to me to involve issues that have more to do with the properties of PRO than with the class of possible relations of coreference versus covariance generally. For some discussion of relevant control interpretations, see Safir 2004.

See also note 9 of chapter 1.

4. This assumes that parallelism refers to LF containing covert syntactic structures, as Kitagawa (1991) has proposed, rather than assuming that the elided portion is constructed by rule from properties of the antecedent. Parallelism enforces matching in some structural sense of a match, and in this schematic way, I also agree with Fiengo and May (1994) (see also Fox 2000). The assumption that parallelism has anything to do with syntactic structures has been challenged by Merchant (1999).

5. Reinhart (1983a, 153) also points out contrasts like (i) versus (ii), but in these cases (the bulk of her examples) it is not obvious that there is any elision of a dependency relation to reconstruct, since the adjunct is not elided in (i).

(i) For *her* seventieth birthday, *Rosa* requested a Stravinsky record and Zelda (did) too.

(ii) For *her* seventieth birthday, I bought *Rosa* a Stravinsky record and Zelda too.

(iii) I bought *Rosa* a Stravinsky record for *her* seventieth birthday, and Zelda too.

In (iii), it is argued, a sloppy reading is available because *for her seventieth birthday* has been elided, but where that phrase is not so obviously elided, as in (i), it is claimed that a sloppy reading is not available. However, it is possible that *for her seventieth birthday* has been moved leftward, leaving a trace in the elided conjunct. Thus, it is predicted that there should be sloppy readings for all cases in both theories. In short, these cases do not speak to the question of whether or not c-command is crucial to bound interpretation. As a matter of judgment, I find the sloppy reading possible for both (ii) and (iii), but not very good in either case, though I do sense a contrast in the direction Reinhart indicates.

6. See Hornstein's (1995, 206n31) comments concerning the conditions under which such sentences are acceptable. Hornstein (p. 25) cites a case where the parallelism established for the ellipsis is not contrastive and treats the sloppy reading as unacceptable, while May (1985, 68, 163n7) accepts similar sentences with the sloppy reading. I believe the sloppy reading is helped along by establishing a contrastive parallel in these cases, as I have done for (13b), which is fully acceptable to my ear. Hornstein (p. 26) also rejects a sloppy reading for *John's mother loves him and Frank's father does too*, and I concur; but here the contrast appears to frustrate parallelism, unlike in (13a), which provides contrast while preserving parallelism. This undermines Hornstein's contention (p. 27) (based on the proposal in Reinhart 1991) that it is necessary to posit QR of names to get a sloppy reading for bare argument ellipsis like *John's mother loves him, and Bill's too*, where parallelism is preserved.

7. Proponents of the CLP will presumably argue that (12) is the general case and (13) and (14) should be licensed by some additional, as yet undiscovered principle or interaction. I do not have an account of why (12) does not permit a sloppy reading, but it seems more promising to have the ranks of bound readings thinned by ancillary factors (perhaps the opacity of such relations for certain prepositions, such as *without*, for (12b)) than to have them augmented by special licensing.

8. I have been careful to use pronoun-SELF in an exceptional Case-marking (ECM) environment, since the paradigm fails when a coargument SELF form is selected, as illustrated in (i).

(i) Everyone loves O.J.
   Orin loves O.J.
   Olive loves O.J.
   Even O.J. loves O.J./*himself.

In coargument contexts, the pronoun-SELF form requires the locally bound reading owing to a condition discussed in Safir 2004, sec. 4.1.

Some find *Even O.J. expects him to be acquitted* less acceptable than (19b) or even (20) for the codependent interpretation; but if there is a difference, the FTIP does not predict it or require it.

9. The existence of such cases, where Principle A still applies to *himself* in the usual way in ECM contexts, but the interpretation is not directly dependent, is exactly what is not expected in Reinhart and Reuland's (1993) theory, which is committed to the idea that the subject of an ECM construction is part of a

syntactic predicate with the subject of the ECM verb, and that predicates marked reflexive must be interpreted as reflexive, as represented by λ-binding. There is nothing reflexive about the interpretation of (20), as a comparison with the cases in note 8 of this chapter makes clear. Similarly, the existence of locality-conditioned SELF forms that do not have directly dependent readings is also inconsistent with Hornstein's (2001, 157) assertion that "reflexive logical form," which he also characterizes as λ-binding, "... is the interpretation that must arise if reflexives are formed via movement." This also compromises Hornstein's broader claim that Principle A (and the binding theory in general) reduces to relations formed by movement. See section 5.1 for further discussion. See also Safir 2004, sec. 5.1, where it is argued that Principle A should not be reduced to A-movement.

Hornstein (p. 171) also suggests that English SELF forms have *de se* semantics by virtue of being derived by movement, and hence bound variable interpretations. Even if it were true that all reflexive interpretations were bound variable interpretations, it would not be true that they are all *de se*. For example, (i) has a guise interpretation (see Safir 2004, chap. 4) by which I, in your shoes, would think I, in my own shoes, so to speak, am intelligent; this is not a *de se* reading, which requires conscious self-ascription.

(i) If I were any one of you, I would think I was pretty smart.

For the same point with different examples, see Chierchia 1989 and C.-T. J. Huang and Liu 2001. Imagine that (ii) is uttered in the following scenario: Professor Jones is currently being evaluated for tenure. He is reading a letter of reference, a letter for which the name of the candidate is blocked out. Unaware that the letter is in fact about him, he concludes that any candidate described in such unflattering terms would never be granted tenure.

(ii) No one expects *Professor Jones* to get tenure. *He* doesn't realize it yet, but *even Professor Jones* doesn't expect himself to get tenure.

Thus, the correct theory of reflexive bound readings should not require them to be interpreted *de se* (a claim that has no sense in any case where the antecedent of the SELF form is inanimate).

10. Reinhart's (1999) notion of covaluation depends on the difference between λ-operators for cases like *Every candidate believes only she voted for her*, such that *her* is not covalued with *only she* because they are bound by different operators. Reinhart further requires that no variable could be simultaneously bound by two operators in order to rule out strong crossover (p. 15n8), which is otherwise not accounted for by Rule I. My account of the latter case does not require binding of one variable by more than one operator to be ruled out, but only requires that *her* cannot depend on *only she*. Unlike my account, however, Reinhart's would appear to exclude split quantified antecedents for pronouns, which are clearly possible.

(i) Each senator told at least one female intern that they would make a good couple.

For cases like (i), there is clearly an interpretation where the value for *they* depends on both quantifiers and on both argument positions that they bind (tellers and tellees). In my account, *they* depends directly on two antecedents, both of them argument positions bound by quantifiers, and neither one excludes binding by the other. Additional stipulations can distinguish the two cases, of course, but it is not obvious that any such stipulations are required in a theory that relies on patterns of dependencies, as mine does, rather than one that must distinguish types of operator binding.

11. This would not be expected if *she* in *only she* did not c-command *herself*. The matter is discussed in some detail in Safir 2004.

Notice that these cases, like the O.J. cases, are further justification not to restate Principle A by reconstituting the notion of binding as "*x* c-commands *y* and *y* is dependent on *x*." A further case involves reciprocals in examples like *The men think they are taller than each other*, which, though perhaps conditioned by the possible scope of *each*, permits the sensible interpretation that each man believes he is taller than the other. See Safir 2004, sec. 7.1.

12. Fox characterizes the sloppy reading as adhering to "structural parallelism," but then the term *referential parallelism* is misleading, since that too depends on a structural parallel that is complete except for the dependency relation.

13. There are cases where covaluation does not involve codependency, however. For example, this account is consistent with addressing the use of *be* in *Superman is Clark Kent* as the assertion of covaluation; the FTIP feeds Pragmatic Obviation to result in an expectation of noncoreference, since the referential values of *Superman* and *Clark Kent* are presumably established independently. By contrast, *Superman is himself*, except on the idiomatic reading (e.g., feeling or appearing as he usually does), does not permit a dependent reading because of the nature of the assertion.

14. Jackendoff (1992 and subsequent work) has argued that the asymmetry in the interpretive possibilities for (39a,b) is evidence that syntactic representations are not rich enough to capture these phenomena and that we should therefore appeal to a level of conceptual structure from which syntax cannot be independent. I argue against this view in Safir 2004, but it is clear enough from the text that the line I take is roughly this: the syntax will not permit the relevant pattern of dependency, so no semantic interpretation that would require such a dependency is a possible interpretation. From this perspective, the semantic asymmetry is predicted without burdening the syntax with any appeal to conceptual structure. Bianchi (2001, 27–31) also appeals to conceptual structure to account for these cases, which is another point where my account diverges from hers. For more on her approach, see chapter 3, note 5.

15. Matters are a little more complicated than this. Preferred Covaluation ensures that covaluation arises from dependency unless dependency is blocked, and so nothing syntactic blocks an animate from depending on a c-commanding inanimate with which it is covalued (and the proxy relation is a covaluation; see Safir 2004). If it does, a form of referential circularity arises, however, because an

animate ends up depending on an inanimate (the proxy) that must depend on a covalued animate. This is illustrated in (i) and (ii).

(i) *Lenin* told the sculptor that *he* was pleased at how *he* towered over the parking lot.

(ii) Unfortunately, *he* fell over in high winds and crushed *his* car.

If *he* of (ii) directly depends on the last *he* in (i) (the proxy reading) and *his* in (ii) could directly depend on *Lenin*, then *his* would not depend on *he* in (ii) and no circularity arises. However, *his* must depend on *he* if Rule H applies, since *his* is covalued with *he*, hence the circularity described. I assume that Rule H applies to proxies because they are not intrinsically unexpected where they are not precluded.

16. This approach to circularity does not cover all of the cases that Higginbotham's does. Examples like [*the author of her book*], where *her* is identified as the author, are not cases where the dependent form is c-commanded by the term it is dependent on, unless there is some appeal to c-command by the head *author* with respect to *her*, a move that requires specific assumptions that do not appear to fit neatly with mine. The same point holds for examples pointed out by Williams (1982, 282) such as *the picture of it*, where *it* is identified with *the picture of it*. In *LGB*, Chomsky treats these as "i-within-i" cases, where an index is contained within a constituent bearing the same index, but Chomsky's account does not extend to cases like (48). I leave the *the picture of it* cases unaccounted for. See Bianchi 2001, 26–27, for an account of circularity essentially like Higginbotham's.

17. This claim is consistent with the Universalist Hypothesis, defended in Safir 1996b, 2004, which does not permit any principle to refer to anaphora unless that principle is universal, under the assumption that *anaphora* refers to the distribution of dependent and codependent identity relations.

Chapter 3

1. The issue did not go unnoticed by Koopman and Sportiche (1983, 143–145), as they discuss cases in Vata where a resumptive pronoun, appearing in a position where an empty category would violate the Empty Category Principle, nonetheless *does* cause WCO effects with other non-c-commanding pronouns that are not inserted to save ECP violations. The Vata pronouns in question do not behave quite as other pronouns in Vata do, and Koopman and Sportiche propose that they bear a special feature that must be licensed, in effect, by Ā-binding. Whatever they must say about such cases will be required in a theory that treats unmarked pronouns as parallel, but otherwise the issue does not affect the reasoning that follows. However, see note 21 of chapter 4.

2. I use the quantifier *each man* in these examples to rule out a gapping account of these conjuncts, where in the second conjunct, *who each man* is gapped in (15a) and *who each man claimed* in (15b). It is not clear to me whether or not it is a possible interpretation for (15a), perhaps under a gapping analysis, for each man to speak to a person and offend some other person—that is, 'I don't know who each man spoke to and who each man offended'. What matters here is that these

sentences are acceptable under an interpretation where for each choice of man, the one he spoke to is the one he offended (in (15a)) or where for each choice of man, the one he claimed to know is the one he claimed to have hired (in (15b)).

3. Approaches that treat conjunction as an adjunction structure treat across-the-board cases as parasitic gap constructions. See Munn 2001 for recent discussion, and for a sideward movement account, Nunes 2001.

4. As noted in chapter 2, if there are quantifiers that have scope across discourse (i.e., that are not sentence bound), then the requirement that bound variables be scoped is less restrictive in its effects. Ruys (2000) argues that in contexts where scope is exceptionally wide (for deeply embedded quantifiers), WCO effects are found, a result he takes to show that crossover effects are fundamentally scopal. This does not follow if WCO is a function of unbounded dependency restrictions independent of scope, as argued in this chapter. If pronouns bound to quantifiers must always be scoped, then wider scope for quantifiers simply renders the distribution of crossover effects more widely visible, not fundamentally scopal.

5. Bianchi 2001, an article that appeared after most of this book was written, deserves mention here since Bianchi has independently proposed that the bulk of crossover effects should be derived from a variant of Higginbotham's principle, formulated in this book as the INP. Moreover, Bianchi extends her version of the INP to cases of indirect dependency in the same way I have here to derive WCO, and she deserves the credit as the first to do it. Nonetheless, my account is justified differently independently of crossover effects and differs from hers in other crucial ways that I will address in chapter 5. For further comments on Bianchi's work, see note 14 in chapter 2 and note 1 in chapter 4.

6. Hornstein (1995, 200n4), who also offers a WCO account based on linking, sees the need for something to force pronouns to depend on the position of the variable at LF, not the quantifier, but he makes no concrete proposal. Hornstein does not assume, contrary to fact, that English permits resumptive pronouns (see, e.g., Safir 1986), nor does he address the fact that resumptive pronouns neutralize WCO. However, my theory, like Hornstein's, does treat the pre-QR position of the quantifier as the key to the process, not multiple $\bar{\text{A}}$-binding, as in the Bijection Principle or PCOB approaches. Hornstein suggests that this reduces the role of QR, which would only be true for my theory if q-variables could be identified in another way. The idea that the bound pronoun must be dependent on the variable left by movement of the quantifier is in some sense a cannibalization of Higginbotham's (1983, 410) accessibility notion, though it is not wedded to his v-chains.

7. This discussion may raise a question concerning the wide scope reading for *everyone* in sentences like *Someone loves everyone*. The matter is discussed in section 3.5.

8. Demirdache (1991) develops Stowell's idea, which is based on a Principle C violation, as one based on the definition of syntactic variable. An intervening index blocks the locality of $\bar{\text{A}}$-binding for the trace. Demirdache also limits the propagation of subordinate indices upward, as I have done for dependency, al-

though her limit on the percolation process is the first maximal projection above the source of the "intrinsic" index, whereas in my account dependency extends to any dominating node that is nominal (see (22)). Since Demirdache's proposals are in the same family as others that depend on local binding of a variable and the use of indices, I will not discuss it here, but I will return to it in section 4.7 with respect to her treatment of resumptives and relative clauses, for which she extends her approach in some interesting ways.

9. See Munn 1992 for an analysis of across-the-board cases that treats gaps in these structures other than the first as parasitic gaps bound by null operators, just as parasitic gaps in adverbs are analyzed in Chomsky 1986. This theory treats the apparent across-the-board extractions in conjuncts as two separate extractions, preserving one-to-one relations between operators and variables, and is thus consistent with the Bijection Principle account. See note 31 of this chapter.

10. See Safir 1984, 606n3, where I attempted to refute Engdahl's (1983) leftness account of these facts by diminishing their importance. Even then, however, I acknowledged that adjuncts could contain pronouns bound to matrix traces for reasons I did not understand (though I speculated). The argument in the text refutes the linear precedence account of these facts, but Engdahl's interpretation of what the facts are is more congenial to my current proposals than the one I attempted in my earlier work.

11. Williams (1997, 587) argues that the contrast between (i) and (ii) follows from adding a precedence requirement on non-c-commanding antecedents for dependent terms.

(i) Anyone can turn *his term paper* in to me now who has written *it*.

(ii) *Anyone can turn it in to me now who has written his TERM PAPER.

However, the test is poorly controlled, as focal stress on *term paper* in (ii) is not much better even if *it* is not coconstrued with *term paper* (e.g., where *it* refers to the textbook for the course). In fact, (i) would be odd with focal stress on *term paper*, and it is unclear why Williams does not contrast focal stress in (i) with focal stress in (ii). As Williams points out, if stress falls on *written*, coconstrual between *it* and *his term paper* is unproblematic, since both forms may depend on previous discourse. However, even if the contrast between (i) and (ii) does reveal a precedence effect, it is not the property that is responsible for crossover effects. Williams argues that for backward dependency, the pronoun must be in a subordinate position within the same clause, as in *His presence in the museum was enough to convict the art thief*. This case, however, exactly contrasts with a WCO case, where replacing *the art thief* with *every art thief* is unacceptable. I have argued that the relation between *his* and *the art thief* is not one of dependent identity in this example.

12. In Safir 1996a, I argued against the linear precedence and dependency–based account on the basis of the contrast between (i) and (ii).

(i) *His* status as omega male prevents **every pup in the litter** from loving *its father*.

(ii) ?*His status as omega male prevents *its father* from loving **every pup in the litter**.

While (ii) is definitely worse than (i), I would predict both of these examples to be excluded in the dependency account I advocate here; however, it is still notable that (i) has only one violation of the INP (*his status as omega male* c-commands *its father*) while (ii) has two (in addition, *its father* c-commands *every pup in the litter*). A precedence account could appeal to the same contrast, arguing for a mildly degraded status for (i). In other words, the contrast between (i) and (ii) does not choose between my account and certain versions of the linear account. I have made a better argument against the linear precedence account on the basis of the absence of WCO in adjuncts, as in (33)–(34).

13. This result should hold in any LF theory where the position of the quantificational antecedent is distinguished from its trace, whether it be by QR, as in the tradition of May (1977) and *LGB*, as assumed here, or in the fashion proposed by Hornstein (1995), which involves the selective deletion of copies of links in interlocking A-chains.

14. Sharvit (1999b) employs a double-indexing system to capture the dependent identity inside the *wh*-trace, indices that are not necessarily borne by any trace-internal pronoun. Rather, she adds a superscript to the trace corresponding to the universal. However, Sharvit is not assuming any particular theory of crossover (any more than Chierchia) and so does not elaborate how this index would induce the effect.

15. For more on functional readings, their relation to pair list readings, and asymmetries that persist between subjects and objects, see Dayal 1996, 105–123, and also note 33 to this chapter. Hornstein (1995, 111–118) gives an interesting account of these cases, but ultimately relies on shadow pronouns that may or may not delete and indices (argument vs. functional indices), which are not necessary in my account. I think Hornstein (in his chapter 7) is right to extend Chierchia's WCO account of functional interpretation to superiority effects (in Hornstein's chapter 7), but I have nothing to say about it here. See Adesola 2003 for an interesting account of the absence of both superiority effects and WCO in Yoruba.

The degree of embedding of the quantifier within the nominal that c-commands the trace is not considered here, and is only relevant insofar as the quantifier contained in the c-commanding nominal can take scope outside the nominal. This corresponds, in Haïk's (1984) theory of indirect binding, to the absence of an upper limit for index percolation. As Sharvit (1999b, 599n7) remarks, "... as formulated, the theory does not impose any limits on index percolation ... [but] in practice, speakers' judgments vary considerably with respect to the possibility of indirect binding when the quantifier is deeply embedded." Sharvit's remarks concern functional relative clauses in Hebrew, but appear to apply more generally to other constructions where functional readings arise.

16. One might appeal to an ellipsis analysis that restores unpronounced structure as in (i) and (ii).

(i) *Someone loves everyone, namely, *his* doctor loves *everyone*.

(ii) Everyone loves someone, namely, *everyone* loves *his* doctor.

However, such an account is insufficiently general, as we will see in section 4.7 when we consider functional relative clauses.

17. Some donkey pronoun anaphora cases pointed out by Haïk (1984) appear to suggest a similar line of argument. Haïk notes contrasts like that between (i) and (ii), where *it* has the interpretation of an E-type pronoun (see note 1 of chapter 2).

(i) ??*Its* offspring have enriched every man who has ever owned *a donkey*.

(ii) *Its* offspring have enriched every man who has ever owned *that donkey*.

However, these cases do not involve the same scopal interactions, but rather work like the conditionals discussed in section 2.2. However one computes the interpretation of *a donkey* within the context of the universal, if the E-type pronoun is dependent on *a donkey*, then *a donkey* cannot be c-commanded by a nominal that contains the E-type pronoun. This is an INP effect like the one in section 2.2, but insofar as there is no crucial appeal to q-variables, it is not, descriptively speaking, a crossover effect.

18. L&S assume the null operator analyses of (41a,b) from Chomsky 1981 and the analysis of parasitic gaps employing a null operator in Chomsky 1986, rather than the one in Chomsky 1982, which did not posit a null operator.

19. Brody (1995, chap. 3) argues that there are indeed parasitic gaps in adjuncts licensed by c-commanding subjects in some circumstances, but the cases he discusses only partially overlap with those environments discussed by Dubinsky and Hamilton that permit epithets anteceded by c-commanding subjects.

20. Postal (1971, 143) originally rejected similar examples, though he suggested that pied-piping of a preposition may improve the judgments, as in the examples on his page 158. (As some of the reconstruction argumentation will show, however, the presence of a pied-piped preposition is not expected to affect crossover effects from the copy theory perspective.) However, Postal (1997), arguing against the Principle C account of SCO, rejects his earlier interpretation of the data and points out that a number of scholars, including Lasnik and Uriagereka (1988, 157), Kuno (1987, 81) (with contrastive stress on a topicalized pronoun), and Pollard and Sag (1994, 247) (with contrastive stress on a topicalized name), all accept examples with similar properties. Williams (1986, 288) and Barss (1986, 275) independently point out that topicalized pronouns are only acceptable if their traces are not clausemates with their antecedents, a judgment they both attribute to Principle B applying to the pronoun locally, but not at a distance.

21. Vehicle change, as introduced in section 1.3, could apply to a SELF form, turning it into a pronoun, as in (i).

(i) *Himsélf*, Louis knew she would never work hard for [*him*]

22. This is not to say that the sets a quantifier quantifies over are not contextually influenced, since they certainly are, as is often observed. For example, *Everyone is here* usually means everyone relevant in the context, not everyone in the world. It is just that context cannot recover all the content of a quantifier.

23. This represents a departure from earlier work of mine (Safir 1984, 1986, 1996a, 1999) in which I assumed that the syntactic definition of variable plays a role in SCO effects.

24. Authier (1993) points out that echo questions and quizmaster questions appear to participate in weakest crossover, although he only considers echo questions nonquantificational (whether they are fronted or left in situ). I assume for echo questions that movement takes place to achieve question scope, but that there is no quantification ranging over a set of possible answers—rather, following Authier, it consists of a placeholder pending identification of the presupposed existence of a unique answer. If so, its trace can be vehicle-changed to a pronoun, with the consequences discussed in chapter 4; but essentially the result is like that for topicalized pronouns. Authier's account of quizmaster questions, (e.g., *Mr. Smith, for $1,000, which secretary of state did the man who appointed him later say t was an imbecile?*) is less congenial to my view, since he considers them quantificational, though he distinguishes dialects that accept these sentences and dialects that do not. For dialects that do accept them, if "dialect" is the right characterization of those speakers that do, he suggests that conventional implicature has a role to play. I leave the matter unresolved.

25. This is the key notion behind Higginbotham's (1980b, 703–704) observations about the absence of WCO effects in nonrestrictive relatives and behind Chomsky's (1982, 92–95) LF′ proposal, particularly as it is adapted to the contrast between restrictive and nonrestrictive relatives in Safir 1986. For further discussion of the differences between restrictive and nonrestrictive relatives with respect to crossover, see Safir 1996a, 1999, Demirdache 1991, and Bianchi 1995. Hornstein (1995) also points out an interesting set of cases that are consistent with the QDC and Rule H as proposed here, but are potentially problematic for the INP (examples from his discussion on pages 103–105).

(i) *His mother gave his picture to every student.

(ii) His mother gave every student his picture.

(iii) *His mother packed his sandwiches for every boy.

(iv) His mother packed every boy his sandwiches.

(v) *His mother introduced every boy to Mary.

(vi) His mother introduced every boy to his teacher.

He argues that the first pronoun in (ii), (iv), and (vi) can depend directly on the second pronoun and that the second pronoun can then depend on the q-variable (in my terms) left by *every student*. The dependency of the first pronoun means that *his mother* is dependent on the second pronoun, which it c-commands, contrary to the INP (though dependency on a c-commanded q-variable may be worse than dependency on a c-commanded pronoun). From my perspective, the first two contrasts pit two violations of the INP against one, and this is the reason they contrast. However, to provide a proper control for the judgments reported in (ii), (iv), and (vi), these sentences should be compared with sentences where *Alice's mother* replaces *his mother*. I would then expect that the counterparts of (ii), (iv), and (vi) with *Alice's mother* would be comparatively better, whereas Hornstein expects no difference at all. I leave the judgment to the reader. The following cases are not susceptible to the same objection:

(vii) Who escorted every boy to Sheila's bus?

(viii) Who escorted *every boy* to *his* bus?

Hornstein (1995, 117–118) points out that (viii) permits a functional answer while (vii) does not. In my account, this is because *his* could depend both on the trace of *who*, which it is not identity dependent on, and on the trace of *every boy*, which it is identity dependent on, without violating Rule H. Thus, a functional reading is predicted to be possible. Notice that Hornstein must assume that *He escorted every boy to his bus* must be ruled out by Principle C applying to quantified DPs, which seems a questionable move, or to their traces, which is even more questionable, as argued in the text.

26. Mulder and Den Dikken (1992) provide an analysis of the *tough*-construction and of parasitic gaps that is quite compatible with the positions taken here. They treat *tough*-constructions as consisting of an adjective selecting a small clause complement, whose predicate is the clause containing the operator. Thus, anything but the q-variable of the operator may depend directly on the small clause subject (which raises to the subject position of the *tough* predicate), or at least as much as Rule H allows. Mulder and Den Dikken also argue that there is no reconstruction into *tough* environments, hence no scope reconstruction, a view consistent with the discussion in chapter 4.

27. This is a serious weakness of Hornstein's (1995) analysis of the weakest crossover cases as involving an operator-external antecedent, in that he provides no account of the absence of SCO effects in most of the weakest crossover environments.

28. Notice that the representations in (59) plausibly violate Rule H as well, depending on the details of how Rule H is formulated, suggesting an alternative path to deriving SCO. However, since WCO does not involve c-commanding intervening pronouns, a Rule H account of SCO will not extend to WCO, although it may provide some insight into why SCO is traditionally (in the literature) perceived to produce more robust contrasts than WCO (hence their names). I will not explore this issue here.

29. Notice that one of the problems with the Principle C account of SCO disappears in the analysis given here without appeal to the DSV theory. Consider the *tough*-movement example (7b), reproduced here with dependency arrows.

(i) *Turley* is tough *Op* for her to count on *t*

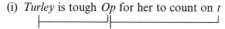

In the Principle C theory, it was necessary to say that the trace acts as a name only within the scope of the operator; otherwise, it would be bound by *Turley* and excluded. In this theory, the trace of the operator is the most dependent form (the only form) available with respect to c-commanding *Turley*, so the FTIP does not rule it out.

It may be necessary to limit the force of Rule H to A-positions. Notice that I assume for (56a,b) that the intervening operator does not have to bind *his* pursuant to Rule H. If there is nothing in the nature of operators from which this can be derived, it is nonetheless a simple amendment to Rule H, one I will not examine here.

30. Elsewhere (Safir 1999, 593), I have used these examples to argue against a dependency account of WCO; but by distinguishing pronouns and q-variables, as the QDC does, and by employing an operator-external antecedent strategy for nonrestrictive relatives, I believe I have overcome the objections made there, as the interested reader can verify.

31. Munn (2001, 374–375) argues that second conjuncts in what are normally taken to be across-the-board extraction do not evidence WCO effects, but do evidence SCO effects. However, he attributes this pattern to his analysis of second conjuncts as adjuncts containing parasitic gaps. If Munn is right about this, then my account of parasitic gap cases readily extends to second conjuncts. At this writing, I have not yet seen Culicover and Postal 2001, which includes Munn 2001, but it promises to shed a great deal of light on these issues.

32. It is now easier to state what is exceptional about PRO gates, namely, that the control relation is not subject to the INP. In *Who did [PRO eating his last seeds] condemn t to starvation*, the *his* appears to be locally dependent on PRO, while PRO is controlled by the direct object. Insofar as PRO is contained in a constituent that c-commands its antecedent, this should be an INP violation, if controllees are really dependent on their antecedents. Thus, in the examples where a PRO gate suppresses WCO, it does so on the assumption that either control of PRO is not a dependency relation (it may be an indistinctness relation) or we must allow PRO, though dependent, to have a special dispensation with respect to the INP (Stowell's (1987) approach faces the same difficulty).

33. Bittner (1998, 57–61) proposes a WCO-specific constraint along these lines, but much of the reasoning she uses to support it is vitiated by the discussion here. In particular, she argues that the functional reading asymmetries pointed out by Chierchia (1991) cannot be captured within the syntactic approach without syntactic representations that make an ad hoc appeal to indices. I concur that the index approach is ad hoc, but I do not assume, as Bittner does, that there are any indices in syntactic representations. The approach to these cases based on the INP in section 3.5 is not based on indices, therefore is not subject to her objection, and provides a more elegant account, without the pitfalls of the semantic approach for those cases where functional readings are sensitive to syntactic properties of pronouns.

Bittner's second argument for a semantics-based WCO principle rests on the acceptability of (i).

(i) At least one woman *he* loved betrayed *every man* I know.

Bittner argues that the semantic type of the antecedent (it is not type *e*) removes the effect, and this seems to be true (although *at most* in place of *at least* in (i) is not well formed to my ear, suggesting that something very quantifier-specific is going on here). I suspect it is related to a quantifier absorption or pair list effect, as in (iii), as opposed to (ii).

(ii) *Which men that you know* swindled which women that *they* loved?

(iii) Which women that *they* loved swindled *which men that you know*?

The paired answer for (ii) is a list for each man of the women he loved and swindled, exhausting that list (see Dayal 1996, 105–123, for a discussion with references); but the answer for (iii) cannot be a list, for each woman or set of women, of the men she/they loved and swindled, since in the latter case, the relevant set of women is still dependent on the choice of man. The answer not possible for (iii) appears to involve a dependency of the subject on an object q-variable, so an INP violation is expected. Also, in contrast to (i), (iv) seems to lack a pair list reading (my thanks to Veneeta Dayal (personal communication) for some very useful discussion of these points).

(iv) ?*Which woman that *he* loved swindled *which man that you know*?

I leave the matter of why (i) permits the reading it does open, but the acceptability of the pattern of dependencies in (i) does not seem to be general.

Chapter 4

1. Bianchi (2001, 20–26) proposes a different account of reconstruction effects based on a refined notion of the distinction between the status of referential terms in the restriction of a quantifier and the status of terms that are in its nuclear scope, based in part on earlier generalizations in Safir 1996a. Safir 1999 appeared after her manuscript was essentially complete, so she chooses not comment on it (see her note 28, page 23), and I will avail myself of the same prerogative here with respect to her paper. Although our approaches have much in common with respect to the INP, they diverge with respect to reconstruction. As mentioned in my note 5 to chapter 3, interested readers should compare our approaches.

2. There is a very subtle prediction that distinguishes the null operator construction with an operator-external antecedent from nonrestrictive relatives. Consider the secondary SCO case in (i) (an example suggested to me by Paul Postal (personal communication)) and the secondary WCO case in (ii).

(i) *Clinton, whose* wife *he* loves, is a poor liar.

(ii) *Clinton, whose* wife *his* daughter loves, is a liar.

In (ii), *whose wife* leaves a copy of the same form as the direct object of *loves* and the *whose* of the lower form is converted to a q-variable. However, *his* can depend directly on *Clinton*, rather than on the q-variable, so no WCO is expected. For (i), the copy of *whose* in its lowest position after *loves* should be a q-variable c-commanded by *he*, which is dependent on *Clinton* (a vacuous operator violation), or else *he* depends on the q-variable, violating the INP. Unfortunately, as I point out in Safir 1999, 333n20, the star on (i) is probably not a representative judgment. Rather, examples like (iii) seem more typical and are acceptable, at least to my ear. I don't know why secondary SCO is more acceptable than it should be here, although I speculate on the difference in my earlier article.

(iii) ?John, *whose* sister *he* truly loves, does not like kids.

A similar example with a parasitic gap (see (iv)) is also difficult to judge, but
I believe coconstrual between *whose* and *he* is less acceptable than coconstrual
between *she* (in place of *he*) and *Mary*, which is the predicted secondary SCO
contrast.

(iv) Do you remember *the guy whose* blind date **Mary** made fun of t before
     he/**she** was even introduced to pg

3. I will not discuss the distribution of A-movement or any of its properties in this
book, but in Safir 2004, sec. 5.1, I argue that vehicle change also can optionally
apply to the traces of A-movement, such that "A-traces" should most often be
understood as pronouns. However, vehicle change is optional in this case too,
since there are constructions, such as the famous quantifier-lowering cases exem-
plified by (i), that can be understood with the scope illustrated in (ii) (but can also
have wide scope for the existential).

(i) Some senator is likely to speak at every rally.

(ii) Likely $\forall x(\text{rally}(x))$ $(\exists y(\text{senator}(y)))$ $(\text{speak-at}(y, x)))$

Insofar as quantifier lowering is understood as scope reconstruction, vehicle
change cannot have taken place in (i) for the reading in (ii).

4. Notice that it is never the case in this account that vehicle change neutralizes
a crossover effect induced by the INP. This is a notable departure from the
theory advanced in Safir 1999, where it was assumed that vehicle change of some
q-variables results in a de facto null resumptive pronoun, with the consequence
that the crossover-inducing effect of that theory (Ā-consistency) is neutralized. I
discuss the neutralizing effect of overt resumptive pronouns in section 4.7.

5. The restriction against converting variables to pronouns is a richer topic than
can be pursued in the main text. For example, a q-variable cannot be reconstructed as a pronoun in (5a) of chapter 3, repeated here as (i), even though the
antecedent VP contains a pronoun in (i) (similarly for (ii)), with the result that a
WCO effect is not avoided. Compare (iii) and (iv), respectively, where there is no
INP violation.

(i) *?Mothers have been known to turn in their sons, but I don't know a single
    boy *who his* mother did [turn in *t*]

(ii) *Every boy is supposed to ask the teacher to help him, but I don't know of a
     single boy *who he* did [ask the teacher to help *t*]

(iii) Mothers have been known to turn in their sons, but I don't know a single
      mother *who t* did [turn in *her* son]

(iv) Every boy is supposed to ask the teacher to help him, but I don't know of a
     single boy *who* did [ask the teacher to help *him*]

On the other hand, Vanden Wyngaerd and Zwart (1991) argue that vehicle change
is unrestricted, introducing pronouns for variables in an interesting set of cases
like (v).

(v) Alfred will kiss any girl that wants him to.

The relevant interpretation, which I agree with Vanden Wyngaerd and Zwart is acceptable, is one where Alfred kisses any x who wants Alfred to kiss x, where x is a girl. These are antecedent-contained deletion cases where *any girl that wants him to* is raised at LF in May's (1985) analysis, leaving a VP containing a trace in the object of *kiss*, ([*kiss t*]), and then [*kiss t*] can be copied after *to*. However, the result is that the variable in [*kiss t*] is then A-bound by the trace of the relative clause subject extraction (the agent of *want*). Vehicle change of *t* to a pronoun (*her*) would save the day, but my restriction on vehicle change won't permit it because *who* is restrictive, hence the trace is a q-variable. I don't know why these cases are different, or if antecedent-contained deletion is playing a crucial role here. Perhaps only one q-variable is permitted per copy set and the restriction on vehicle change of q-variables to pronouns only restricts the copy that is actually converted. If so, even though the object of *kiss* in the moved VP would have to be converted to a q-variable, the lowest VP could contain a pronoun in place of the variable after *kiss*, hence resolving the problem with (v), perhaps without harm to my analyses of nonelliptical constructions, though the issues are complex. Brody (1995, 116–127) also argues for vehicle change, but would ultimately reject the notion that vehicle change can apply to names (constants). The theory he proposes does not allow any nonphonetic displacement relevant to the binding theory before LF, so he appeals to chain formation rules where quantified phrases remain in situ and are related to scope markers in the positions that would be landing sites for QR in other theories. He then sees replacement of the in-situ quantified phrase with a variable as a way of resolving antecedent-contained ellipsis without yielding infinite regress. Too many assumptions distinguish Brody's theory from mine to enter into these differences here, but with regard to the matter at hand, it is not obvious that Brody's approach is any better equipped to account for (v).

6. These considerations may also bear on the choice between two vehicle change options for (i), shown in (iii) and (iv), as opposed to the derivation competing with (i), shown in (ii) (bracketed portions of these examples are not pronounced).

(i) *Phil's* mother *he* could never get *his* wife to appreciate [*Phil's* mother]

(ii) *His* mother *he* could never get *his* wife to appreciate [*his* mother]

(iii) *Phil's* mother *he* could never get *his* wife to appreciate [her]

(iv) *Phil's* mother *he* could never get *his* wife to appreciate [*his* mother]

Both (iii) and (iv) are outcomes that could arise from the numeration in (i) after vehicle change, while (ii) results from a different numeration. It would appear, modulo the use of vehicle change when a competing derivation will do, that many successful outcomes are possible, and this may be why secondary SCO induced by the FTIP is even less marked for names in nonlocal contexts than primary SCO is.

7. I am assuming here that quantifiers do not pied-pipe other material at LF, following Chomsky's (1995, 377) suggestion that it may be only the quantifier (the quantifier features, as he puts it) that moves, thereby inducing what I call a q-variable. If my account were to permit pied-piping at LF, then in examples like (i), names contained in the pied-piping quantified phrases could be replaced in

their lower copy positions by vehicle change after QR, predicting neutralization of Principle C effects, contrary to fact.

(i) *He* loves [everyone but *Arnold*]

This assumption creates problems for any analysis of antecedent-contained deletion built along the lines proposed by May (1985), as pointed out by Hornstein (1995, 53ff.); but I will not explore the matter here.

8. I draw heavily from Safir 1999 in various parts of this section, especially my discussion of (26), but the general perspective on dependency proposed here is radically different from my earlier proposals.

9. See Safir 1999, 610, for a brief discussion of a restriction based on a logophoric effect posited by Kuno (1997).

10. As mentioned in note 6 to this chapter, in cases where both vehicle change and a competing numeration with a pronoun are available, the vehicle-changed option is less preferred; this may be the origin of the imperfect acceptability of some of the examples in (26a–j).

11. All of the contrasts in this section are discussed in more detail and with a wider variety of examples and references in Safir 1999, so I restrict my discussion here to sketching how that earlier analysis may be adapted to fit the dependency-based account I am defending here.

12. In Safir 1999, I argue that both copies are retained at LF and unaccountably fail to cite Brody's (1995, chap. 4) proposal to the same effect. Moreover, some of Brody's earlier published arguments for this position anticipate arguments in Safir 1999 and should have been properly cited. I am now less committed to the idea that both copies are retained, particularly in cases of Ā-movement by a non-operator, where a topicalized name, for example, is not a potential A-antecedent for anything, unless vehicle change applies to the copy in situ.

13. These problems are not minor. See Wiltschko 1993, Borsley 1997, and Büring and Hartmann 1997 for critiques of Kayne's analysis and Åfarli 1994 and Bianchi 1995 for work supporting the promotion analysis for restrictive relatives. It is also not clear what is predicted when a restrictive relative clause extraposes. If such cases involve base-generated right adjunction, as Rochemont and Culicover (1990) and Wiltschko (1997) argue (as opposed to Büring and Hartmann), then they cannot involve promotion and WCO should be absent when a quantifier is embedded in the relative clause head.

(i) [*Whose* pictures] did you ship to Bill [which *his* mother hated]

(ii) [*Whose* pictures which *his* mother hated] did you ship to Bill

I find the judgments difficult here, but if (i) and (ii) are both excluded, then either the relative clause extraposition construction must arise by a promotion analysis (with the possibility that *whose pictures which*, which is a constituent in Kayne's analysis, could somehow be appropriately partitioned) or else the correlation among copy sets, late adjunction, and crossover effects does not arise uniquely from copies created by movement. If only (i) is acceptable, then it might be argued that a right-adjunction-without-movement analysis is possible for extraposition cases and that the absence of promotion in these cases predicts the absence of WCO. Other problems peculiar to Kayne's analysis include positing extraction of *famous author* from the presumed underlying prenominal possessive phrase *who (famous author)'s books* in examples like *that famous author, glowing reviews of whose books we recently read in the newspaper.* These considerations raise an interesting set of challenges for the promotion analysis, but to examine them any further would take me too far afield.

Note also that it is not obvious that the promotion analysis is appropriate for nonrestrictive relatives, as the clause portion of nonrestrictive relatives is generally an island to outside quantificational binding, as noted in Safir 1986, 672–673, where some counterexamples are also mentioned. See also Bianchi 1995.

14. I give transcriptions, glosses, and translations of the Hebrew examples as written in the sources, without attempting to reconcile them.

15. Typically, there are morphological effects on the shapes of complementizers, as discussed by McCloskey (1979, 1990) for Irish and Shlonsky (1992) for Palestinian Arabic. My remarks in the text are written with Shlonsky's analysis of Hebrew in mind, in that he extends his analysis of contrasting complementizer forms in Palestinian Arabic to Modern Hebrew, where there is no visible morphology on complementizers distinguishing resumptive pronoun structures from gap structures. (I do not assume, however, as Shlonsky argues, that pronouns are inserted as a last resort, since they do not preserve the same range of interpretations that traces do, even in Hebrew, as argued in the text.) I will not attempt to defend the promotion analysis here for the cases in Hebrew where there is a gap in the relative. For the cases that have a resumptive, I assume there is a null operator in Spec,CP on which the resumptive pronoun is dependent, although this is not necessarily crucial. See Borer 1984, however, for argumentation against a base-generated null operator analysis for Modern Hebrew resumptive pronoun structures.

16. Sells (1984, 79–82) points out that there is a residual linear precedence effect in Hebrew that permits conjunction of clauses in relative clauses where the first conjunct contains a trace and the second a pronoun, but not vice versa. I agree with Sells that this effect in Hebrew is not at the core of the phenomenon. It is possible, however, that conjunctions are asymmetric structures, or are at least optionally so, and if they are, then one might hope that these asymmetries in the behavior of gaps can be derived. Munn (1992, 2001) proposes an asymmetric theory of this sort (see note 9 of chapter 3), but I do not have a concrete proposal to make for these examples. Demirdache (1991) points out a similar asymmetry for parasitic gaps (following Sells), such that a resumptive pronoun in direct object position can support a parasitic gap inside a subject relative, but cannot support a gap inside a following adjunct. See note 19 to this chapter.

17. One might appeal to a chain-binding solution of the sort proposed by Barss (1986), whereby there is an intermediate Spec,CP to the left of ʔ*im* where ʔ*acmo* could be anteceded. I reject this analysis for English, and I do not believe it is necessary to appeal to it here.

18. It is clear that a functional reading for a resumptive pronoun should not be ruled out in principle, though in many instances it is difficult or impossible. In English, a functional reading for a relative clause is not easily achieved unless the relative appears in a specificational equative sentences, as in (i).

(i) The bill that every man fears is his tax bill.

(ii) ??The bill that every man fears reaches him in April.

As Sharvit points out, Hebrew differs from English in that a functional reading for a relative clause gap is possible in Hebrew outside of specificational contexts, but the answers to the questions in (56) already show that resumptive pronouns can support functional readings in principle. Sharvit (1999b, 588, (3)) illustrates this further by showing that restrictive relative clauses with resumptive pronouns do support functional readings in specificational equative sentences in Hebrew. The connectivity effects that have been observed to hold in specificational pseudo-clefts are not well behaved from the perspective of the theory proposed here, or of any other. For discussion of the issues, see Sharvit 1999a and Heycock and Kroch 1999.

19. Aoun and Choueiri (2000) propose an analysis of epithets with a related structure, such that a pronoun is embedded in the DP containing the epithet and it is the pronoun that permits the epithet to act as a bound variable or a resump-tive in a relative clause. On the basis of contrasts between Lebanese and Moroc-can Arabic, they argue that the ability of an epithet to be a bound variable or resumptive is a function of whether or not, in a given language, a pronoun of the right sort can also be embedded in the epithet DP. Demirdache (1991, 57–59) cites some cases, based on a paradigm from McCloskey 1990, whereby a resumptive pronoun is blocked from local Ā-dependency by an epithet, but this appears to depend on whether or not the epithet is a successful resumptive or not. In English, an epithet can be resumptive, as in *Do you remember that guy who we could never be sure whether the bastard would do his job or not?* If the epithet *the bastard* is resumptive, then it can still antecede *his*, but *his* can be resumptive also if *the bastard* refers to some other individual. Clearer distinctions are required for Hebrew and Irish with respect to whether or not epithets can ever be resumptive in those languages, and if so, whether or not this patterns with their ability to act as bound variables (see McCloskey 1990 and Demirdache 1991, 57–59, for attempts to explore these relations).

Recall also from note 16 of this chapter that direct object resumptive pronouns in Hebrew can license parasitic gaps embedded in subject position. This may be explicable on an analysis like (60b) (for those resumptive pronouns not embedded in islands).

20. Aoun and Benmamoun (1998, 594–595) reject an analysis close to the one in the text in favor of a slightly different one. They argue that the left-dislocated phrase is base-generated (merged) in the Spec,CL node, assuming the clitic to be a head, generated higher than V, and they assume that Spec,CL is coindexed with the null argument position (e.g., the direct object). They reject the idea that the left-dislocated phrase starts in the argument position because it obligatorily

reconstructs to a position that appears to be higher than the direct object. The main line of their argument is that the obligatory reconstruction is the result of PF movement, such that the left-dislocated phrase is in fact in situ at LF (which in my account would mean that it is not doubled at LF and perhaps not subject to vehicle change). They assume PF movement of the left-dislocated phrase because it is insensitive to intervening Ā-binders that do not form islands, while overt syntactic movement of the other sorts (topicalization and question movement) is sensitive to intervening Ā-binders. Clitic left-dislocation outside of an island shows no reconstruction effect. These two facts (regarding islands and reconstruction) are taken to support the view that clitic left-dislocation that violates islands is not movement. I am employing the same sort of reasoning here. In a more recent paper that appeared after this chapter was largely written, Aoun, Choueiri, and Hornstein (2001) propose an analysis quite consistent with the one I propose schematically in the text, and I refer interested readers to their approach.

21. The resumptive pronoun that saves what used to be considered ECP violations in Vata (see note 1 of chapter 3) also induces WCO effects in relation to other pronouns in the structure that are not resumptive (Koopman and Sportiche 1983, 142). Such cases become quite interesting from this perspective, and similar questions arise for the Swedish cases, discussed by Engdahl (1984), where subject resumptive pronouns that appear to save ECP violations can, in the right environments, also license parasitic gaps.

Chapter 5

1. Hornstein (2001) attempts to justify sideward movement as an account of control relations, another form of coconstrual. His theory is challenged by Culicover (2001), who argues that the choice of controller is better predicted by lexical semantic factors than by syntactic ones, and by Landau (2000, chap. 2), who demonstrates that the coconstruals that arise in obligatory control often involve only partial identity with the antecedent. For example, *Wanda wanted to meet at six* requires a reading where Wanda is only one of the participants in the act of meeting, while *Wanda meets at six* is quite impossible. Hornstein (p. 39) takes it to be a virtue of his system that partial obligatory control cases are predicted not to exist, contrary to fact. Landau demonstrates that there must be a theory of control that allows for such cases, and Hornstein's movement theory of coconstrual does not appear to have the right properties. See also note 3 to this chapter.

2. It is perhaps worth noting that no attempt is made to show that this would be an advance in our understanding of islands, but neither is it immediately clear that it is a backward step, since so much would have to be rethought.

3. An idiom chunk argument would be interesting confirmation, for example, if one could be constructed.

(i) ??We were hoping for *headway*, and John said they had made *it*.

(ii) *We were surprised by *the shit* because we didn't expect *it* to hit the fan.

(iii) *We were surprised by *so much advantage* because we didn't expect *it* to be taken of John.

Predicates like *hoping for* and *surprised by* permit notoriously nonspecific thematic selection, so if the idiom chunks are licensed by the interpretation they can receive in the idioms where they originate under the movement account, then it is not obvious, particularly under Kayne's (2002) account where doubling is involved, why thematic roles compatible with their positions of origin are not licensed in their landing sites. If so, the movement theory is not supported by this evidence. It is not clear, if these cases do not count, how the movement theory of coconstrual could ever be independently motivated for intersentential movement.

See also Nunes 2001, where Nunes offers an account of sideward movement and supports it with considerations independent of anaphora, though what appears to be his best evidence concerns the distribution of parasitic gaps, which receive an alternative account in chapter 4. It is not clear to me that Nunes intends for sideward movement to be intersentential, but I suspect he does not assume that it is; if it were, it might undermine his theory of across-the-board movement. It would not be hard to restrict derivation building to sentence grammar, I suspect, if we were to confine Move and Merge to operations on a unique numeration and condition the output to contain a node γ such that γ dominates every form in the numeration. The MAC theory does not appear to be restricted in this way. As Nunes's paper appeared after most of this book was written, I will not evaluate it here.

4. I am inclined to give both of these theories the benefit of the doubt as concerns backward coreference, but there are significant doubts. The distinction made in the theory I have proposed is that backward coreference is generally possible where neither the FTIP nor the INP is violated. Sometimes backward coreference is awkward because pronouns are normally dependent, and there is no previous mention for the pronoun to depend on; there is a sense of missing something until the right referent comes along (as in the Count Marzipan discourse of section 2.5). On the other hand, if previous discourse has introduced a referent, then codependency on previous mention is possible, and backward coreference is quite natural. Many speakers accept backward coreference for (i)–(iii) without a preceding discourse, but these coconstruals are certainly possible when there has been a previous mention.

(i) The picture that *his* mother placed beside her bed indicated to *John* how deeply she felt.

(ii) That picture of *him* proved that *John* was guilty.

(iii) A cousin of *his* gave *John* up to the police.

Backward coreference is possible in Hornstein's MAC theory, if all that must be avoided is a violation of the extension requirement.

(iv) The fact that *he* was not there on time does not indicate that *David* is guilty.

(v) [$_\alpha$ David was not there on time] [$_\alpha$ is guilty]

In Hornstein's theory, (15a) could be derived by sideward movement to the right, extending the α constituent. However, it is not obvious that it can generate cases like *Her mother loves Mary*, especially felicitous with stress on *loves*, if Hornstein's account of the unacceptability of *His mother loves everyone* (p. 202n81) is to be believed. For Kayne's theory, matters are considerably murkier, since he appears content to exclude backward coreference altogether (a different interpretation of the facts than the one given here, to say the least), apparently on the wings of the theoretical commitment that movement can never be rightward. If so, *rightward* would have to be defined by some presupposed notion of precedence that ensures that constituents which are unconnected at the point in the derivation where movement applies are merged in the right linear order at a later point in the derivation. This is an anticipatory global relation of the sort that recent theories of derivational economy have sought to avoid. Kayne could avoid the problem altogether and admit backward coreference if he were willing to abandon his global notion of "rightward."

5. Hornstein (p. 180) claims to derive the exclusion of (i) from the extension requirement on sideward movement.

(i) **His* mother loves *everyone*.

This is excluded because there is no movement into the object of *loves* because that would not constitute an extension of a phrase marker, although even this result requires qualifications about the derivation of the VP (see Hornstein 2001, 202n81; and on the problem noted in the text, see p. 203n82). See also note 4 to this chapter on the global notion of "rightward," which raises similar issues.

6. Kayne (2002, 145) provides an account for Principle B effects by introducing a stipulation that doubled constituents of the form [*John* [*him*]] must move to a position in the clause higher than the θ-position where *John* could receive a θ-role. Then the only way that *John* could receive a θ-role where a pronoun is a clausemate is by moving down, which is indeed excluded by the fundamental restriction on movement in his theory. He offers no independent evidence that the stipulated movement should be required or why it should be required only of constituents of this type, other than to facilitate his account of Principle B. This vitiates his claim that Principle B effects "follow, in a derivational perspective, from basic properties of pronouns and basic properties of movement" (p. 134). Kayne's account of Principle A effects is to say that a pronoun embedded in a SELF form, as in [[*John* [*he*]] *self*], is somehow permitted to avoid the stipulated movement, but he admits (p. 148) that he has no account of why c-command and locality should restrict the distribution of pronoun-SELF forms in English.

7. Hornstein (2001, 205n88, 219) suggests that examples like (i) are instances where a SELF form can have a non-c-commanding genitive antecedent.

(i) The men's books attacked/defamed/criticized each other.

However, in this instance, it is far from clear that *each other* is not anteceded by *the men's books*, such that books criticize books and not men. If there is a 'men' reading, it would appear to arise insofar as the books can express the attitudes of their authors. If we choose a head noun that cannot easily be imagined to express an attitude, the genitive antecedent reading is hopeless.

(ii) In the pileup, the men's cars crushed each other.

Only the 'cars crushing cars' reading is possible for (ii). Such cases bring to mind the famous subcommand cases of Chinese, where in examples like (ii), possessives appear to be possible as antecedents for forms like *ziji* (see Tang 1989), but even these cases are restricted by locality effects associated with blocking concerning logophoric interpretations, person, and distributivity (see C.-T. J. Huang and Liu 2001). As mentioned in the text, sideward MAC-Move is impervious to locality in such cases.

8. For additional argumentation against the MAC theory based on the distribution of syntactic anaphors, see Safir 2003.

9. Epstein's First Law does not actually achieve its goal, because it only requires that there be *some derivational point* where α and β are dominated by the same node. If α moves to a position β, thereby relating those two positions in separate trees, the two trees could be merged at a later point and sideward movement would still be possible (see Brody 1997 for a related critique). For this reason, Epstein et al. (1998) introduce derivational sisterhood as a condition on checking, which has the unique effect of blocking movements to positions that do not c-command the position they originate in. As I have formulated it, Insularity requires a mutual dominating node *at the point in the derivation where α and β are related*. Although I plan to explore the force of Insularity in subsequent work, I leave further discussion of the notion aside here.

Chomsky (1995, 189) proposes a restriction on PF designed to ensure a similar result:

At each point in the derivation, then, we have a structure Σ, which we may think of as a set of phrase markers. At any point, we may apply the operation Spell-Out, which switches to the PF component. If Σ is not a single phrase marker, the derivation crashes at PF, *since PF rules cannot apply to a set of phrase markers* and no legitimate PF representation π is generated. [emphasis added]

The MAC theory, as Kayne states it, technically meets Chomsky's PF condition, since Kayne assumes that a conjunction-like operation (but really just discourse relatedness) connects all sentences that involve any coconstrual, even across speakers, as described in the text. If Kayne's liberal notion of conjunction is not assumed, then Chomsky's principle still permits sideward movement as long as the PF condition of a single tree is met, but movement across unconnected trees would appear to be excluded. Chomsky's condition is thus less restrictive than Insularity; but on the other hand, Insularity does not ensure that if more than one structure is formed from a single numeration, then they must all be gathered into a single tree—Insularity permits this as long as no rule of syntax relates the two trees. The status of numerations in relation to the trees formed by them deserves more study, however. The theory proposed here (particularly the FTIP) only requires establishment of the numeration at LF, since before that point, direct selection from the lexicon (as in Chomsky 1995, chap. 3) would be adequate to construct trees without any preconceived numeration. At LF, the numeration must be held constant for the FTIP to apply coherently, but not before that point. Thus, any convergent tree that consists of legitimate LF objects (chains are of the right form, etc.) would be well formed. Chomsky's condition would only be needed to apply to two or more trees (after all lexical phonetic features are already in the trees) that are merged subsequent to Spell-Out in the covert component (i.e., separate trees in PF, a single tree at LF). It is not clear that such a case would not be prevented from occurring by features that must be checked at PF, but I leave the matter open.

Appendix

1. I assume here that scrambling is derived by some sort of movement and not by base generation (see appendix note 11) or by base generation and lowering, as proposed by Bošković and Takahashi (1998). I remain partial to the role of the extension requirement in derivations. For a critique of Bošković and Takahashi 1998, see Bailyn 2001.

2. There are many mysteries associated with what has been called rightward movement, even in English, that I will also set aside. Culicover (1992) reports cases where relations between double complements do not always reconstruct, as in (i).

(i) You should give *everyone his* paycheck.

(ii) *His paycheck you should give *everyone*.

(iii) *His* paycheck *everyone* should give me.

Many find the topicalizations in (ii) and (iii) awkward even without bound variable interpretation, but (ii) is clearly worse than (iii). Culicover suggests that quantifiers in VP at the surface do not escape VP at LF, so that they never bind a subject or any pronoun that is outside of VP, including topicalizations containing pronouns. Presumably, then, there is no reconstruction in this account, and subjects are assumed to bind into topicalized constituents at LF. Culicover suggests this might be a general account of WCO. Such an account leaves us with no way to represent wide scope for the universal in *Someone saw everyone*, however (as Culicover appears to acknowledge in his footnote 2). Moreover, Culicover assumes that WCO effects arise uniquely in quantificational environments, a view I have criticized as too narrow in chapter 2. Most pressingly for my concerns, a number of problems remain unresolved, such as the patterns in (iv)–(vii).

(iv) *After all the stolen dogs were recaptured, Ellen gave *its* owner *every dog*.

(v) We returned *every dog* to *its* owner.

(vi) We returned to *its* owner *every dog that had been captured*.

(vii) I introduced to *every student her* immediate neighbor.

Superficial precedence does not explain (vi), though reconstruction would, but the opposite is true of (vii). Larson's (1988) structures for double complement cases do not predict (vi) and (vii), and so at minimum these would require some clarification. Culicover's proposal does not predict (iv), where VP scope for *every dog* should allow it to bind *its*.

3. Kidwai (2000, 117) suggests that there is no focus in the preverbal position unless scrambling has taken place. See her note 3 on page 117 for some discussion and references on the relation between focus and scrambling.

4. The Hindi examples in this appendix are drawn from a variety of sources whose orthography is not consistent, although I cite them from Kidwai 2000 as

often as possible to preserve what consistency I can. To avoid the effort of concordance, and because I don't believe it makes any difference for the issues I discuss, the orthography for each example is based (roughly) on the reference from which it is cited.

5. For reasons that will become clearer in subsequent notes, the disposition of scrambling of VP-internal arguments that land to the right of the subject of the same clause will not be examined in the main text. See also appendix note 2.

6. The matter is carefully discussed by Dayal (1993), who argues that even in the dialects where *apne* is not strictly subject oriented, such as that reported by Mahajan (1989), it is still the case that the pronouns are anti–subject oriented and that *apne* embedded in a subject is dispreferred for a coreferent reading with the leftward scrambled object—in other words, (5b) is better with a pronoun in place of *apne*. Dayal treats this usage of *apne* as independent of Principle A (LAL, in my account) and licensed by other (rather unclear) factors. She also points out that the more permissive dialect Mahajan reports also allows *apne* embedded in an indirect object to be anteceded by a leftward-scrambled direct object (all to the right of the subject, apparently within VP); but in that case as well, a pronoun is much preferred.

7. As mentioned in appendix note 6, where his interpretation of the data is disputed, Mahajan (1989) claims that *apni* can be anteceded by the indirect object in (6a) but not in (6b) (for similar effects in Scandinavian, see Safir 2004, sec. 5.2.4). I suspect that once arguments based on the possessive anaphor in Hindi are set aside, as in appendix note 6, the evidence against A-binding is thin at best. Still unexplained, however, is the contrast between (i) and (ii): (ii) is not acceptable with the reading indicated, for which Dayal (1993) appeals to an ad hoc linear precedence effect. I have nothing to say about such cases.

(i) raam-ne [*uskii* kitaab] *mohan-ko* lautaaii
     Ram-su his   book   mohan-io returned
     'Ram returned *his* book to *Mohan*.'

(ii) raam-ne *mohan-ko* [*uskii* kitaab] lautaaii
     Ram-su Mohan-io his   book   returned
     'Ram returned *his* book to *Mohan*.'

8. In reconstruction environments, the LF movement responsible for subject orientation would be movement of the lower copy of *apni* in *apni kitab* to the Tense-related position discussed in Safir 2004. I am assuming that if one copy of *apni* satisfies LAL, then the others do not matter because copies are indistinct, as noted in the text (see (8)). Thus, I am not required to assume that one of these copies has to delete, though I leave the matter open.

9. Dayal (1993), reporting work by Jones (1993), accepts examples like (i) where the fronted direct object antecedes the reciprocal.

(i) ?jaun aur meri-ko [ek   duusre-ne] dekhaa
    John and Mary-do each other's-su saw
    'John and Mary saw each other.'

In this instance, subject orientation is weak, if a factor at all, suggesting that all that is wrong with (9b) is that the anaphor is subject oriented. The distinction holds in a number of other languages that Dayal (1993, fn. 11) cites; but also see an example cited by Franks (1995, 21) where a scrambled accusative in Russian can bind a complex reciprocal in indirect object position.

10. This difference may be further evidence that the INP should be reduced to a constraint on semantic composition, in which case we would not expect it to have any influence on the syntactically based FTIP. See section 3.7.

11. There is a tradition in the scrambling literature that treats variation in word order, particularly in the Germanic mittelfeld (to the right of the subject and left of the verb), as base generation rather than movement of any sort. Evidence for these proposals should be largely consistent with the assumption that the marked orders (if marked they are) arise by A-movement leaving no copy (see, e.g., Neeleman 1994, chap. 3). Most of the reconstruction data, however, relies on picture nominals (as is the case with Neeleman's Dutch and German examples), and these cases are suspect as evidence for reconstruction even in those languages. Neeleman also provides German examples in which an indirect object is scrambled to the immediate left of a locative PP containing *sich* (an anaphoric pronoun) with an acceptable result (whereas *sich* is excluded when the indirect object is not scrambled leftward), yet *sich* is normally subject oriented. Such cases require deeper inquiry, but they also suggest that the relevant factors may not be entirely structural. See appendix note 7.

References

Adesola, Oluseye. 2003. Operators and pronouns: Superiority effects. Ms., Rutgers University.

Åfarli, Tor. 1994. A promotion analysis of restrictive relative clauses. *The Linguistic Review* 11, 81–100.

Aoun, Joseph, and Elabbas Benmamoun. 1998. Minimality, reconstruction, and PF movement. *Linguistic Inquiry* 29, 569–597.

Aoun, Joseph, and Lina Choueiri. 2000. Epithets. *Natural Language and Linguistic Theory* 18, 1–39.

Aoun, Joseph, Lina Choueiri, and Norbert Hornstein. 2001. Resumption, movement, and derivational economy. *Linguistic Inquiry* 32, 371–403.

Authier, J.-Marc. 1993. Nonquantificational *wh* and weakest crossover. *Linguistic Inquiry* 24, 161–168.

Bailyn, John Frederick. 2001. On scrambling: A reply to Bošković and Takahashi. *Linguistic Inquiry* 32, 635–658.

Baltin, Mark. 1982. A landing site theory of movement rules. *Linguistic Inquiry* 13, 1–38.

Barss, Andrew. 1986. Chains and anaphoric dependence: On reconstruction and its implications. Doctoral dissertation, MIT.

Berman, Steve, and Arild Hestvik. 1997. Split antecedents, noncoreference and DRT. In *Atomism and binding*, ed. by Hans Bennis, Pierre Pica, and Johan Rooryck, 1–29. Dordrecht: Foris.

Bianchi, Valentina. 1995. Consequences of antisymmetry for the syntax of headed relative clauses. Doctoral dissertation, Scuola Normale Superiore, Pisa.

Bianchi, Valentina. 2001. Antisymmetry and the Leftness Condition: Leftness as anti-c-command. *Studia Linguistica* 55, 1–38.

Bittner, Maria. 1998. A crosslinguistic semantics for questions. *Linguistics and Philosophy* 21, 1–82.

Borer, Hagit. 1984. Restrictive relatives in Modern Hebrew. *Natural Language and Linguistic Theory* 2, 219–260.

Borsley, Robert. 1997. Relative clauses and the theory of phrase structure. *Linguistic Inquiry* 28, 629–647.

Bošković, Željko, and Daiko Takahashi. 1998. Scrambling and last resort. *Linguistic Inquiry* 29, 347–366.

Brody, Michael. 1995. *Lexico-Logical Form: A radically minimalist theory.* Cambridge, Mass.: MIT Press.

Brody, Michael. 1997. Towards perfect chains. In *Elements of grammar: A handbook of syntax,* ed. by Liliane Haegeman, 139–167. Dordrecht: Kluwer.

Büring, Daniel, and Katharina Hartmann. 1997. The Kayne mutiny. In *Rightward movement,* ed. by Dorothee Berman, David LeBlanc, and Henk van Riemsdijk, 59–79. Amsterdam: John Benjamins.

Burzio, Luigi. 1989. On the non-existence of disjoint reference principles. *Rivista di Grammatica Generativa* 14, 3–27.

Burzio, Luigi. 1991. The morphological basis of anaphora. *Journal of Linguistics* 27, 81–105.

Burzio, Luigi. 1996. The role of the antecedent in anaphoric relations. In *Current issues in comparative grammar,* ed. by Robert Freidin, 1–45. Dordrecht: Kluwer.

Chierchia, Gennaro. 1989. Anaphora and attitudes *de se.* In *Semantics and contextual expression,* ed. by Renate Bartsch, Johan van Benthem, and Peter van Emde Boas, 1–31. Dordrecht: Foris.

Chierchia, Gennaro. 1991. Functional WH and weak crossover. In *Proceedings of the Tenth West Coast Conference on Formal Linguistics,* ed. by Dawn Bates, 75–90. Stanford, Calif.: CSLI Publications.

Chomsky, Noam. 1976. Conditions on rules of grammar. *Linguistic Analysis* 2, 303–351.

Chomsky, Noam. 1977. On *wh*-movement. In *Formal syntax,* ed. by Peter Culicover, Thomas Wasow, and Adrian Akmajian, 71–132. New York: Academic Press.

Chomsky, Noam. 1981. *Lectures on government and binding.* Dordrecht: Foris.

Chomsky, Noam. 1982. *Some concepts and consequences of the theory of government and binding.* Cambridge, Mass.: MIT Press.

Chomsky, Noam. 1986. *Barriers.* Cambridge, Mass.: MIT Press.

Chomsky, Noam. 1995. *The Minimalist Program.* Cambridge, Mass.: MIT Press.

Chomsky, Noam, and Howard Lasnik. 1995. The theory of principles and parameters. In *The Minimalist Program,* Noam Chomsky, 129–166. Cambridge, Mass.: MIT Press.

Cinque, Guglielmo. 1990. *Types of Ā-dependencies.* Cambridge, Mass.: MIT Press.

Culicover, Peter. 1992. A note on quantifier binding. *Linguistic Inquiry* 23, 659–663.

Culicover, Peter. 1997. *Principles and parameters.* Oxford: Oxford University Press.

Culicover, Peter. 2001. Control is not movement. *Linguistic Inquiry* 32, 493–512.

Culicover, Peter, and Paul M. Postal, eds. 2001. *Parasitic gaps.* Cambridge, Mass.: MIT Press.

Dahl, Östen. 1974. How to open a sentence: Abstraction in natural language. In *Logical grammar reports 12.* University of Götenberg.

Dayal, Veneeta. 1993. Binding facts in Hindi and the scrambling phenomenon. In *Theoretical perspectives on word order in South Asian languages,* ed. by Tracy Holloway King and Gillian Ramchand, 237–261. Stanford, Calif.: CSLI Publications.

Dayal, Veneeta. 1996. *Locality in* wh-*quantification.* Dordrecht: Kluwer.

Demirdache, Hamida. 1991. Resumptive chains in restrictive relatives, appositives and dislocation structures. Doctoral dissertation, MIT.

Déprez, Viviane. 1989. On the typology of syntactic positions and the nature of chains: Move α to the specifier of functional projections. Doctoral dissertation, MIT.

Dobrovie-Sorin, Carmen. 1990. Clitic doubling, *wh*-movement, and quantification in Romanian. *Linguistic Inquiry* 21, 351–398.

Doron, Edit. 1982. The syntax and semantics of resumptive pronouns. In *Texas Linguistic Forum* 19, 1–48. Austin: University of Texas.

Dubinsky, Stanley, and Robert Hamilton. 1998. Epithets as antilogophoric pronouns. *Linguistic Inquiry* 29, 685–693.

Elbourne, Paul. 2001. E-type anaphora as NP-deletion. *Natural Language Semantics* 9, 241–288.

Engdahl, Elisabet. 1983. Parasitic gaps. *Linguistics and Philosophy* 6, 5–35.

Engdahl, Elisabet. 1984. Parasitic gaps, resumptive pronouns, and subject extractions. Ms., University of Wisconsin, Madison.

Epstein, Samuel David. 1999. Unprincipled syntax: The derivation of syntactic relations. In *Working minimalism,* ed. by Samuel David Epstein and Norbert Hornstein, 317–345. Cambridge, Mass.: MIT Press.

Epstein, Samuel David, Erich M. Groat, Ruriko Kawashima, and Hisatsugu Kitahara. 1998. *A derivational approach to syntactic relations.* Oxford: Oxford University Press.

Evans, Gareth. 1980. Pronouns. *Linguistic Inquiry* 11, 337–362.

Fiengo, Robert, and Robert May. 1994. *Indices and identity.* Cambridge, Mass.: MIT Press.

Fox, Danny. 1998. Locality in variable binding. In *Is the best good enough?,* ed. by Pilar Barbosa, Danny Fox, Paul Hagstrom, Martha McGinnis, and David Pesetsky, 129–155. Cambridge, Mass.: MIT Press.

Fox, Danny. 1999. Reconstruction, binding theory, and the interpretation of chains. *Linguistic Inquiry* 30, 157–196.

Fox, Danny. 2000. *Economy and semantic interpretation.* Cambridge, Mass.: MIT Press.

Franks, Steven. 1995. *Parameters of Slavic morphosyntax.* Oxford: Oxford University Press.

Franks, Steven, and Tracy Holloway King. 2000. *A handbook of Slavic clitics.* Oxford: Oxford University Press.

Freidin, Robert. 1986. Fundamental issues in the theory of binding. In *Studies in the acquisition of anaphora*, ed. by Barbara Lust, 1:151–188. Dordrecht: Reidel.

Grodzinsky, Yosef, and Tanya Reinhart. 1993. The innateness of binding and coreference. *Linguistic Inquiry* 24, 69–102.

Gurtu, Madhu. 1985. Anaphoric relations in Hindi and English. Doctoral dissertation, CIEFL, Hyderabad.

Haïk, Isabelle. 1984. Indirect binding. *Linguistic Inquiry* 15, 185–223.

Hardt, Daniel. 1999. Dynamic interpretation of verb phrase ellipsis. *Linguistics and Philosophy* 22, 185–219.

Heim, Irene. 1993. Anaphora and semantic interpretation: A reinterpretation of Reinhart's approach. SfS-Report-07-93. Tübingen: University of Tübingen.

Hellan, Lars. 1988. *Anaphora in Norwegian and the theory of grammar.* Dordrecht: Foris.

Heycock, Caroline. 1995. Asymmetries in reconstruction. *Linguistic Inquiry* 26, 547–570.

Heycock, Caroline, and Anthony Kroch. 1999. Pseudocleft connectedness: Implications for the LF interface level. *Linguistic Inquiry* 30, 365–397.

Higginbotham, James. 1980a. Anaphora and GB: Some preliminary remarks. In *NELS X*, ed. by John T. Jensen, 223–236. Ottawa: University of Ottawa, Cahiers Linguistiques d'Ottawa.

Higginbotham, James. 1980b. Pronouns and bound variables. *Linguistic Inquiry* 11, 679–708.

Higginbotham, James. 1983. Logical Form, binding, and nominals. *Linguistic Inquiry* 14, 395–420.

Higginbotham, James. 1985. On semantics. *Linguistic Inquiry* 16, 547–593.

Higginbotham, James. 1989. Reference and control. *Rivista di Linguistica* 1, 301–326. Reprinted in *Control and grammar*, ed. by Richard Larson, Sabine Iatridou, Utpal Lahiri, and James Higginbotham, 29–48. Cambridge: Cambridge University Press (1992).

Hornstein, Norbert. 1995. *Logical Form.* Oxford: Blackwell.

Hornstein, Norbert. 2001. *Move! A minimalist theory of construal.* Oxford: Blackwell.

Huang, C.-T. James. 1983. A note on the binding theory. *Linguistic Inquiry* 14, 554–561.

Huang, C.-T. James, and C.-S. Luther Liu. 2001. Logophoricity, attitudes and *ziji* at the interface. In *Syntax and semantics 33: Long-distance reflexives*, ed. by Peter Cole, Gabriella Hermon, and C.-T. James Huang, 141–195. San Diego, Calif.: Academic Press.

Huang, Yan. 1991. A neo-Gricean pragmatic theory of anaphora. *Journal of Linguistics* 27, 301–335.

Huang, Yan. 1994. *The syntax and pragmatics of anaphora: A study with special reference to Chinese.* Cambridge: Cambridge University Press.

Jackendoff, Ray. 1992. Mme Tussaud meets the binding theory. *Natural Language and Linguistic Theory* 10, 1–31.

Jones, Doug. 1993. A-binding and scrambling in Hindi: Reflexives vs. reciprocals. Paper presented at the Workshop on Theoretical Issues in Ergative Languages, Rutgers University.

Kamp, Hans, and Uwe Reyle. 1993. *From discourse to logic.* Dordrecht: Kluwer.

Kayne, Richard S. 1994. *The antisymmetry of syntax.* Cambridge, Mass.: MIT Press.

Kayne, Richard S. 2002. Pronouns and their antecedents. In *Derivation and explanation in the Minimalist Program*, ed. by Samuel David Epstein and T. Daniel Seely, 133–183. Oxford: Blackwell.

Kidwai, Ayesha. 2000. *XP-adjunction in Universal Grammar: Scrambling and binding in Hindi-Urdu.* Oxford: Oxford University Press.

Kitagawa, Yoshihisa. 1991. Copying identity. *Natural Language and Linguistic Theory* 9, 497–536.

Koopman, Hilda, and Dominique Sportiche. 1983. Variables and the Bijection Principle. *The Linguistic Review* 2, 139–160.

Kuno, Susumu. 1987. *Functional syntax.* Chicago: University of Chicago Press.

Kuno, Susumu. 1997. Binding theory in the Minimalist Program. Ms., Harvard University.

Landau, Idan. 2000. *Elements of control.* Dordrecht: Kluwer.

Larson, Richard. 1988. On the double object construction. *Linguistic Inquiry* 19, 335–391.

Lasnik, Howard. 1976. Remarks on coreference. *Linguistic Analysis* 2, 1–22. Reprinted in *Essays on anaphora*, Howard Lasnik, 90–109. Dordrecht: Kluwer (1989).

Lasnik, Howard. 1999. *Minimalist analysis.* Oxford: Blackwell.

Lasnik, Howard, and Tim Stowell. 1991. Weakest crossover. *Linguistic Inquiry* 22, 687–720.

Lasnik, Howard, and Juan Uriagereka. 1988. *A course in GB syntax: Lectures on binding and empty categories.* Cambridge, Mass.: MIT Press.

Lebeaux, David. 1990. Relative clauses, licensing, and the nature of derivation. In *Proceedings of NELS 20*, ed. by Juli Carter, Rose-Marie Déchaine, Bill Philip, and Tim Sherer, 318–332. Amherst: University of Massachusetts, GLSA.

Lebeaux, David. 1998. Where does binding theory apply? Ms., NEC Research Institute.

Levinson, Stephen. 1987. Pragmatics and the grammar of anaphora: A partial pragmatic reduction of binding and control phenomena. *Journal of Linguistics* 23, 379–434.

Levinson, Stephen. 1991. Pragmatic reduction of the binding conditions revisited. *Journal of Linguistics* 27, 301–335.

Mahajan, Anoop. 1989. The A/A-bar distinction and movement theory. Doctoral dissertation, MIT.

Mahajan, Anoop. 1997. Rightward scrambling. In *Rightward movement*, ed. by Dorothee Berman, Devid LeBlanc, and Henk van Riemsdijk, 185–213. Amsterdam: John Benjamins.

May, Robert. 1977. The grammar of quantification. Doctoral dissertation, MIT.

May, Robert. 1985. *Logical Form*. Cambridge, Mass.: MIT Press.

McCloskey, James. 1979. *Transformational syntax and model theoretic semantics*. Dordrecht: Reidel.

McCloskey, James. 1990. Resumptive pronouns, A'-binding and levels of representation in Irish. In *The syntax and semantics of modern Celtic languages*, ed. by Randall Hendrick, 199–248. San Diego, Calif.: Academic Press.

Merchant, Jason. 1999. The syntax of silence: Sluicing, islands and identity in ellipsis. Doctoral dissertation, University of California at Santa Cruz.

Mulder, René, and Marcel den Dikken. 1992. Tough parasitic gaps. In *NELS 22*, 303–317. Amherst: University of Massachusetts, GLSA.

Munn, Alan. 1992. A null operator analysis of ATB gaps. *The Linguistic Review* 9, 1–26.

Munn, Alan. 2001. Explaining parasitic gap restrictions. In *Parasitic gaps*, ed. by Peter Culicover and Paul M. Postal, 369–392. Cambridge, Mass.: MIT Press.

Neeleman, Ad. 1994. Complex predicates. Doctoral dissertation, Utrecht University.

Nunes, Jairo. 2001. Sideward movement. *Linguistic Inquiry* 32, 303–344.

Pesetsky, David. 1998. Some optimality principles of sentence pronunciation. In *Is the best good enough?*, ed. by Pilar Barbosa, Danny Fox, Paul Hagstrom, Martha McGinnis, and David Pesetsky, 337–383. Cambridge, Mass.: MIT Press.

Pesetsky, David. 2000. *Phrasal movement and its kin*. Cambridge, Mass.: MIT Press.

Pollard, Carl, and Ivan Sag. 1994. *Head-Driven Phrase Structure Grammar*. Chicago: University of Chicago Press.

Postal, Paul. 1971. *Cross-over phenomena*. New York: Holt, Rinehart and Winston.

Postal, Paul. 1993. Remarks on weak crossover effects. *Linguistic Inquiry* 24, 539–556.

Postal, Paul. 1997. Strong crossover violations and binding principles. Ms., New York University.

Reinhart, Tanya. 1976. The syntactic domain of anaphora. Doctoral dissertation, MIT.

Reinhart, Tanya. 1983a. *Anaphora and semantic interpretation*. Chicago: University of Chicago Press.

Reinhart, Tanya. 1983b. Coreference and bound anaphora: A restatement of the anaphora questions. *Linguistics and Philosophy* 6, 47–88.

Reinhart, Tanya. 1991. Elliptic conjunctions: Non-quantificational LF. In *The Chomskyan turn*, ed. by Asa Kasher, 360–384. Oxford: Blackwell.

Reinhart, Tanya. 1997. Strategies of anaphora resolution. OTS Working Paper. Utrecht: Utrecht Institute of Linguistics (UiL OTS).

Reinhart, Tanya. 1999. Strategies of anaphora resolution. OTS Working Paper. Utrecht: Utrecht Institute of Linguistics (UiL OTS).

Reinhart, Tanya, and Eric Reuland. 1991. Anaphors and logophors: An argument structure perspective. In *Long-distance anaphora*, ed. by Jan Koster and Eric Reuland, 283–321. Cambridge: Cambridge University Press.

Reinhart, Tanya, and Eric Reuland. 1993. Reflexivity. *Linguistic Inquiry* 24, 657–720.

Riemsdijk, Henk van, and Edwin Williams. 1981. NP-Structure. *The Linguistic Review* 1, 171–217.

Rochemont, Michael, and Peter Culicover. 1990. *English focus constructions and the theory of grammar*. Cambridge: Cambridge University Press.

Ross, John. 1973. Nouniness. In *Three dimensions of linguistic theory*, ed. by Osamu Fujimura. Tokyo: Tokyo Institute for Advanced Studies of Language.

Ruys, E. G. 2000. Weak crossover as a scope phenomenon. *Linguistic Inquiry* 31, 513–539.

Safir, Ken. 1984. Multiple variable binding. *Linguistic Inquiry* 15, 603–638.

Safir, Ken. 1986. Relative clauses in a theory of binding and levels. *Linguistic Inquiry* 17, 663–689.

Safir, Ken. 1992. Implied noncoreference and the pattern of anaphora. *Linguistics and Philosophy* 15, 1–52.

Safir, Ken. 1996a. Derivation, representation, and resumption: The domain of weak crossover. *Linguistic Inquiry* 27, 313–339.

Safir, Ken. 1996b. Semantic atoms of anaphora. *Natural Language and Linguistic Theory* 14, 545–589.

Safir, Ken. 1997. Symmetry and unity in the theory of anaphora. In *Atomism and binding*, ed. by Hans Bennis, Pierre Pica, and Johan Rooryck, 340–377. Dordrecht: Foris.

Safir, Ken. 1999. Vehicle change and reconstruction in Ā-chains. *Linguistic Inquiry* 30, 587–620.

Safir, Ken. 2003. Anaphors, movement and coconstrual. In *Grammatik i fokus. Grammar in focus: A festschrift for Christer Platzack, November 18, 2003*, ed. by Lars-Olof Delsing, Cecilia Falk, Gunlög Josefsson, and Halldór Sigurðsson. Lund: Lund University, Department of Scandinavian Languages.

Safir, Ken. 2004. *The syntax of anaphora*. Oxford: Oxford University Press.

Sag, Ivan. 1976. Deletion and Logical Form. Doctoral dissertation, MIT.

Saito, Mamoru, and Hajime Hoji. 1983. Weak crossover and Move α in Japanese. *Natural Language and Linguistic Theory* 1, 245–259.

Schachter, Paul. 1973. Focus and relativization. *Language* 49, 19–46.

Sells, Peter. 1984. Syntax and semantics of resumptive pronouns. Doctoral dissertation, University of Massachusetts, Amherst.

Sharvit, Yael. 1999a. Connectivity in specificational sentences. *Natural Language Semantics* 7, 299–339.

Sharvit, Yael. 1999b. Resumptive pronouns in relative clauses. *Natural Language and Linguistic Theory* 17, 587–612.

Shlonsky, Ur. 1992. Resumptive pronouns as a last resort. *Linguistic Inquiry* 23, 443–468.

Stowell, Tim. 1987. Adjuncts, arguments and crossover. Ms., UCLA.

Tang, Chih-Chen Jane. 1989. Chinese reflexives. *Natural Language and Linguistic Theory* 7, 93–121.

Toman, Jindřich. 1998. A discussion of resumptives in colloquial Czech. Ms., University of Michigan.

Ueyama, Ayumi. 1998. Two types of dependency. Doctoral dissertation, University of Southern California.

Vanden Wyngaerd, Guido, and Jan-Wouter Zwart. 1991. Reconstruction and vehicle change. In *Linguistics in the Netherlands, 1991*, ed. by Frank Drijkoningen and Ans van Kemenade, 151–160. Amsterdam: John Benjamins.

Vergnaud, Jean-Roger. 1974. French relative clauses. Doctoral dissertation, MIT.

Wasow, Thomas. 1979. *Anaphora in generative grammar*. Ghent: E. Story-Scientia.

Webelhuth, Gert. 1992. *Principles and parameters of syntactic saturation*. Oxford: Oxford University Press.

Williams, Edwin. 1977. Discourse and Logical Form. *Linguistic Inquiry* 8, 103–139.

Williams, Edwin. 1978. Across-the-board rule application. *Linguistic Inquiry* 9, 31–43.

Williams, Edwin. 1982. The NP-cycle. *Linguistic Inquiry* 13, 277–295.

Williams, Edwin. 1986. A reassignment of the functions of LF. *Linguistic Inquiry* 17, 265–299.

Williams, Edwin. 1994. *Thematic structure in syntax*. Cambridge, Mass.: MIT Press.

Williams, Edwin. 1995. Ellipsis. Ms., Princeton University.

Williams, Edwin. 1997. Blocking and anaphora. *Linguistic Inquiry* 28, 577–628.

Wiltschko, Martina. 1993. Extraposition in German. *Wiener Linguistische Gazette* 48–50, 1–30.

Wiltschko, Martina. 1997. Extraposition, identification and precedence. In *Rightward movement*, ed. by Dorothee Berman, David LeBlanc, and Henk van Riemsdijk, 59–79. Amsterdam: John Benjamins.

Index